HUME'S SYSTEM

HUME'S SYSTEM

An Examination of the First Book of his Treatise

DAVID PEARS

OXFORD UNIVERSITY PRESS

*This book has been printed digitally and produced in a standard specification
in order to ensure its continuing availability*

OXFORD
UNIVERSITY PRESS

Great Clarendon Street, Oxford OX2 6DP

Oxford University Press is a department of the University of Oxford.
It furthers the University's objective of excellence in research, scholarship,
and education by publishing worldwide in

Oxford New York

Auckland Bangkok Buenos Aires Cape Town Chennai
Dar es Salaam Delhi Hong Kong Istanbul Karachi Kolkata
Kuala Lumpur Madrid Melbourne Mexico City Mumbai Nairobi
São Paulo Shanghai Singapore Taipei Tokyo Toronto

with an associated company in Berlin

Oxford is a registered trade mark of Oxford University Press
in the UK and in certain other countries

Published in the United States
by Oxford University Press Inc., New York

ISBN 0-19-875100-1
ISBN 0-19-875099-4 (pbk)

To Maisley

Preface

HUME is an empiricist and a naturalist. His empiricism evidently makes him a precursor of John Stuart Mill, Ernst Mach, and Bertrand Russell. What is not so widely recognized is that his naturalism makes him a precursor of Ludwig Wittgenstein, even if there is in this case no direct influence.

Hume's empiricism is expressed in his axiom that all our ideas are derived from impressions. His naturalism goes further and deals with the various ways in which we combine our ideas when we are thinking, and especially when we are forming beliefs or making inferences.

His aim was to establish the science of the human mind (today psychology) on firm foundations, and then to use it to solve the main problems of philosophy. This may strike us as an ill-judged project, because we are now so accustomed to the idea that philosophy and science — even the scientific investigation of the mind — are two separate disciplines. However, in his day the separation was far from complete, and in any case, even now there is nothing to prevent a philosopher from putting the two disciplines in contact with one another and finding that the scientific facts about human modes of thought help him towards a solution of the philosophical problems. That is the aim of Hume's naturalism. One of its developments, his theory of causal inference, runs parallel to Wittgenstein's naturalistic account of the foundations of logic and descriptive language.

Hume investigated thought rather than language. That is one difference between his naturalism and Wittgenstein's. Another difference is that he is less confident that his naturalism really does settle all the difficult philosophical issues that he discusses. In several cases he admits that his treatment leaves a gap between what we seem to believe and what we can legitimately believe, and between the ideas that we seem to have and the ideas that we can legitimately have. When he makes these admissions, he is not necessarily implying that anything not covered by his treatment is speculative or spurious. He is uneasily aware that the results yielded by his science of human nature might turn out to be too niggardly and even genuinely sceptical in the final assessment.

But were his results really sceptical? T. H. Green and several other nineteenth-century British critics believed that they were, and assumed that this was Hume's view of them too. Consequently, they interpreted his whole philosophy as an elaborate *reductio ad absurdum* of the empiricism that he had taken over from Locke and Berkeley. More recently Norman Kemp Smith[1] and Barry Stroud[2] have argued that this view of his philosophy is neither accurate nor the view taken by Hume himself.

This controversy about the interpretation of Hume's philosophy will be pursued in this book. The question at issue—whether he is a sceptic or only a cautious naturalist—surfaces most conspicuously in his treatment of the three most difficult problems tackled in the first book of the *Treatise*, causation, personal identity, and perception.

This book will divide into two parts. First, there will be an exposition of the main lines of Hume's theory of the human mind. Then there will be an examination of the application of the theory to the three difficult problems and an assessment of its achievement.

One last point remains to be made in this Preface. Hume's theory of the mind has two aspects which must always be carefully distinguished from one another. His account of the derivation of ideas from impressions is offered as an answer to the question 'What ideas may we legitimately have?' (or perhaps the question is better put like this, 'Which of the ideas that we seem to have are genuine ideas?'). But his account of the connections between ideas and the way in which they function in thinking is offered mainly as an answer to a different question, 'What may we legitimately believe?' It is important to appreciate the difference between these two questions. His response to the first one runs parallel to a linguistic philosopher's theory of meaning, while his response to the second one is an investigation of the evidence available to us and it makes a direct contribution to the theory of knowledge. In this book the two questions will be kept separate from one another, and meaning will be taken before truth and the evidence for truth.

Both aspects of his theory of mind will be explained before the theory is applied to the three difficult problems and its achievement

[1] *The Philosophy of David Hume* (London: Macmillan, 1949).
[2] *Hume* (London: Routledge and Kegan Paul, 1977).

is assessed. The final verdict will be that it is astonishing that a theory that is so simple—almost primitive—produced such profound insights when it was applied to causation, personal identity, and perception.

Contents

PART I

HUME'S THEORY OF MIND

I

A General Account of Hume's Theory of Mind

THE point from which I shall start is a point made in the Preface: Hume's theory of mind is intended to help us towards answers to two distinct questions: 'What ideas may we legitimately have?' and 'What may we legitimately believe?' The first of these two questions is concerned with the origin of our ideas, and the second is concerned with the connections between our ideas and the various ways in which we combine them in thinking, and especially in belief.

The first thing that needs to be done is to develop these questions in more detail and to appreciate how Hume saw them. This is worth doing, because Hume's treatment of the first question runs parallel to a linguistic philosopher's theory of meaning: ideas correspond to words and Hume's empiricist account of the derivation of ideas from impressions corresponds to an empiricist account of the way in which words get their meanings from the things to which they are applied. If an idea is not derived from impressions either directly by copying a single impression, or indirectly by combining ideas which are themselves direct copies of impressions, then, according to Hume, it is a spurious idea, one that we may not legitimately have—or perhaps we should say that it is one that we do not really have but only seem to have. Similarly, in an empiricist account of the way in which a word gets its meaning, like Russell's theory of knowledge by acquaintance, either the word must be attached to something with which we are acquainted, or else it must be shown to combine other words in its definition and each of these other words must be attached to things with which we are acquainted. If neither of these conditions is met, the word lacks meaning.

There is a striking similarity here between Hume's account of the derivation of ideas from impressions and Russell's account of a word's derivation of its meaning from the object of acquaintance to which it is applied: ideas, we may say, are the elements out of which thoughts are constructed, just as words are the elements out of which sentences are constructed.

The similarity can be illustrated by comparing two quotations, one from Hume and the other from Russell:

Every proposition that we can understand must be composed wholly of constituents with which we are acquainted.[1]

That is Russell's principle of acquaintance: if we lack acquaintance with the objects from which the words in a proposition derive their meanings, then we will not be able to understand the proposition, and—he might have added—if there are no such objects, it will have no meaning. Now compare a remark made by Hume in his *Abstract of the Treatise of Human Nature*:

... when he [our author] suspects that any philosophical term has no idea annexed to it (as is too common) he always asks *from what impression that pretended idea is derived?* And if no impression can be produced, he concludes that the term is altogether insignificant.[2]

The similarity becomes even more striking when we notice that Hume's indirect method of deriving ideas from impressions relies on definitions recording the division of a complex idea into its simple components.[3] For this is very close to the leading idea of Russell's logical atomism, that words signifying complex things can be defined, and the process of definition can be continued until we reach indefinable words which signify simple things.

However, it is important not to be over-impressed by this similarity. For when we look back at Book I of the *Treatise*, we shall miss the richness of its philosophy if we interpret it entirely from a later linguistic point of view. Hume's treatment of ideas packs a wealth of detail into a deceptively simple theory and it presents some very sophisticated insights in a framework that is almost primitive. So the next thing that needs to be done is to enumerate some of the complexities' which would be overlooked by anyone who mistakenly supposed that his theory of ideas amounts to no more than a theory of meaning.

---

[1] B. Russell, *The Problems of Philosophy*, 1st edn., 17th impression (London: Oxford University Press, 1950), 58.

[2] *An Abstract of the Treatise of Human Nature*, in *A Treatise of Human Nature*, ed. P. H. Nidditch (Oxford: Clarendon Press, 1989), 648–9.

[3] *An Enquiry concerning Human Understanding*, VII. i.

There are three such complexities. The first and most important is, of course, the second part of the theory, about which more will be said in a moment. That is the part which deals with the way we combine ideas in thinking and especially in belief. It is a direct contribution to the theory of knowledge, and is mainly concerned with truth and evidence for truth, rather than with meaning.

It is not entirely concerned with truth, however, because it does contain a certain contribution to the topic of meaning. For the combination of ideas in thoughts corresponds to the combination of words in sentences. Also, the combination of ideas in an inference corresponds to the combination of two sentences connected by the word 'therefore'—for example, this would be the structure of a causal inference. So anything that Hume has to say about these combinations of ideas is going to be, at least in part, a contribution to the topic of meaning.

However, that is merely a qualification. This part of the theory of ideas really is mainly concerned with belief, truth, and evidence. That is the point which is rightly emphasized by Kemp Smith and Stroud, but it should be emphasized without exaggeration—i.e. without suppressing the qualification.

The next two things that would be overlooked by anyone who took Hume's theory to be exclusively concerned with meaning, affect the first part of the theory—the part that deals with the derivation of ideas from impressions. One of them is an ambiguity in something that might be said about Humean ideas. It might be said that ideas occur in thinking, whereas impressions occur in sense-perception.[4] But this could mean that ideas are combined to form individual thoughts, like the thought that it is raining today or the thought that it will be sunny tomorrow. Alternatively, the word 'thinking' might be used more generally to cover all the operations of the mind except perceiving.

If 'thinking' means 'having individual thoughts', then the combination of ideas to form those thoughts will be like the combination of words to form sentences, and anything that Hume says about this kind of combination of ideas will be like the syntactical part of a linguistic philosopher's theory of meaning.[5] But if 'thinking' covers operations of

[4] There are, according to Hume, also impressions of reflection, which arise within the mind without any operation of the senses at the time when they arise (see *Treatise*, pp. 7–8). But here we are concerned only with impressions of sensation.

[5] In fact, Hume says very little about this kind of combination of ideas. He discusses the combination of several ideas to produce a complex idea, but the *Treatise* does not contain a separate discussion of the combination of several ideas to produce a thought.

the mind which are not so purposively directed, like day-dreaming, then an examination of the role of ideas in this further area will show that it often has no connection with meaning. This is another important point which would be overlooked by anyone who took this part of Hume's theory of ideas to be exclusively concerned with meaning.

In order to see the importance of this point, it is necessary to go back to the beginning and ask what kind of thing a Humean idea really is. The answer is that it is a replica of a sense-impression and is, therefore, an image. You look up at the sky and get a visual impression of an expanse of blue, which then leaves in your mind, as a kind of residue, a mental image which copies it more faintly. That mental image is a Humean idea.

This explanation can be applied to the point that was made above. An image of this kind may occur in your mind later in either of the two ways that have just been distinguished. It may occur in the course of your day-dreaming, or, perhaps, among the images that parade before your mind before falling asleep. In that kind of case the image will not have any meaning, and it will not be contributing anything to any thought. It will just be itself, a datum. The second way in which the same image may occur can be illustrated by the following episode: you ask yourself what colour a sapphire is and the same image of blue comes into your mind, but this time it comes as the visualization that answers your question. In this case the image has a meaning. Maybe you are not thinking that a sapphire is exactly that shade of blue, but only that it is some shade of blue. If that is what you are thinking, then the image is functioning as your abstract, general idea of blue, and Hume's explanation of its function will be a contribution to the topic of meaning.[6]

The point is a simple one. Although this function of images, to carry meanings, is a prominent one in Hume's theory, he also allows for their occurring in the other way which has nothing to do with meaning. This other way, their occurrence as data, is important too and it would be overlooked by anyone who took this part of his theory of ideas to be exclusively concerned with meaning.

The third point that would be overlooked by anyone who interpreted his theory exclusively as a semantic theory is connected with the previous one. His account of the derivation of ideas from impressions runs parallel to a linguistic philosopher's theory of meaning, and it is

This is because he treated the latter kind of combination merely as a special case of the former kind. See below, pp. 55–7.

[6] Hume's account of abstract general ideas is discussed below, pp. 27–30.

strikingly similar to Russell's empiricist theory of meaning based on knowledge by acquaintance. Given this similarity, we might expect Hume's argument for his account of the derivation of ideas to start from premisses about meaning. Perhaps, like Russell, he might have started by making a connection between meaning and denoting. However, he does not argue in that way at all. His argument is simply based on observation of what actually happens in people's minds. It is, according to him, just a matter of fact that in every person's mind each idea is preceded by an impression of the same kind (or else, if it is a complex idea, the ideas that are combined in its definition will, as a matter of fact, be preceded by impressions of the same kind as themselves).[7] He then proceeds to argue that in all these cases the occurrence of the impression, which is the first-comer of its kind, causes the occurrence of the later idea. So the idea is always derived from the impression, but, it appears, only as a matter of contingent fact.[8]

The connection between this point about Hume's argument for his view of the derivation of ideas from impressions and the previous one is evident. The previous point was that ideas do not always carry meanings, because they sometimes occur as mere data—i.e. as objects in their own right. Now if ideas occur in these two different ways, any argument for the derivation of all ideas from impressions will have to cover both kinds of occurrence—not only ideas occurring as bearers of meaning, but also ideas occurring as data in day-dreaming and in trains of hypnagogic imagery. Here we have an explanation of the way in which Hume argues for his view of the derivation of ideas from impressions. An argument starting from premisses about meaning would be too narrow in its scope, because it would fail to cover ideas which occurred not as bearers of meaning but as data. This is a further point that would be missed by anyone who took his theory of ideas to be exclusively concerned with meaning.

It may be objected that I am understating the case against the semantic interpretation of Hume's theory of ideas. For what I have just said may suggest something more than the need to qualify that interpretation by adding that ideas also occur as data, and that any argument for their derivation from impressions must cover that kind of occurrence too. It may suggest that his account of the derivation of ideas has nothing whatsoever to do with meaning and that the semantic

---

[7] See above, p. 4, for this alternative.

[8] There is a good discussion of this argument in B. Stroud, *Hume* (London: Routledge and Kegan Paul, 1977), 20–7. It will be examined below, pp. 21–4.

interpretation of it is a complete misunderstanding inspired by modern Positivism.

That, I think, would go too far, and I am prepared to stick to the intermediate interpretation of the theory—that, in part, it shares the concerns of a modern theory of meaning, but that it also has other concerns. A full defence of this interpretation will be given in succeeding chapters. However, there are two points in its favour that can be made immediately.

First, if we ask what use Hume makes of his view of the derivation of ideas, the answer will be that he uses it exactly like a modern empiricist theory of meaning. He makes that very clear in the passage quoted above from the *Abstract*: a term is 'altogether insignificant' if the supposed idea to which it is annexed is not derived from any impression.[9]

The most perspicuous example of this way of using his account of the derivation of ideas is his treatment of the philosophical thesis that we have an idea of causal power that is not derived from experience:

We must produce some instance, wherein the efficacy is plainly discoverable to the mind, and its operations obvious to our consciousness or sensation. By the refusal of this, we acknowledge, that the idea is impossible and imaginary . . . [10]

If we have really an idea of power, we may attribute power to an unknown quality. But as 'tis impossible, that that idea can be deriv'd from such a quality, and as there is nothing in known qualities, which can produce it; it follows that we deceive ourselves, when we imagine we are possest of any idea of this kind, after the manner we commonly understand it.[11]

If we have really no idea of a power or efficacy in any object, or of any real connexion betwixt causes and effects, 'twill be to little purpose to prove, that an efficacy is necessary in all operations. We do not understand our own meaning in talking so, but ignorantly confound ideas, which are entirely distinct from each other.[12]

There is a second point in support of the intermediate interpretation which can be made quickly. The reason why Hume puts his thesis about the derivation of ideas on a broad basis is that he wants to establish the science of the human mind on firm foundations before using it to solve the main problems of philosophy.[13] So the broad

---

[9] See above, p. 4.   [10] *Treatise*, pp. 157–8.   [11] Ibid. 161.
[12] Ibid. 168. He means that we have a very scaled-down idea of power derived from experience, and that we confuse it with a more grandiose (pseudo-) idea of power inherent in objects but not derived from experience.
[13] See Preface, p. vii.

argument from the observed facts comes first, and it is only later, when he is applying its general conclusion to particular philosophical problems, that we find him challenging his opponent to produce a genuine idea of some disputed entity or to explain what he means by the term for it.

That completes the list of things that would be overlooked by anyone who interpreted Hume's theory of ideas as a theory entirely concerned with meaning, i.e. as a psychological version of a semantic theory. It is at least, but not exclusively, that kind of theory.

It is also possible to push the interpretation of his theory of ideas too far in the opposite direction and to treat it as predominantly a theory of belief and only minimally a theory of meaning. It evidently cannot be treated as a theory exclusively concerned with belief. Hume's explicit use of it to eliminate terms that are 'altogether insignificant' makes that extreme interpretation impossible.[14] But moves in that direction have been made by several philosophers.

Norman Kemp Smith's study *The Philosophy of David Hume*[15] put Hume's naturalistic theory of belief in the foreground of the *Treatise*. Barry Stroud went further in 1977[16] and argued that Hume attached much less importance to his account of the derivation of ideas from impressions. According to Stroud, the theory of ideas was the inherited framework on which he constructed his naturalistic system, and demonstrations of meaninglessness based on the thesis that genuine ideas must be derived from impressions were of minor importance.

Stroud's interpretation is avowedly a reaction against the view that the *Treatise* is a work of demolition which relies on a theory of meaning very like that of the Logical Positivists of the 1930s. But why must the reaction be so extreme? A one-sided view is better replaced by a balanced view. We can allow that Hume's theory of truth and evidence provides much of the weight behind his attacks on his adversaries without reducing the weight of his theory of meaning quite so far, and we can admit the importance of his constructive work without denying the importance of the demolition that preceded it.

In two recent books Edward Craig[17] and Galen Strawson[18] have

---

[14] See above, p. 4.
[15] (London: Macmillan, 1st edn. 1940, 2nd edn. 1949).
[16] *Hume.*
[17] *The Mind of God and the Works of Man* (Oxford: Clarendon Press, 1987).
[18] *The Secret Connexion: Causation, Realism, and David Hume* (Oxford: Clarendon Press, 1989).

taken the ideas behind Stroud's interpretation further. Craig argues that, when Hume tackles a difficult problem, like personal identity, he does not always use his theory of the derivation of ideas, and when he does use it, he soon switches to his theory of belief, thus indicating where his true interest lies. Strawson argues that Hume's treatment of causation is not what Logical Positivists take it to be. For Hume allows the meaningfulness of the general hypothesis that physical objects possess causal powers, thus indicating that he does not hold a regularity theory of causation, and he only denies the possibility of our giving the hypothesis any specific content. His view is that, when Hume challenges his opponents to produce the impression from which the idea of causal necessity is derived, he is only concerned with causation so far as we know it, or, as he would put it in the *Treatise*, causation in so far as it relates things within our minds. In this restricted field he does insist that all our thoughts must have specific content, and he uses his theory of the derivation of ideas to show that the specific content of our idea of causal necessity falls far short of what his opponents claim that it is. But in the other field, causal relations in the physical world, Strawson thinks that he allows that we have an understanding of the hypothesis that objects have causal powers, but denies that we have any way of discovering them. This denial is the true centre of his treatment of causation, and it gives his theory of belief, on which it is based, much greater importance than his theory of the derivation of ideas.

These interpretations will not be examined in detail in this book. In the chapters that follow my particular points of disagreement with them will sometimes be indicated.[19] Here I only want to make two general points. First, my rejection of these interpretations is not a reversion to the naïve 'positivistic' reading of the *Treatise*, which downgrades the importance of the theory of belief and takes the whole book to be deploying an empiricist theory of meaning. It is surely possible to see two separate thrusts in Hume's strategy, one against the meaningfulness of his opponent's views and the other against their credibility, and to attribute equal importance to each of them. Secondly, if Hume sometimes blurs the distinction between his two lines of argument, that is not hard to understand. For his view is that both meaning and truth are founded on impressions and it proved extremely difficult for him to keep the two functions of the foundation distinct simply because it is extremely difficult.

---

[19] See below, pp. 91–3 and 194–5.

The best way to launch a balanced interpretation of Hume's theory of ideas is to take the distinction drawn above, between what it has to say about the understanding of meaning and what it has to say about the apprehension of truth, and to apply it to some simple examples. So let us now take three kinds of judgement and ask what Hume's theory has to tell us, first about their meaning, and then about the evidence that leads us to hold them true. The first kind is a singular judgement of immediate perception, the second is a singular judgement of memory, and the third a singular causal inference.

A typical singular judgement of immediate perception would be 'This is blue'. At this stage we need not ask any questions about the world outside our minds, and we can take it that the word 'this' makes a reference to a particular sense-impression and then the phrase 'is blue' goes on to describe it. What psychological counterpart of this sentence does Hume's theory of ideas provide?

The answer, surprisingly, is 'None'. He saw no need for any psychological counterpart of a sentence about a present sense-impression. You have the impression and why would you want to duplicate it with an idea? If you objected that you needed to register your sense-impression in thought, and, therefore, had to bring in an idea, he would probably have replied that you do not need to bring in an idea to register your impression at the time, but only afterwards in memory. So in such cases ideas do not have any role to play, not even as bearers of meaning.

Nevertheless, he is quite explicit about our apprehension of truth in such cases. For he says that 'since all actions and sensations of the mind are known to us by consciousness, they must necessarily appear in every particular what they are, and be what they appear'.[20] All possibility of mistake is ruled out, and yet the truth that we always succeed in attaining is not a property of any record in our minds. Perhaps we should take him to have supposed that immediate sensory knowledge is intuitive, or, to put it in another way, that sense-impressions are self-intimating and, as it were, speak for themselves.

His account of memory is less sketchy and it does provide us with some sort of psychological counterpart for the sentence 'That was blue'. He allows that memory involves ideas, and one of their functions is to take over the role played by the descriptive part of the sentence, the phrase 'was blue'. The idea which takes over this role in his

[20] *Treatise*, p. 190.

psychological theory is an image serving as the abstract general idea of blue. But he offers nothing to take over the referential function of the word 'That'. In a case of recollection, we must assume that the context supplies the reference: you ask yourself what colour that sense-impression was, and your memory simply responds with the image serving as the abstract general idea of blue, in much the same way that it might have responded with the general word 'blue'.[21]

There are many complications in Hume's account of memory. For example, images often occur in memory-situations in the other way, as data rather than as bearers of meaning. In such cases the subject is not making any attempt at recollection, but is merely the passive recipient of an image which he may find problematical. But the discussion of these and other complications can wait until later.

What about the truth of a recollection and our reason for holding it true? Hume's answer is that it is true if the idea matches the earlier impression, and that our reason for holding it true is that it is 'strong and lively'. He probably meant that we find that it is stubborn and resists alteration. But those characteristics will serve as an indication of truth only in a context in which a question has been asked. Otherwise the stubbornness and resistance to alteration might merely show that the idea was an obsession.

Hume's account of singular causal inference is more elaborate than his account of singular memory claims. This is hardly surprising, because it is a more complicated matter and his treatment of it is the centre-piece of the book.

His main point is introduced as a point about meaning but it soon develops into a point about evidence and truth: the idea of causal necessity is not derived from any sense-impression—we do not pick it up by observing necessity at work in the world outside our minds: it is derived from an impression of reflection—we pick it up by feeling a natural process operating within our minds. So when we suppose that there is real causal necessity outside our minds we are projecting outwards something that really belongs within, namely an internal impression of constraint.[22]

---

[21] This, of course, merely shifts the problem to another point. For what happens in your mind when you ask yourself about 'that sense-impression'? However, something is gained, because it is, at least, clear that the context in which the image occurs is essential to Hume's theory of memory when it is applied to recollection.

[22] As he puts it, 'the mind has a great propensity to spread itself on external objects' (*Treatise*, p. 167).

He does not mean that there is no external basis for our causal inferences: there is, as he says, the constant conjunction of this kind of cause with that kind of effect.[23] Nor does he mean that what we feel in our minds is anything more than the so-called 'force of habit': we are accustomed to seeing the red ball on the billiards table move when it is struck by the white ball, and so this time, when we see it struck, we feel ourselves pushed along the track of the two associated ideas—i.e. from the idea of impact to the idea of movement. That is all. The mental process is just another example of the repetition of a couple, like the external process which it reflects. The only difference is that we ourselves go through the mental process and feel its inevitability, such as it is. This is the central experience of causal inference and so we tend to exaggerate its status: we blow it up and project it outwards on to the external world, where it gives us the illusion of an intelligible real power lodged in the nature of things.

Suppose that you have this idea of causal necessity, derived in the way that Hume describes. What does it enable you to do? First, it enables you to understand the possibility that two events are related as cause and effect. For example, you watch something that you have never seen before—a drop of sulphuric acid hits a sheet of paper and a hole appears in the paper with blackened edges and fumes. It occurs to you that the hole is produced by the drop, but you do not actually make this judgement, because you have never had the experience that would lead you to make it. You merely consider the possibility that this is a case of cause and effect. You strongly suspect that it is, but you suspend judgement. The experience that you lack is, of course, experience of the constant conjunction of these two kinds of event.[24]

Hume passes over these cases, where you understand a causal sentence but do not assert it, and hurries on to the cases that interest him more, where you not only understand the causal sentence but also assert it. I have separated the two stages—the understanding of meaning and the apprehension of truth—because that is the only way to get a clear view of what is happening on Hume's crowded stage. Meaning must come before truth.

So what would Hume have said about this first stage, if he had

---

[23] He says more than this about the evidence in the external world on which singular causal inferences are based, but this is only an introductory sketch. The full account is given below, pp. 66–70 and 81–3.

[24] Or, of course, you might make the judgement on the ground that there is, apparently, nothing else in the immediate vicinity to cause the hole to develop.

paused to deal with it? I think that he would have said that when you received this unfamiliar pair of sense-impressions, you did not feel yourself pushed along any associational track leading from the first item in the pair to the second item. In fact, the second item, the burning of the hole, came as a complete surprise to you. Of course, now that it has actually happened, you have the idea of being pushed along a track connecting the two, but not the impression, and you did not feel any impression of being pushed at the time.

The second stage, where you do make the causal inference, is examined by Hume in full detail. Here you see the drop of acid hit the paper, and your causal inference is a shot at the truth. You make it, because this time, we may suppose, you have already noticed this particular conjunction, and it has been constant in your experience, and so it has established an associational track in your mind. Consequently, as soon as you get the first impression, of the acid hitting the paper, it draws into your mind by association the second idea, of the opening up of the hole. If your inference is correct, you will find that you will immediately get an impression to match the second idea.

One more point is needed to complete this sketch of Hume's account of singular causal inferences. When the second idea is drawn into your mind, it has strength and liveliness bestowed on it by the first impression, and this strength and liveliness make it an idea of belief. It is like an idea of memory, which is also strong and lively, but the difference is that an idea of memory is referred to the past and gets its strength and liveliness directly from the past impression, whereas this idea of belief gets its strength and liveliness indirectly, by association with a present impression, and is referred to the future.

Further details and comments will have to wait until later. The only point that needs to be added now to this introductory sketch is that Hume's account of causal necessity is naturalistic and, we can now say, anthropocentric, like Wittgenstein's account of logical and mathematical necessity. In both cases the suggestion is that we start with the idea that we are under the constraint of some force which operates on us from outside our minds, but the truth is that the necessity, such as it is, is constituted by the fact that certain processes of thought come naturally to us.

In this introduction, no details have been given of the other two difficult problems, personal identity and perception. They are difficult for the same reason that the problem of causation is difficult: they seem to demand more resources than Hume is prepared to allow that we have. In all three cases, the same question arises. Is his treatment sceptical, or does it cover everything that we may legitimately claim to understand and believe?

2

The Derivation of Ideas from Impressions

IN the analysis of Hume's account of the derivation of ideas, which is the topic of this chapter, there are two points to look out for. Both were made in the previous chapter, but it is worth repeating them before starting the analysis. First, an idea, like a mental image of blue, may occur not as a bearer of any meaning, but as something less than that, a mere datum, for example, which just floats into your mind in day-dreaming. Secondly, when this same idea does occur as a bearer of meaning, when, for example, you use it to recall that sapphires exhibit that distinctive shade of blue, it is often, at the same time, more than a bearer of meaning. In fact, in this particular case it is evidently more than a bearer of meaning, because you are making the general memory-judgement that those jewels exhibit this colour. You do not confine yourself to thinking that they might exhibit this colour. You believe that they actually do so.

So if we think of Hume's account of the derivation of ideas as a theory of concept-formation, taking whatever images occur to be bearers of meaning, we must remember that they may be less than that, as in the first case mentioned above, and also that they may be more than that, as in the second case.

There are two more preliminary points that need to be made before his account of the derivation of ideas is analysed. First, we need to look at the difference between a concept and an image. This is important, because, though Hume's ideas are always images (or, at least, definite things in the mind, like images, which are the objects of inner sense),[1] they are sometimes, but not always, concepts, and this is an ambiguity that needs to be explained.

---

[1] The qualification is needed because he must have realized that not everybody is capable of getting images across the whole range of sensory properties with which he is familiar.

If we ask what is involved in having a concept of a quality like blue, the first requirement that springs to mind is that you should be able to recognize blue things when you see them. We will discover later that that is not all that is involved in having the concept of blue,[2] but even that amounts to more than getting an image of blue when your eyes are shut. For you might get such an image *before* you acquired the ability to recognize it, or anything else, as blue. That shows up the difference between getting an image of a sensory quality and possessing the concept of it.

Secondly, we need to look at the difference between singular ideas and general ideas. Now a philosopher might set out to draw this distinction among ideas by searching for something in the image itself which would indicate singularity or generality. But Hume, following Berkeley, claims that there is never anything in the image itself, never anything intrinsic to it, which could possibly make it general. For whenever an image occurs in a person's mind, it occurs as a particular mental item. Of course, a visual image will have a colour, and that colour may happen to be blue. But that will not show that it is the general idea of blue: it might be the general idea of colour, or, to go to the more specific end of the scale, it might be the general idea of the determinate shade, sapphire-blue. The image cannot fix the range of its own application as a concept. It follows that general ideas must owe their generality to something outside themselves, something extrinsic to them.

Hume, again following Berkeley, attributes their generality to the fact that they are 'general in their signification'. So this image of a determinate shade of blue may signify blue-in-general, rather than its own determinate shade. The details of this theory will be given later,[3] but the point to be made about it now is that it is a functional theory: the extrinsic factor which gives an idea its generality is its function. Here, as in many other places in his theory of mind, Hume is exploiting the difference between two of the ways in which an image can occur, as a mere datum and as a bearer of meaning, and he makes it clear that the difference does not lie in the image itself, but in its function (or lack of function).

This explanation of the generality of general ideas leaves a loose end. What gives a singular idea its singularity? It cannot be the

---

[2] See below, pp. 27–30.   [3] See below, pp. 27–30.

particularity of the image itself, because *all* images are particular. So here we might expect Hume to rely on the fact that singular ideas are 'singular in their signification'—another functional theory.

However, that is not what we find. We find, instead, something rather surprising: Hume simply does not allow for any simple singular ideas in his theory. That is to say, he offers us no ideas to serve as counterparts of demonstrative words, like 'this', or of names, like 'Paris', used by someone in the city. It is true that he claims that he himself has a singular idea of Paris, but it is a complex idea, and he explains it by saying that it is 'such an idea of that city, as will perfectly represent all its streets and houses in their real and just proportions'.[4] This shows that he does not intend the idea of Paris to be the counterpart of the word 'Paris' used demonstratively by someone actually in Paris, but, rather, to be the counterpart of a definite description of Paris as 'the city with such and such streets and houses', used by someone no longer in Paris as a way of identifying the city for another person in conversation. This is really what we ought to have expected, because his view was that ideas are not needed at the actual moment of perception,[5] and afterwards, in memory, a singular idea could not possibly be the counterpart of a demonstrative, but only of a definite description.

After this introduction to Hume's theory of the derivation of ideas from impressions, we need the theory itself. He states it very briefly: '*all our simple ideas in their first appearance are deriv'd from simple impressions, which are correspondent to them, and which they exactly represent*'.[6] This is a compressed statement, and it contains two distinct points. First, every simple idea has an impression that it resembles (and vice versa, but, the fact, if it really is a fact, that every simple impression has an idea that resembles it[7] does not play any important role in his system). Secondly, in any such couple it is the impression that comes first. Adding these two points together, and relying on Hume's account of causation,[8] we may say that in each couple it is the impression that causes the idea, or, putting it the other way round, that the idea is derived from the impression.

Hume applies this theory to impressions of reflection as well as to

---

[4] *A Treatise of Human Nature*, ed. P. H. Nidditch (Oxford: Clarendon Press, 1989), 3.
[5] See above, p. 11.
[6] *Treatise*, p. 4.
[7] Ibid. 3.
[8] See above, pp. 12–14.

impressions of sensation, but when he formulates it in his first chapter, he uses only impressions of sensation to illustrate it. So the kind of illustration that he uses at first would be my impression of blue when I look up at the sky, and not the impression of necessitated transition that I feel when I infer that it will be a dry day.

The theory seems straightforward enough and even a bit superficial. However, it does have certain intricacies and the key to them is his concept of simplicity. It is noteworthy that it is only our simple ideas which, according to him, must have been derived from resembling ·impressions. Complex ideas need not have been derived in that direct way, because another alternative is available for them. He himself had seen Paris and so his complex idea of Paris was derived directly from a complex impression that it resembled. But neither he nor anyone else had seen the New Jerusalem, and so that idea would have to be derived from impressions in an indirect way: it would have to be constructed out of simple ideas, and then it is those simple ideas that would need to have been derived directly from the simple impressions which they resembled.[9] An idea which was not derived from impressions in either of these two ways would be a spurious idea, one that we should not have — or, perhaps, could not really have.

This is a challenging conclusion and the key to the argument for it is the distinction between simple and complex ideas. What exactly is this simplicity which makes it necessary for ideas which exhibit it to be derived directly from impressions that they resemble? And if this direct derivation really is necessary for them, what kind of necessity is that?

This question, about the kind of necessity that Hume's theory is supposed to have, is an important one. When it was discussed in the previous chapter, it was pointed out that he presents his theory of derivation as a psychological theory based on observation, and his reason for doing this was said to be that he wants to establish it on a broad base before applying it to the three difficult problems, causation, personal identity, and our perception of the world around us. He thought that if he built up his theory in this way, he would be able to cover all occurrences of images, not only when they are bearers of meaning but also when they are mere data.

However, this psychological approach does have a certain disadvantage:

---

[9] There are two versions of this thesis, one strong and the other weak. The weaker thesis would be that it is psychologically necessary for simple ideas to be derived from simple impressions that they resemble, while the stronger thesis would be that it is logically necessary.

the necessity of the derivation for which he argues will be weaker than it would have been if he had confined himself to images functioning as bearers of meaning and if he had argued for the derivation a priori. Evidently, the broad empirical argument is appropriate to images in general, while a narrower, a priori argument would be appropriate to images functioning as bearers of meaning or concepts.[10]

But let us go back to the crucial question about simplicity, leaving the question about the necessity of Hume's thesis for later consideration. What exactly is simplicity?

Hume gives as examples of simple ideas the idea of the taste of pineapple and the ideas of specific shades of colours.[11] When he calls these ideas 'simple', he means that they cannot be divided. The kind of division that he has in mind is phenomenological. For his method is to ask what simple ideas can be discerned in a complex idea, like the idea of an orange. The answer in this case might start with the idea of the colour, and then go on to the idea of the taste, and so on. According to him, these would both be simple ideas, because it is not possible to discern further ideas contained in them. The process of phenomenological division has to stop when simple ideas are reached.

Although this method is phenomenological, it is really quite like the modern method of logical analysis. For when he is describing the combination of simple ideas to form complex ones, he says that they are put together in ways which are recorded in definitions.[12] So his phenomenological division of ideas follows lines laid down by definitions until it reaches indefinables. That is how Russell too and Wittgenstein in his early period saw the task of logical analysis.

When Hume treats complex ideas as divisible into parts, he is thinking metaphorically. The division of the idea of an orange into parts may be like, but does not run parallel to, the physical division of the orange itself into parts. However, the metaphor is a powerful one, and it has a profound effect on his philosophy. It makes him concentrate on the kind of definition which gives a list of the intrinsic features of the thing whose complex idea is being analysed. So the special colour of an orange and its special taste are both intrinsic to it, and the kind of definition that guides his phenomenological analysis is a conjunctive definition listing those and other intrinsic features of the thing.

His concentration on this kind of definition, reinforced by the

---

[10] See above, pp. 5–6.   [11] *Treatise*, pp. 2 and 5.
[12] See above, p. 4.

metaphor, drives him to atomism.[13] For it makes him neglect the lateral connections of any thing whose idea is under analysis. For example, the colour blue is related to other colours in certain ways shown on the colour-circle, and particular shades of blue also exhibit relations with one another. If he had undertaken his phenomenological analysis in a more holistic spirit, he would have attached just as much weight to extrinsic connections of this kind as he does to the intrinsic features of things. But concentrating, as he does, on conjunctive definitions which list intrinsic features he can only divide and sub-divide until he reaches phenomenological atoms.

If we now look again at Hume's text, we find something very surprising. After he has offered his theory of the derivation of ideas from impressions, apparently as a universal truth with no exceptions, he notes a 'contradictory phænomenon, which may prove that 'tis not absolutely impossible for ideas to go before their correspondent impressions'.[14] The counter-example that he suggests is the case of a person familiar with all the shades of blue except one, of which he has never had an impression. Could such a person get an idea of this further shade of blue? Hume is inclined to think that he could get an idea of it, because he could fill in the blank between the two shades on either side of it. However, he is not in the least worried by this possibility, because 'the instance is so particular and singular, that 'tis scarce worth our observing, and does not merit that for it alone we should alter our general maxim'.[15]

This is very surprising. Why is he not worried by this counter-example to his 'general maxim'? The explanation will take us through many of the important questions already raised about the interpretation of his theory.

Hume's amazing calm when he faces the counter-example to his 'general maxim' is discussed by Stroud in his book *Hume*.[16] Stroud points out that the 'general maxim' is only based on psychological observation, and only offered as a matter of fact established by the science of human nature. Such things are never more than contingently so, and it is always conceivable that they could have been otherwise. In any case, Stroud adds, Hume is only saying that we can

---

[13] It is not the only force driving him to atomism (see below, pp. 107–9), but it is a very important one.
[14] *Treatise*, p. 5.
[15] Ibid. 6.
[16] (London: Routledge and Kegan Paul, 1977), 33–5.

see that it would be possible for someone to get a simple image which was not derived from an impression that it resembled: he is not saying that this ever actually happens. However, Stroud concludes his discussion by admitting that these considerations do not remove the puzzle.

They fall far short of removing the puzzle. It is quite true that Hume treats his thesis about the derivation of ideas as a contingent truth, and that, in itself, is not puzzling. For his aim, as already explained, was to establish it on the broadest possible basis, extending it to all images regardless of their function or status. However, when he admits that it would be possible for there to be a counter-example to his thesis, he does not mean that this is a remote possibility which has never been realized: he means that, when he reflects on the possibility, his thought-experiment reveals that there is nothing to stop its realization, and he treats this as 'a proof that the simple ideas are not always derived from the correspondent impressions'.[17]

Stroud points out that empirical generalizations are often subject to exceptions—water does not always boil at 212° Fahrenheit, the monsoon does not always arrive, etc. But such considerations are no help to Hume, because he is going to use his 'general maxim' polemically—for example, he is going to argue that there is no sense-impression from which the idea of causal power as something inherent in objects could possibly be derived. If he has already conceded that there are exceptions to his 'general maxim', an adversary who believes that we do have such an idea of causal power can claim that this is just another exception. Perhaps this criticism will not get Hume's adversary very far, but the point is that Hume's carelessness about counter-examples does invite the criticism. So the next question that must be asked is this: 'Did he have a good reason for thinking that the criticism is not damaging?'

In most of the remainder of this chapter I shall sketch and comment on three lines of defence which he might have used. One of them will turn out to be a bad option, but the other two will be better, and, together, they might offer him some prospect of success, but, as will become apparent, only at a certain cost. The suggestion behind my analysis of his strategic position is going to be that he was too ready to accept empiricism, almost as an intuition, and that this made him careless about the details of his formulation of it, but that, in spite of

[17] *Treatise*, p. 6.

this, his position was a strong one, giving him real ground for confidence.

First, he might have *defined* an 'impression' as 'the first-comer of its kind'. Stroud points out that there are remarks which suggest that that was what he was doing. For example,

Those perceptions, which enter with most force and violence, we may name *impressions*; and under this name I comprehend all our sensations, passions and emotions, as they make their first appearance in the soul.[18]

But Stroud also points out that, if primogeniture were being offered in this passage as a definitory property of impressions, 'the connection between having an impression and perceiving or feeling would have been severed'.[19] For, on that interpretation, nothing could properly be described as 'a completely new kind of visual idea' because the complete novelty would entail that it must be an impression rather than an idea. It would then follow that impressions could occur in situations where neither outer sense nor inner sense were operating. This cannot be right, because Hume evidently believed that he could distinguish impressions from ideas independently of the order of their occurrence. No doubt, it is difficult to see exactly what independent distinction he had in mind—in this passage he implies that it turns on a difference in 'force and violence', but there are obvious problems about that.[20] However, the difficulties certainly should not persuade us that he must have meant the connection between being an impression and being the first-comer of its kind to be definitional. That would be a bad line of defence, because it would lead very quickly to a dead end.

A second, quite different line of defence would rely on the tacit restriction of his thesis about the derivation of ideas to cases where the idea was an image functioning as a bearer of meaning. This would put his thesis on a narrower basis, and that, as already explained, would be a disadvantage. However, it might have the more than compensating advantage of making it invulnerable to the counter-examples which have just given the wider version so much trouble. For in all the suggested counter-examples the ideas would be images occurring not as bearers of meaning, but as data.

Suppose, for example, that a man blind from birth had novel

---

[18] Ibid. 1, quoted by Stroud, *Hume*, p. 30. Cf. *Treatise*, p. 275: 'Original impressions or impressions of sensation are such as without any antecedent perception arise in the soul.'

[19] *Hume*, p. 31.   [20] See below, pp. 36–7, 41–2, and 44.

experiences when the visual centre in his brain was artificially stimulated. Suppose too that, after surgery had given him the sense of sight, he claimed that his earlier experiences had been what he now realized were occurrences of images of various colours. Is it not obvious that those images did not occur as bearers of meaning but only as problematical data? So are they not irrelevant to Hume's thesis, if, as we are assuming, its range has been restricted precisely in order to exclude such images from its scope?

I think Hume could reasonably claim to be able to deal with this kind of case in this way. However, there is a certain complication that he would have to face. Someone might object that the patient was mistaken when he claimed that his earlier experiences were occurrences of *images*: in fact, they were occurrences of *impressions*. The patient's only reason for calling them 'images' would have been that during his period of blindness he assumed that he was not receiving sensory input. But even at that time the experimenter knew that he *was* receiving sensory input, and now he himself knows that he was. So were they not really impressions?

This is not a suggestion that need give Hume any anxieties. For, of course, if they were impressions, the attempt to find a counter-example to his unrestricted thesis would have failed right from the start.

We may conclude that this option — restricting his thesis to images functioning as bearers of meaning — provides Hume with a good defence, but only up to a certain point, because it is not a defence that can be used against the example of the idea of the shade of blue derived from no previous matching impression. Here the idea really might be an image functioning as a bearer of meaning, and so the defensive restriction of the thesis would not preserve it from the counter-example.

Is there some third defence which Hume could fall back on at this point? Perhaps there is no need for him to abandon his empiricist theory of the derivation of *concepts*. If we can take it that he has given up any claim to extend the theory to images occurring as mere data, and has restricted its scope to images functioning as bearers of meaning, it may be that all that he now needs to do, in order to save it, is to allow that they may be derived from impressions in more ways than the two that he describes.

His official view is that an idea (which we are now taking to be a bearer of meaning or, to put the assumption in another way, a concept) must *either* be a direct copy of a simple impression, *or else* be a combination of other ideas, themselves copies of simple impressions, where the method of combination is recorded in a conjunctive definition listing intrinsic features of the thing whose idea is being analysed. Perhaps what he needs to do now is to add a third way in which an idea may be derived from impressions. He can allow an idea to be derived, as it were, laterally from other ideas in the group to which it belongs. This would relax the conditions imposed on derivation by his official view and make them more realistic. Yet it would preserve the empiricist character of the theory, because it would still require the derivation of any idea to start from impressions. The difference would be that a new and even less direct line of derivation would now be permitted — a big change in his theory, but one that is consistent with its point.

This problem, and the various ways in which Hume might have tried to solve it, if he had faced it squarely, may seem to be rather parochial. It has a certain fascination for students of Hume, but has it really any great philosophical importance?

There seem to be three things that make it important. First, it is a very clear illustration of the functional character of concepts. When a concept manifests itself as a particular image occurring in a person's mind at a particular time, it cannot just be identified with that image. Anyone who says that it *is* the image will have to add that it is only the image with its special function, which is the function of bearing the meaning *blue* (or *sapphire-blue*, or perhaps, more generically, *coloured*).[21] This is a point of general importance, because functionalism is a plausible theory in many other areas of the philosophy of mind. It is a theory which opposes our inveterate preference for explanations which appeal to mental objects with intrinsic powers. We so easily forget that the power of one of these images is almost entirely bestowed on it by the way in which we use it. Wittgenstein, in his later writings, argued at length against our stubborn prejudice in favour of intrinsic powers. The point on which he insisted in this particular case was not merely that the image must have a function, but also that its function is the use that we make of it.[22]

The second thing that gives this Humean problem a more far-reaching importance is that it is a good example of the kind of difficulty that we get into on the borderline that runs between philosophy and

---

[21] The question of which meaning the image bears will be discussed in the last part of this chapter, on abstract general ideas. See below, pp. 27–30.

[22] See Wittgenstein, *Philosophical Investigations*, tr. G. E. M. Anscombe, 3rd edn. (Oxford: Blackwell, 1958), pt. I, §§ 139–41.

science. In this case the science is psychology. Now in Hume's day no sharp line had been drawn between philosophy and science and he often uses the word 'philosophical' to mean 'scientific'. Even when the two disciplines were distinguished, it was a long time before psychology split off as an independent science. So it was entirely natural for him to develop his philosophy as a science of the mind. However, there is a difficulty about proceeding in this way.

The difficulty is that the philosophical aspect of a problem will need to be treated in a different way from its psychological aspect. The derivation of ideas is a topic for psychology, when ideas are taken as images occurring as mere data; but when they are taken as images functioning as bearers of meaning, it is a topic for philosophy. Hume picks up both problems in one handful and his commentators have to tease them apart. This tendency to lump philosophy and science together is not just an idiosyncrasy of Hume's. It was extreme in his case, but it is a perennial risk and it too is the subject of many warnings by Wittgenstein.[23]

The third thing that gives a more general importance to Hume's theory of the derivation of ideas from impressions is that it is an early, particularly clear illustration of the opposition between atomism and holism. An atomist, like Hume, would take the idea of each thing separately, and if he found that an idea was complex, a combination of other simpler ideas, he would break up the combination. But how would he decide where to make the cuts between one component and another? How would he even know what sort of component to look for?

His method is predetermined by his original assumption, that the idea of each thing should be taken separately. For that implies that there is no point in looking for lateral, or extrinsic, connections between one idea and others in the same group. So his strategy is to look for the intrinsic properties of the complex thing whose idea is under analysis. Each of those intrinsic properties will have an idea corresponding to it, and each of these ideas will be a component of the complex idea that is being analysed.

This method leads inevitably to the problem of the interpolated idea of the shade of blue. The problem is not the peripheral nuisance that Hume takes it to be. It is a clear instance of the central problem of atomism, and he is not in a position to deal with it dismissively, in the way that he hopes. He has to adopt the third defence sketched

---

[23] e.g. see *Philosophical Investigations*, pt. I, §§ 191–4.

above, and that amounts to a renunciation of atomism (but not of empiricism).

The problem is not just Hume's problem. It is worth observing that the logical atomism of Russell and Wittgenstein ran into exactly the same impasse, and that they too were both forced to retrace their steps and develop a more holistic theory which allowed for lateral connections. Russell defined a simple word as one whose meaning can only be learned through acquaintance with the thing denoted by it. Then are words for determinate shades of colour simple? He thinks that they are, and that, of course, commits him to a view which exactly parallels Hume's view: the meaning of the word 'sapphire-blue' can only be learned through seeing the colour, which is just like saying that the idea of sapphire-blue can only be derived from a sense-impression of the colour. Wittgenstein pushed this logical atomism even further: because words like 'sapphire-blue' evidently do have lateral connections, with other colour-words, he denied that they are simple and looked for other more convincing examples. But genuine simplicity proved unattainable and he soon abandoned his atomism in favour of holism.[24] Hume should have done the same.

One more thing is needed to complete this account of Hume's theory of the derivation of ideas from impressions. Something was said earlier in this chapter about abstract general ideas, but not enough, and some more details now have to be added.

First, it should be noted that there are two reasons for calling general ideas abstract. One is that *all* ideas are mental and, therefore, abstract rather than concrete. The other reason is confined to general ideas: a general idea, unlike a singular idea, is not a mechanical copy of an impression but is acquired by selective abstraction. You look down on Paris from a plane and get a complex impression of it: according to Hume, your singular idea of Paris is just a mechanical copy of this impression, and no selection or abstraction is needed before you can acquire it.[25] But a general idea has to be acquired in a different way. We observe a globe of white marble and then, later, a globe of black marble: in each case the round shape is inseparable from the colour in

---

[24] See Russell, 'The Philosophy of Logical Atomism', in *Logic and Knowledge: Essays 1901–1950*, ed. R. C. Marsh (London: Allen and Unwin, 1956), 193–5, and Wittgenstein, *Tractatus Logico-Philosophicus*, 6.3751, and 'Some Remarks on Logical Form', *Proceedings of the Aristotelian Society*, suppl. vol. 9 (1929), 162–71; repr. in *Essays on Wittgenstein's Tractatus*, ed. R. Beard and I. Copi (London: Routledge and Kegan Paul, 1966), 31–7.

[25] See above, p. 18.

the impression, but we can view the shape and the colour 'in different aspects, according to the resemblances, of which they are susceptible. When we wou'd consider only the figure of the globe of white marble, we form in reality an idea both of the figure and the colour, but tacitly carry our eye to its resemblance with the globe of black marble.'[26] This relies on our capacity for selective attention: we can, at will, see the impression merely as a member of the set of impressions of round things, in spite of the fact that none of them could have that shape without having some colour.

That is Hume's account of the perception of qualities and our acquisition of general ideas of them. We are then in a position to use these general ideas in thought, and some account is needed of what goes on in our minds on such occasions. Here, as already explained, Hume takes over Berkeley's thesis 'that all general ideas are nothing but particular ones, annexed to a certain term, which gives them a more extensive signification, and makes them recall upon occasion other individuals, which are similar to them'.[27] The particularity of general ideas follows directly from the assumption that they are images: an image, like the impression from which it was derived, can only be an image of a triangle by being a particular image of a specific triangle, perhaps an isosceles one. Mechanical copying will never yield generality, which must, therefore, come from elsewhere, and Hume says that it comes from the term to which the idea is annexed. This term, he thinks, gives the idea its generality.

This needs some comment, but first it is necessary to draw attention to a problem, noted by Hume, and to his solution to it. The problem is 'that the very same idea [i.e. the identical image] may be annex't to several different words, and may be employ'd in different reasonings'.[28] For example, one and the same image of an isosceles triangle may serve in a thought about isosceles triangles or in a thought about triangles in general. But what gives the image these two different functions on two different occasions? Hume's answer to this question is that it is the two terms, each calling up by association a different set of images, which keep the two lines of thought distinct.[29]

Here we have an ingenious explanation of our acquisition and use of general ideas. However, it cannot be the right explanation, because it

---

[26] *Treatise*, p. 25. [27] Ibid. 17.
[28] Ibid. 21. [29] Ibid. 21–2.

represents thinking as a more passive process than it really is. This is easily seen. Consider a person running through a geometrical proof in his mind, using an image of an isosceles triangle to think about triangles in general, because he is trying to prove a theorem about all triangles. It is certainly true that he will have no trouble giving his image the wider signification. But, as Hume sees, that cannot simply be an effect of the association of ideas. For this image stands at the intersection of several different lines of associated ideas, each following up a different similarity and giving the image a different signification. So something is needed to give it the signification 'triangle in general', and Hume suggests that it is the word that plays this role.

But what is it that gives the *word* its general signification? Hume's explanation will remain incomplete until this question has been answered. However, he has made some progress by bringing in words. For the word 'triangle', unlike the image that the thinker is using, does select a single signification, the one that the thinker wants. But does it achieve this effect by the passive operation of the association of ideas?

Surely not, and if Hume had examined the function of words more closely, he would have come to see that, in a piece of directed thinking (as opposed to day-dreaming), words do not occur in our minds by mere association, just as they do not occur in our sentences by mere association when we are speaking. Meaning cannot be explained without bringing in the concepts of choice and intention and drawing on the nature of activities rather than the nature of passive processes.

When Hume relies on words to solve the problem of the multiple significations of images, he is really exploiting the active character of directed thought. But he exploits it without acknowledging it, because he does not even ask himself what gives a word its selective power. He merely helps himself to the selectivity of words in order to get out of a difficulty, and he does not inquire into the origin of their selectivity. So it would be a fair verdict on this part of his theory of mind that it tacitly relies on unexamined features of language. He follows his chosen psychological path under the guidance of language, but never stops to examine the features of the guide.

If he had been going to examine them, he would have had to go back and take another look at the way in which we acquire general ideas. He would have needed to ask himself how we set up the general words which are going to be so useful later when we are employing the general ideas in thinking. The answer would have to be that we select the different lines of resemblance radiating out from the white marble sphere, or whatever the object happens to be, and that we attach a different word to each of them and thereafter intentionally maintain the attachments. These are all things that we do, activities.

It is interesting to observe that, in his account of the acquisition of general ideas, Hume points out that we 'consider the figure and colour [of the sphere] together . . . but still view them in different aspects, according to the resemblances, of which they are susceptible'.[30] Is this a passive seeing-as, or is it the more active kind of seeing-as, where we choose to see the object in one way rather than another? The answer would have been plain if he had gone on to consider the setting up of general words attached to general ideas. Anyone who was faced with that task would deliberately think of one of the lines of resemblance, and attach a word to it. He would also deliberately continue to maintain the use of each word with its own original meaning. These are activities. It is worth adding that later, when this person was employing the word in a piece of directed thinking, he would choose it to express his thought. For that kind of thinking is a clear case of an activity. So here too Hume's passive model of the mind is inadequate.

These inadequacies are conceded by his tacit reliance on the guidance given by language. So the best strategy for an interpreter is to offer him a dilemma: either dispense with that guidance or scrutinize it. If he dispenses with it, this part of his theory of mind will disintegrate. If he scrutinizes it, this part of his theory of mind will need to be changed by the substitution of active for passive processes. This is a strategy that will often be used in the chapters that follow.

[30] *Treatise*, p. 25.

3

Memory

THE previous chapter was mainly concerned with ideas or images as bearers of meanings. However, the point was made that they sometimes occur as something less than that, namely as mere data, and that they sometimes occur as something more than that, namely as would-be bearers of truth.[1] This chapter and the next one will deal with occurrences of both these further kinds, especially the second kind. For the topics to be discussed in them, Hume's accounts of memory, belief, and existence, will throw light on the transition from the theory of ideas developed as a psychological analogue of a theory of meaning to the theory of ideas developed as a psychological analogue of a theory of truth and evidence.

It may seem surprising that three such disparate topics should all contribute to making this transition intelligible. So perhaps it would be best to begin by describing some of the connections of thought that are going to be traced in these two chapters.

The discussion will start from the fact that ideas or images can occur in the three different ways that have just been mentioned. Their occurrence as mere data, for example, in day-dreaming and in sequences of hypnagogic imagery, is relatively unproblematical, and the only difficulty is to keep this kind of occurrence clearly separated from the other two. It is here that Hume's discussion of memory first becomes relevant. For when he speaks of 'ideas of memory', he often has in mind the straightforward kind of case in which an image just floats into a person's mind, presumably as the result of some previous experience, but without any reference to the particular occasion of it. These cases are not hard to understand, but he does not mark them off from the next kind of case, where the image functions as a bearer of meaning. Nor does he mark them off from the third kind of case, where it also functions as a would-be bearer of truth, or separate the

[1] See above, pp. 16–17.

second and third kinds of case from one another. It is not just that he is unsuccessful at drawing these distinctions: he does not make any attempt to draw them.

This deficiency in his treatment of memory is very clear. For it is obvious that memory is not always manifested in stray images, but often brings thoughts about one's past, and that those thoughts must have been put together in ways that gave them meanings. For example, you may ask yourself whether you really locked the front door when you left home. That is a question with a reference to your own past and, therefore, a question for your memory, but, before you answer it, you must understand it. Then you will answer it, if you can, by making the memory-judgement, that you did lock it. Suppose now that your memory-question and the answer that you give it in your mind both involve images.[2] Then we will want to know what Hume has to say about the occurrence of the images at the two different stages, one involving the understanding of a meaning and the other a claim to truth. It will emerge later in this chapter that, unfortunately, he fails to distinguish the occurrences of images at these two stages both from their first kind of occurrence, as mere data, and from one another. The second of these two failures is a particularly clear example of his general failure to mark the transition from his theory of ideas developed as a psychological analogue of a theory of meaning to its development as a theory of truth and evidence.[3]

This deficiency in Hume's theory of ideas is connected with another point made at the end of the previous chapter. It was noted there that when he is developing the theory, he tacitly relies on the guidance provided by the words that express the ideas. The example given was the use that he makes of the 'term annexed to a general idea' to solve the problem of the multiple 'general significations' of a single image.[4] Here, in the fusion of the two entirely different functions, the bearing

[2] Hume's apparent assumption that all memory involves images is, of course, an exaggeration.

[3] Memory-judgements are immediate and not based on evidence, but Hume takes on the task of finding a property of memory-images which will serve as a criterion of their truth. His failure to give a clear indication of the transition from meaning to truth is an important feature of his theory of ideas and it has encouraged the two extreme interpretations, one of which underestimates his concern with truth while the other underestimates his concern with meaning. See above, pp. 4–10.

[4] Another example is his use of definitions to guide his analysis of complex ideas. He never stops to examine different kinds of definition, or to ask himself why he is always guided by conjunctive definitions listing the intrinsic properties of the things defined. See above, pp. 4 and 20–1.

of meaning and the bearing of truth, we have a much more far-reaching example of the same tendency to exploit the guidance provided by language without stopping to look at the features of the guide. If he had looked more closely at the way language works, he would never have made the transition from meaning to truth in the realm of ideas without marking it clearly and explaining it.

The next chapter will deal with the other two topics, belief and existence. Hume's account of belief has an obvious relevance to the transition from ideas as bearers of meaning to ideas as would-be bearers of truth. He gives a very sketchy account of the meanings of the ideas that are involved in beliefs, because he is in a hurry to get on to the question that he finds more interesting, namely the question of the evidence for them and how it generates them. Some of the details of this part of his theory of ideas were given at the end of Chapter 1 in the introductory remarks about singular causal inferences.[5] That was just another way of approaching the same topic, under a different name. For his theory of belief and his theory of causal inference are one and the same theory. This may seem surprising, but the reason for it is simple: he held that all belief is inferential and that the only kind of inference which takes us beyond what is perceived at the moment is causal.[6]

Perhaps it would be useful to include in this introductory section a few more details of this particularly rapid transition from ideas as bearers of meaning to ideas as would-be bearers of truth. The best way to do this would be to pick up some of the points made in the review of singular judgements in Chapter 1.[7]

It was pointed out there that a thought always has a certain internal complexity: in Hume's system a reference is made to a sense-impression and something is said about it. Now when an image functions as a bearer of meaning, it corresponds only to what is said about the impression—the predicate—and so something else is needed to effect the reference to it. This is a problem which does not arise for Hume in cases of immediate perception, because he treats perceptual knowledge as intuitive (as if impressions identified themselves and spoke for themselves).[8] But it does arise for him in the case of memory, because memory requires the target of reference to be picked out from

---

[5] See above, pp. 12–15.
[7] See above, pp. 11–15.
[6] See below, pp. 70–4.
[8] See above, p. 11.

the person's past. However, he offers no solution to it in this case, and he seems to assume that the context in which the image occurs—perhaps a particular task of recollection—will supply the reference that he needs. In the third case, singular causal inference, or belief, things work out rather better for him. For in his analysis of what we observe on the billiards table he might perhaps claim that the impression of the white ball's impact on the red one yields the required reference to the red one, and enables the observer first to consider the possibility that it may now move, and, secondly, to infer that it will now move. So in this case he may be able to provide the reference that is needed both for the thought that occurs and for the belief which it becomes.

At this point it is worth asking a general question about his procedure. Why does he attach so little importance to the internal structure of these singular thoughts? If composition is essential to all thoughts, his neglect of it is surprising. It is all the more surprising in a philosopher who was so concerned with the kind of external connection between two thoughts which is expressed in a singular causal inference. If he analysed the structure of molecular thoughts, why did he leave the structure of atomic thoughts unanalysed?

An easy answer to this question would be that his psychology is primitive. What it corresponds to in language is not full sentences but only single words. To put it in another way, he describes a style of thinking more like the style that we might attribute to animals without speech. A dog is hungry and it has an image of the spot where it buried the bone,[9] and it searches for a sense-impression to match the image, etc.

But that is hardly an explanation of Hume's strange neglect of the composition of thoughts. If we want an explanation, we must go to the last of the three topics, existence, which will be discussed in the next chapter. In his brief treatment of it, he claims that there is no difference between the idea of X and the idea of X as an existing thing. In one way he is right: *existence* is not an idea like others, to be added to the list of the intrinsic properties of a thing and included in its conjunctive definition.[10] However, from this he drew the mistaken conclusion that the only difference between thinking of a thing and judging that it exists lies in the strength and liveliness of your idea of it. That cannot be right. When you think of a thing, all that is required is that

---

[9] Or, at least, such an image is the most that we could attribute to the dog.

[10] See Kant, *Critique of Pure Reason*, trans. N. Kemp Smith (London: Macmillan, 1929), pp. 500–7 ('The Impossibility of an Ontological Proof of the Existence of God').

the idea of it should occur in your mind, but the composition of a complex idea out of simple ones will never amount either to the thought 'This is how things may be' or to the belief 'This is how they are'. The elements of this kind of thought are put together in a different way, as a possible shot at the truth, and the belief is the actual shot. His failure to appreciate this difference seems to be the explanation of his neglect of the composition of thoughts: he believed that it was adequately covered by his account of the composition of complex ideas.[11]

This introduction to the three topics, memory, belief, and existence, has tried to show how they are all connected with the transition from images as bearers of meaning to images as would-be bearers of truth. These two functions of images must be kept distinct from one another, and both must be kept distinct from their mere occurrence as data without any function. Hume does not succeed in marking these distinctions properly, and his failure is illustrated very clearly by his treatment of the three topics. In spite of this failure, he succeeded in achieving profound insights when he went on to investigate the three difficult problems, causal necessity, personal identity, and our knowledge of the world outside our minds. So the final verdict will be that his psychological apparatus was primitive, but the results that he achieved with it brilliant.

The first of the three topics is memory, and it will occupy the rest of this chapter. Hume approaches it by asking how we distinguish between ideas of memory and ideas of imagination. Part of his answer is that 'memory preserves the original form, in which its objects were presented', whereas 'the imagination is not restrain'd to the same order and form with the original impressions'.[12] However, he is aware that 'this difference is not sufficient to distinguish them in their operation, or make us know the one from the other; it being impossible to recall[13] the past impressions, in order to compare them with our present ideas, and see whether their arrangement be exactly similar'.[14] What is needed is a contemporary property possessed by ideas of memory but not by ideas of imagination, a property which we can immediately observe in the ideas the moment they occur.

---

[11] See below, pp. 55–9, for the details of this difficult phase in Hume's theory of mind.

[12] *A Treatise of Human Nature*, ed. P. H. Nidditch (Oxford: Clarendon Press, 1989), 9.

[13] i.e. impossible to bring back.

[14] Ibid. 85.

His suggestion is 'the superior force and vivacity' of ideas of memory.[15] In his first treatment of the topic, he says that, when an impression reappears in the mind as a memory, 'it retains a considerable degree of its first vivacity, and is somewhat intermediate betwixt an impression and an idea',[16] but in his second treatment of it, he speaks of *impressions* of memory and not *ideas* of memory.[17] Whichever term he uses for them, the criterial property, which shows that they belong to memory rather than to imagination, is always force and vivacity, strength and liveliness. Memory 'paints its objects in more distinct colours, than any which are employ'd by the latter'.[18] 'When we remember any past event, the idea of it flows in upon the mind in a forcible manner.'[19]

It is worth remarking that the last two quotations specify the criterion in very different ways. The first one explains 'force and vivacity' as a *pictorial property* of an image, namely distinctness of colours, whereas the second one explains it as a *behavioural property*, or feature of the way in which the image enters the mind: 'it flows in upon the mind in a forcible manner'. Hume shows the same ambivalence about specifying the criterion in his second discussion of memory.[20]

Both discussions are very dense and impacted. So the first thing that needs to be done is to shake them out and let in some air and daylight. We may start from the distinctions, already drawn, between the three ways in which images may occur in the mind.

The first kind of occurrence of an image or idea was occurrence as a mere datum. This sort of thing happens in day-dreaming but not in directed thinking. Now, according to Hume, all ideas are derived from previous impressions, either as a direct record or after some rearrangement and shuffling. So it looks as if, when he marks off ideas of memory from those of imagination, he is merely marking off ideas that are derived as a direct record from the remainder that are derived by rearrangement.

---

[15] *Treatise*, p. 85.   [16] Ibid. 8.   [17] Ibid. 84.
[18] Ibid. 9.
[19] Ibid.
[20] Ibid. 85. He speaks of the 'lively colours' of ideas of memory, but he also describes a case of recollection in which someone suddenly becomes convinced that this is how it was, and then 'the very same ideas now appear in a new light, and have, in a manner, a different feeling from what they had before. Without any other alteration beside that of the feeling, they become immediately ideas of the memory, and are assented to.' (This case is described in a passage in the Appendix which, Hume says, should be inserted at this point in the main text. See pp. 627–8.)

However, that cannot really have been his intention. If it had been his intention, his answer to the question about the derivation of our ideas could have been put very simply like this: 'They are all memories.' For, it makes no difference to his empiricism that some of them are shuffled memories and others unshuffled memories. But he *does* say that it makes a difference—the difference between memory and imagination.

It follows that he must have been thinking of a narrower set of memory-situations. But which narrower set? The most plausible suggestion is that he was thinking of cases where a definite reference is made to something in the past experience of the person who remembers. This is certainly the kind of case he is describing in his second discussion of memory: 'It frequently happens, that when two men have been engag'd in any scene of action, the one shall remember it much better than the other, and shall have all the difficulty in the world to make his companion recollect it.'[21]

But where in his theory of ideas is there any explanation of the definite reference to the past experience of the person who remembers? He must be relying on definite reference to mark off the kind of memory-situation with which he is concerned, but he seems to be taking it from the context, without ever explaining it or trying to integrate it into his own psychological theory. So the two men in the example given in his second discussion of memory talk about the past 'scene of action', and the one who remembers it more clearly succeeds in reminding the other of the details.[22] But what is *it*? The definite reference is fixed only by the context and within Hume's theory there is no psychological analogue of the linguistic devices that fix it in real life.

This is a clear example of the consequences of failing to allow for the complexity of singular atomic thoughts. One essential element, the definite reference, in this case to an occasion in the past, is left out. Hume could have incorporated it in his theory only if he had looked more carefully at the way language works and modelled his psychology more closely on its working. This is a serious fault, because the excluded element, definite reference to the past, is essential to the specification of the narrower set of memory-situations with which he

---

[21] Ibid. 627. It is this conversation between two men which ends in the way described in the passage cited in the previous note.

[22] Ibid.

was concerned. He cannot have intended his account of memory to cover *all* occurrences of ideas derived directly, and without rearrangement from impressions. For, if he did not restrict the set of such occurrences by tacitly presupposing definite references to the past, his account of memory would merely be a restatement of his empiricist theory of the derivation of ideas, and, in that case, there would be no need to exclude those complex ideas which do not, as they stand, match complex impressions but result from the rearrangement of simple ideas matching simple impressions.

At this point we need to take care not to exaggerate the criticism. A qualification is needed, because, although a definite reference to the past is needed for some memories in the restricted set, it is not needed for all of them. It is needed for cases of recollection, like the one described in his second discussion of memory. But in that kind of case the image is not a mere datum but a bearer of meaning and a would-be bearer of truth. If we looked at cases of memory in which images occur as mere data, we might find that his account fared better.

Let us see. When an image or idea occurs as a mere datum, are we to take Hume to mean that it is *always* a memory unless it is the result of rearrangement? If so, his account of memory would merely be a restatement of his empiricism in an unnecessarily restricted field. The restriction—to unrearranged ideas—would be inexplicable in a general statement of his empiricist theory of the derivation of ideas. So, as before, he needs some way of picking out a narrower set of ideas occurring as mere data, a narrower set which really will count as memories in some stronger sense (parallel to, but different from the sense in which the set of ideas occurring in cases of recollection count as memories).

Now when an image occurs as a mere datum, what makes it a memory in a stronger sense cannot be a definite reference to the past, as it was in cases of recollection, because in this kind of case there is no definite reference to the past. However, the person who gets the image will sometimes feel that there is an indefinite reference to the past, and that might give Hume the narrower set of memory-situations that he evidently needs at this point. For example, an image of a particular human face floats into your mind while you are day-dreaming and it strikes you as familiar. That means that it strikes you as a face that you have seen somewhere before, and so it supplies the indefinite reference to the past that Hume needs at this point.

Notice, incidentally, that you would probably then go on to ask yourself, 'Where have I seen this face? Whose is it?' That would be a question of recollection and the answer to it would be a *definite* reference to someone in your past experience. Here, of course, the image comes first, and the definite reference is dredged up as the solution to the problem of recollection. In Hume's other example, the conversation between the two men, the definite reference came first, and the man with the weaker memory then tried to dredge up *images* as the solution to his problem of recollection.[23] The two examples exhibit opposite directions of fit, and the second type is, perhaps, commoner.

There is also another interesting case, lying on the same line as the stray image of a face that strikes you as familiar, but further out on it. Suppose that the image does *not* strike you as familiar, and a friend asks you to draw it on paper, looks at the drawing, and tells you that it is the face of someone at school with you long ago. Then this image too is a memory of a kind, but further out on the familiarity-line, because it did not strike you as familiar, although, perhaps, it ought to have done so.

So here we have the qualification that needs to be made to the criticism of this part of Hume's theory: he has to pick out some narrower set of memory-situations than the set that he explicitly picks out, but he does not have to require a definite reference to the past in every case. Such a reference is not needed when an image occurs as a mere datum, and for *those* occurrences the feeling that there is an indefinite reference to the past is sufficient but not absolutely necessary.

Let me sum up this discussion of reference to the past. In cases of recollection, there is a definite reference to something in the past, but in Hume's account of memory this reference is simply borrowed from the context, and it is not achieved by any psychological device within his system. However, images that occur as mere data do not have either of the two functions of images used in recollection: they are not bearers of meaning and they do not contribute to any shot at the truth. So, naturally, they are not associated with definite references to things in the past. They are never a solution to a problem, but, if anything, they pose one, for example, 'Where have I seen this face before?'

It is, however, important that on some occasions the person who has an image will feel that there is an indefinite reference to the past, though, of course, he will not feel this in every case of an image which

---

[23] See above, n. 20.

has not been rearranged. So unless Hume's account of memory simply repeats his account of the derivation of ideas—which it does not, because, if it did, there would be no need to confine it to unrearranged ideas—he must restrict its scope, and the most plausible restriction would be to cases where there is either a definite reference to something in the past or else the feeling that there is an indefinite reference.

Cases of recollection evidently rely on images occurring not only as bearers of meaning but also as would-be bearers of truth. But before we investigate recollection, there are three more points that need to be made about the first kind of occurrence of images, as mere data.

First, it would be quite wrong to look for a *pictorial* property of such images which would serve as an indication that they were unrearranged copies of complex impressions. For example, it would be absurd to claim that the pictorial property, *distinctness of colours*, played that role. How could it possibly do that, if the original impression was dim, as it might well happen to be? Secondly, in any case, we know that what does play this role is the relational property, *striking the person as familiar*. Thirdly, it would be a mistake to infer that this relational property is going to play a similar role, or indeed any role, in cases of recollection, where images occur not as data, but as bearers of meaning and would-be bearers of truth. The magnitude of this mistake will emerge in what follows.

Perhaps the best way to approach the question, how Hume's account of memory applies to recollection, is to start from the way in which he sees the problem of memory. He sees it as the problem of distinguishing ideas of memory from ideas of imagination. But what is this distinction which he takes to be marked by these words, 'memory' and 'imagination'? The trouble is that there are two different distinctions that could be drawn with the words, and it is not clear which one he has in mind.

One distinction is between remembering and imagining regarded as two things that we do, two different activities. For example, my wife visits me in hospital and asks me to remember what happened when I drove through the red stop-light. Alternatively, suppose that I am luckier and do not hit another car, and she gives me a lecture on dangerous driving, and says 'Imagine what would have happened if that other car had had slightly faster acceleration.' I am obviously being asked to do two different things in these two scenes, and this is one of the distinctions between remembering and imagining.

The other distinction is a subdivision of cases where I am trying to remember. I may remember the accident correctly, in which case my wife would say 'Good, at least you remember that.' Alternatively, I may get it all wrong, in which case she would say 'No, you are just imagining that it happened like that.' This is a different use of the verb 'to imagine', because what it means here is 'to suppose incorrectly'; and it is also a different use of the verb 'to remember', because what it means here is 'to remember correctly'. So here is a different distinction marked by the verbs 'to imagine' and 'to remember'. It is one thing to distinguish two activities, and quite another thing to take one of them and distinguish between its correct and its incorrect performance.

Which of these two distinctions was Hume thinking of when he looked for the difference between ideas of memory and ideas of imagination? Surprisingly, that is not at all clear. Sometimes he is evidently thinking of the activity of imagining and deliberate fiction, for example, 'The fables we meet with in poems and romances'[24] and 'the case of liars; who by frequent repetition of their lies, come at last to believe and remember them, as realities'.[25] Here he is trying to mark the difference between this kind of activity and the activity of remembering, which, at this stage, might be correct or incorrect. At other times, he is clearly thinking of remembering correctly: for example, in the conversation between the two men 'the one shall remember it much better than the other'.[26]

Now Hume only offers a single criterion to distinguish ideas of memory from ideas of imagination, namely strength and liveliness. But it is impossible to rely on a single criterion to mark two different distinctions. It follows that the most charitable interpretation of his procedure is to take him to be concerned with the difference between remembering correctly and *both* the other two things, remembering incorrectly and deliberate fantasizing.

This is not a pedantic criticism. On the contrary, it strikes at one of the central weak points of his system, its failure to start with questions about meaning and settle them first, before going on to questions about truth. In the case of memory, he is mainly concerned with truth, but he tries to extend his criterion of truth backwards to cover the prior problem of meaning. This attempt is doomed to fail for the reason that

[24] *Treatise*, p. 10.
[25] Ibid. 86. This is an interesting type of case, which starts with deliberate fantasizing but ends with acceptance and the speaker's mistaken impression that he is remembering what actually happened.
[26] This is how the passage quoted above, n. 20, begins. See *Treatise*, pp. 627–8.

has just been given; it is impossible to use the same criterion to solve these two entirely different problems. But there is also another, more profound error underneath that one: if you use an image in a piece of deliberate fantasizing, that will be a fact about the way you mean it, and it is a mistake to expect that fact to be marked by *any* property of the image—least of all by one of its pictorial properties.[27]

There is a well-known argument designed to show that this would be a mistake. Suppose that you try to imagine a dragon, a fictitious animal, but you are unsuccessful, because your image comes out as an image of an iguana, a real animal. The first point to notice is that even though what you were engaged in doing ended in failure, there is no doubt at all that you really were engaged in doing just what you would have said, if asked, namely imagining a dragon. Exactly the same verdict would be given in the parallel case, where you were engaged in drawing a dragon on paper but only succeeded in producing a picture of an iguana.

Now, to go back to your mental image, what makes it an image of a dragon, even if it is incorrect? The answer must be 'your intention'— that is what you are engaged in imagining, a dragon. It would be a mistake to look for pictorial properties of the image to serve as criteria for your description of your image when you are getting it. It would be a mistake, because you might be very bad at getting an image of a dragon. Similarly, it would be a mistake to judge what you were engaged in drawing by the result.

This point must not be exaggerated. There will obviously be a lot of correlation between intention and achievement. But the achievement is not the *criterion* of the intention. So no *pictorial* property of the image that you get will ever be a decisive indication of what you were engaged in imagining.

Then how do you know whether you are engaged in imagining rather than remembering? You do not need any criterion for that. You just *mean* your mental image in one way rather than the other. This is the point that Hume misses completely, and then tries to cover by extending his answer to the question of truth back to the prior question of meaning.

It is interesting to observe that, when he was faced by another problem about meaning, the meaning of an image functioning as a

---

[27] See above, p. 36, for an explanation of the difference between pictorial and behavioural properties of images.

general idea, he realized that it cannot depend entirely on the pictorial properties of the image.[28] However, that was because he realized that a single image could not possibly match all the various instantiations of the general idea. Here, in the analysis of imagining, the reason for the inadequacy of the pictorial properties of the image is quite different. Your image of a dragon is not required to achieve the impossible feat of multiple match: it is just that the image is your fallible achievement, and, therefore, not a sure indication of what you were engaged in doing.

Before we move on from meaning to truth, let us pause to review the points made about the meanings of recollections which Hume either covers inadequately or does not cover at all. First, memory-judgements of this kind, like any other judgements, have a certain minimal complexity of structure. For they need to offer not only a description (in Hume's theory an image playing a descriptive role), but also a definite reference to something in the past to which the description is being attached. There is nothing in his theory to cover this aspect of recollection. Secondly, the making of a memory-judgement of this kind is something that a person does, an activity. Hume does try to cover this point, by distinguishing the activity of recalling how things were from the very different activity of imagining how they might have been. However, he tries to pick out the activity by using as its criterion a property of the images involved.

There are two things wrong with this. First, the image is the recollector's achievement and it is a mistake to use any of its properties as a criterion of the activity in which he is engaged. Secondly, even if a property of images could be offered as a criterion of the activity, it could not possibly be the *same* property as the one that is offered as a criterion of correctness or truth.

Finally, there is the problem of truth, and the question whether any contemporary criterion of accuracy is available to a person trying to recollect something from his past. Hume proposes 'force and vivacity' of image to play this role. Henceforth we may ignore his misguided attempt to extend this criterion backwards to deal with the prior problem of meaning. How does it fare simply as a criterion of truth?

The first thing that needs to be done is to pick up a question of interpretation that was posed earlier in this chapter.[29] Does he intend

---

[28] See above, p. 28.   [29] See above, p. 36.

'strength and vivacity' to be a *pictorial property* of images, namely distinctness of colours, as he suggests in his first discussion of memory,[30] or does he intend it to be a *behavioural property*, a feature of the way an image enters the mind ('it flows in upon the mind in a forcible manner')?

It can easily be demonstrated that no pictorial property of images can possibly serve as a criterion of truth. All that is needed is an adaptation of an argument used above.[31] Whatever pictorial property is proposed as a criterion of truth, it may well happen that the thing in the past lacked that property. For example, you are told that memory 'paints its objects in more distinct colours',[32] and then you are asked to recall a dim and foggy scene. What can you do? If you get an image that satisfies this criterion of truth, it will fail to match the original scene and, therefore, it will be false. If, on the other hand, you get a true image, matching the original scene, this criterion will tell you that it is false. But that is absurd. Therefore, the only hope for this part of Hume's theory lies in the other interpretation of 'strength and vivacity'.

The source of the absurdity is interesting. When someone uses an image in an attempt to recall a scene from his past, the image functions as part of an internal memory-judgement — 'This is how it was . . . IMAGE'. So the *meaning* of the judgement will depend on the pictorial properties of the image. It follows that the *truth* of the judgement cannot be settled by the presence of any *single* pictorial property serving as a *general* criterion of accuracy. For that would produce the absurd consequence that a memory-judgement involving an image *with* this chosen property could not be false, while one involving an image *without* it could not be true. If the pictorial properties of images contribute to the various meanings of different internal memory-judgements, then it is not going to be possible for any single pictorial property to serve as a general criterion of their truth. Again, Hume's neglect of meaning wrecks his account of truth.

The remedy is to switch to the other interpretation of 'strength and vivacity'. They are features of the way images enter the mind. When Hume's account of memory is taken in this way, it works much better. You ask yourself what a particular acquaintance of yours looks like, and you get an image in response to your self-addressed question. If this image is stubborn and difficult to alter, if it maintains itself as your

---

[30] *Treatise*, p. 9. [31] See above, p. 40. [32] *Treatise*, p. 9.

pictorial answer to the question, that is a fairly good indication of its accuracy. What more could we reasonably expect?

However, this criterion of truth works only in the context of a question that has been asked. If a certain image kept recurring as a datum and you could not get rid of it, that would not be any indication of its truth. For what would it be true of? There would be no definite reference and so no possibility of truth, and the stubbornness of the image would merely indicate an obsession.

4

Belief and Existence

HUME'S theory of belief is naturalistic. He wanted to determine how much we may legitimately believe, and he thought that the way to do this was to start by inquiring what belief is, and how it works. When we know what belief is and what it actually does, we will be better able to establish the limits of what it can do. Here, as elsewhere, the solution to philosophical problems is to be extracted from the science of the human mind.

In the Preface the point was made that Hume's theory of mind has two distinct aspects. On the one hand, he faces the question 'What ideas may we legitimately have?' ('Which of our ideas are genuine?'), and here his answer runs parallel to a modern theory of meaning. On the other hand, he faces the question 'What may we legitimately believe?', and here his answer makes a direct contribution to the theory of knowledge. Some commentators see the second question as the key to his philosophy and attach less importance to the first one,[1] but the interpretation offered in this book gives the two questions parity and argues that Hume's answers to them are closely interdependent.[2]

So in the examination of belief in this chapter the same line will be taken as in the examination of memory. The aim will be to exhibit the connections between the two inquiries, one into meaning and the other into truth and evidence, and to show that here too Hume made the transition to the second one before he had dealt fully with the first one.

The explanation of his theory of belief must start with some indication of its scope. He held that all belief is inferential and that the only kind of inference that takes us beyond what we perceive at the moment is causal inference.[3] His arguments for this view will be given later.[4] In

---

[1] See above, pp. 4–10.
[2] See above, pp. 10–15.
[3] See above, p. 33.
[4] See below, pp. 69–74.

effect, it draws a very sharp line between belief and immediate judgement. Memory is immediate and, therefore, strictly speaking, not an example of belief.[5] Perceptual judgements, which scarcely figure in Hume's system, would also be immediate.[6] Belief begins when we venture out from what is immediately given along lines of causal inference.

Like any scientist starting in a new field, Hume has to give a precise account of the object of his investigation, and he has to explain how it works. So he divides this part of the *Treatise* into two chapters, one 'Of the Nature of the Idea, or Belief',[7] and the other 'Of the Causes of Belief'.[8] Naturally, his treatment of such a central topic as belief spreads itself through other chapters,[9] but the essence of it is given in these two. We may follow his division of the subject and begin with the question 'What is belief?' That will occupy the rest of this chapter and the question about the causes of belief will be taken up in the next one.

We are all familiar with the cycle of starting, continuing, and ceasing to believe things, but it is not at all easy to say what this believing is. Hume draws heavily on his theory of ideas when he answers the question. His answer is that belief is 'a lively idea produc'd by a relation to a present impression'.[10] His arguments for this conclusion are intricate and will need careful analysis. But, first, let us ask how his account of belief is related to his account of memory, examined in the previous chapter.

This question will have to be dealt with in two stages. First, we need to discover his view of the content of a belief, and then we go on to ask how believing latches on to the content.

A belief is, for Hume, the conclusion of a causal inference, and so the content of a belief will.be whatever psychological counterpart his system provides for such conclusions. What it provides is an idea, a complex idea, perhaps, but still only an idea, and not a complete internalized judgement.

[5] Hume does not always speak so strictly. On p. 86 of the *Treatise* he talks about 'the *belief* or *assent* which always attends the memory and senses'.

[6] See above, p. 11.

[7] *A Treatise of Human Nature*, ed. P. H. Nidditch (Oxford: Clarendon Press, 1989), 94–8.

[8] Ibid. 98–106.

[9] See especially *Treatise*, pp. 10–13, 'Of the Connexion or Association of Ideas', pp. 13–15, 'Of Relations', and pp. 86–94, 'Of the Inference from the Impression to the Idea'.

[10] Ibid. 97. He restates this conclusion with rather less confidence, but without altering it, in the Appendix to the *Treatise*, pp. 624–7.

Suppose a person present with me, who advances propositions, to which I do not assent ... notwithstanding my incredulity, I clearly understand his meaning, and form all the same ideas, which he forms. My imagination is endow'd with the same powers as his; nor is it possible for him to conceive any idea, which I cannot conceive; or conjoin any, which I cannot conjoin.[11]

Identity of content, which is needed for disagreement as well as for agreement, is assured by identity of idea.

We need not dwell on the fact that, in Hume's system, the content of a belief is merely a cluster of ideas and not an internalized proposition. This fact will become important in a moment, when we look at his arguments for his view, but now, when we are only trying to understand what his view amounts to, it is enough to observe that what he leaves out is the singular reference which is needed to pin the inference on to the world. This is the same fault that was found in his account of the content of memory. The judgement 'It will move'—a causal inference—needs a mechanism for securing a definite reference, just like the judgement 'It did move', based on memory. The only difference between the two cases is that, if an idea is to serve as the content of a memory-claim, there must be something in the context, perhaps the asking of a question of recollection, to supply the required reference; whereas, in a causal inference, the reference may, perhaps, be gathered from the premiss.[12]

The second question was 'How does believing latch on to its content?' Hume's answer is the same as it was for memory. Belief is not a separate idea, but a special property of another idea, the idea which fixes the content of the belief, and this special property is liveliness. The difference between an idea as the content of a memory and an idea as the content of a belief is simply that in the case of memory the liveliness is achieved by the idea immediately, whereas in the case of belief it is transferred to the idea from a present sense-impression along the track formed by an association.[13]

The arguments for this view of the nature of the idea of belief will be given in a moment. Meanwhile, it is worth observing that Hume makes it absolutely clear that the liveliness of an idea of belief is not a pictorial property. In fact, he uses an argument like the one used in the previous chapter to show that, in the case of memory, the liveliness of an image

[11] *Treatise*, p. 95.
[12] See above, pp. 12, 33–4, and 37. Of course, the suggestion that the definite reference may be gathered from the premiss merely shifts the problem to another point.
[13] See above, pp. 12–15.

could not be a pictorial property, because, if it were, the content of the memory-claim would be changed by the actual remembering.

When you wou'd any way vary the idea of a particular object, you can only encrease or diminish its force and vivacity. If you make any other change on it, it represents a different object or impression. The case is the same as in colours. A particular shade of any colour may acquire a new degree of liveliness or brightness without any other variation. But when you produce any other variation, 'tis no longer the same shade of colour. So that as belief does nothing but vary the manner, in which we conceive any object, it can only bestow on our ideas an additional force and vivacity.[14]

The use of the word 'brightness' is unfortunate here, but Hume is clearly trying to formulate the principle that content remains unchanged through all vicissitudes of belief, disbelief, and suspension of belief.[15]

These remarks about the idea of belief confirm the interpretation of his theory of memory given in the previous chapter. It was argued there that, if strength and liveliness were pictorial properties of memory-images, it would be futile asking a person to recollect a dim, foggy scene, using an image.[16]

It is, nevertheless, difficult to be sure exactly what non-pictorial property of images Hume has in mind. Sometimes he uses words like 'brightness' which are more appropriate to a pictorial property. However, he immediately backs away from this implication and calls the property that he has in mind *'solidity*, or *firmness*, or *steadiness'*, which

gives [the ideas of belief] more force and influence; makes them appear of greater importance; infixes them in the mind; and renders them the governing principles of all our actions.[17]

In the next chapter, 'Of the Causes of Belief', he calls it, rather disarmingly,

that certain *je-ne-scai-quoi*, of which 'tis impossible to give any definition or description, but which every one sufficiently understands.[18]

---

[14] *Treatise*, p. 96.
[15] See the passage paraphrased above, ch. 3 n. 20. Cf. p. 94, where he says, 'When I think of God ... as existent, and when I believe him to be existent, my idea of him neither encreases nor diminishes.'
[16] See above, pp. 43–4.
[17] *Treatise*, p. 629. This passage in the Appendix should be inserted, Hume tells us, in the text near the end of the section 'Of the Nature of the Idea, or Belief'.
[18] Ibid. 106.

Finally, in the Appendix to the *Treatise*, he again stresses the effect of this property of ideas of belief on our actions:

They strike upon us with more force; they are more present to us; the mind has a firmer hold of them, and is more actuated and mov'd by them ... In short, they approach nearer to the impressions, which are immediately present to us ... [19]

It is clear that he wanted to avoid the notion that strength and vivacity are pictorial properties of ideas of belief. However, it is not so clear why his positive account of the properties is so elusive. He is quite sure that *he* knows which properties he means, but curiously unconcerned by his inability to specify them. He even comes near to saying that they are unique.[20]

I confess, that 'tis impossible to explain perfectly this feeling or manner of conception. We may make use of words, that express something near it. But its true and proper name is *belief*, which is a term that every one sufficiently understands in common life.[21]

However, this would be a confession of a failure of the science of the human mind. For, as he says later in the Appendix to the *Treatise*,

... if it be not analogous to any other sentiment, we must despair of explaining its causes, and must consider it as an original principle of the human mind. If it be analogous, we may hope to explain its causes from analogy, and trace it up to more general principles.[22]

A clue to his difficulty may be found in his remarks about the effect of belief on action. This aspect of belief has led many philosophers to treat it as dispositional: to put their point very roughly, to believe something is to behave as if it were so. Now this treats belief as a state which persists through time, instead of treating it in Hume's way as a mental event or occurrence. It also connects belief with action and so, at least, reduces the burden of explanation placed by Hume on the phenomenology of the mental occurrence that he tries to identify.

So perhaps his mental occurrences are *not even a necessary part* of the analysis of belief. This would not mean that they never occur, but only that they are never essential. What is essential is the behavioural sequel, the deployment of the disposition in appropriate circum-

---

[19] *Treatise*, pp. 624–5.
[20] Or *sui generis*, as philosophers in this predicament sometimes say.
[21] Ibid. 629. See above, n. 18.
[22] *Treatise*, p. 624.

stances. To believe something is to hold it true, but to hold to its truth in one's actions. Images may well occur at the beginning, when the dispositional state is established, and they may even occur insistently, but, if they are not essential, it will be a mistake to seek for the essence of belief in any of their properties. Instead of saying, as Hume does, that there must be ideas 'which approach nearer to impressions', we may say that the believer must behave in much the same way that he would have behaved if he had received impressions.[23]

If this is the right way of looking at belief, it explains Hume's inability to specify the properties of its ideas or images. For in many cases nothing of this kind will occur, and, even when it does occur, the only property which it can possibly possess in order to explain the behavioural sequel *in every case* would be *whatever property causes the sequel*. But that shows that, even when these occurrences can be found, their phenomenology is not really explanatory.

Here we have the reason why Hume found it so difficult to give a positive account of belief: he was looking in the wrong place. His phrase 'idea of belief' is, after all, ambiguous. No doubt, it can be interpreted to mean, within the privacy of the believer's mind, *the idea, or the special property of ideas, experienced by him at the moment of forming a belief.* But it can also be given a public interpretation: it would then mean *the concept of belief, as we all apply it to each other on behavioural grounds.* Hume's conception of the science of the human mind—something to be investigated in isolation from the body—concentrates his attention entirely on the first interpretation, and excludes the second one. It is then not surprising that he runs into an impasse. The same fault, with the same result, can be found in his account of personal identity.[24]

The next, and last, topic under the heading *The Nature of Belief* is the way Hume argues for his view. When we have dealt with that, we can move on, in the next chapter, to *The Causes of Belief.*

Hume's arguments for his view of the nature of belief are intricate and hard to analyse. The difficulty is that he is thinking in a framework, the theory of ideas, which is no longer a natural framework for us. A considerable effort of imagination is required of us if we are going to succeed in seeing the problem in the way that he saw it.

The problem, as he saw it, was the threat of conflict between two

---

[23] This way of treating belief owes much to Wittgenstein's rejection of Naïve Empiricist appeal to a special experience. See Wittgenstein, *Philosophical Investigations, passim.*

[24] See below, pp. 135–47.

different principles. One was the principle that content, which is fixed by ideas, must remain unchanged through all vicissitudes of belief, disbelief, and suspension of belief.[25] The other was the principle that anything that goes on in the mind must be explained by the occurrence of impressions or ideas. Now in the case of belief the explanation is more likely to be the occurrence of an idea (though, as will appear in a moment, Hume does think it worth considering the possibility that belief might be explained as an impression of reflection).[26] The threat of conflict arises because he does not see how to segregate the belief-idea—if he finds that the second principle forces him to introduce such an idea—from the ideas that fix the content of the belief. This threat drives him to adopt, in a rather panicky way, the solution that belief is explained not by the occurrence of a special idea, but by a special property of the ideas that fix its content.

One point can be made immediately about his conception of the threatened conflict and his resolution of it. He assumes, without question, that the explanation of belief will be phenomenological: it can only be explained as the occurrence of a special idea or impression, or a special property of ideas. This assumption has just been questioned,[27] but the only way to understand this phase of Hume's thinking is to let it stand and see what follows.

We may now set to work on the details of his argumentation. Suppose that someone did suggest that to believe something was to have a special idea *about* it. This would be an example of intentionality (in Brentano's sense of the term), and, though Hume allows for intentionality, he never finds himself able to explain it. How would this special idea remain segregated from the ideas that fix the content and yet be directed on to them?

In fact, Hume uses two different arguments against the hypothesis of a special idea of belief.

First, he implies that there would be no way of segregating this idea from the content-ideas.

But as 'tis certain there is a great difference betwixt the simple conception of the existence of an object, and the belief of it, and as this difference lies not in the parts or composition of the idea, which we conceive; it follows, that it must lie in the *manner*, in which we conceive it.[28]

---

[25] See above, pp. 47–8.
[27] See above, pp. 50–1.
[26] See below, pp. 53–5.
[28] *Treatise*, pp. 94–5.

This argument immediately follows the remark,

> When I think of God . . . as existent, and when I believe him to be existent, my idea of him neither encreases nor diminishes;[29]

and it is followed, in its turn, by his two clearest statements of the principle that content must remain unchanged through all belief-vicissitudes.[30] The implication is clear: if belief did consist in a special idea in the mind of the believer, there would be no way of segregating it from the content-ideas, and the principle of constancy of content would be violated. This is an argument which impressed Hume only because he had no way of explaining intentionality.

His second argument against the hypothesis of a special idea of belief is different. The central point on which his theory of belief differs from Descartes's is that he thinks that belief is completely constrained by evidence and does not depend at all on the will. But

> The mind has the command over all its ideas, and can separate, unite, mix, and vary them, as it pleases; so that if belief consisted merely in a new idea, annex'd to the conception [i.e. to the content-ideas], it wou'd be in a man's power to believe what he pleas'd.[31]

This might suggest that to believe something must be to have, instead of a special idea, a special impression of reflection, which would not be subject to the will.

Hume considers this suggestion in the Appendix to the *Treatise*, where he says that the only alternative to his view that belief consists in the strength of liveliness of its content-ideas would be to say that

> belief, beside the simple conception, consists in some impression or feeling, distinguishable from the conception. It does not modify the conception, and render it more present and intense: It is only annex'd to it, after the same manner that *will* and *desire* are annex'd to particular conceptions of good and pleasure.[32]

This alternative would avoid making belief depend on the will, as it does in Descartes's theory. The special impression which it proposes would occur automatically in response to the evidence *just as*, according to Hume, the impression called 'will' or 'desire' occurs

---

[29] Quoted above, n. 15.
[30] Quoted above, pp. 48–9.
[31] This argument is developed in the Appendix to the *Treatise*, pp. 623–4.
[32] Ibid. 625.

automatically in response to an idea of something good or pleasurable. There is here only an *analogy* with the will and it is an analogy only with an *automatic* response of the will.[33]

Hume argues at length against this alternative in the Appendix to the *Treatise*.[34] His main objection is that

It is directly contrary to experience, and our immediate consciousness. All men have ever allow'd reasoning to be merely an operation of our thoughts or ideas; and however those ideas may be varied to the feeling, there is nothing ever enters into our *conclusions* but ideas, or our fainter conceptions.[35]

He may be making two points here. He says that, if there were such an impression it would 'enter into our *conclusions*'. This may mean that the principle of the constancy of content would be violated by a special impression of belief in the same way that he had argued that it would be violated by a special idea of belief. If so, this argument, like the other one, convinced him only because he had no way of explaining intentionality. But it is not an argument that is available to him at this point, because, although he cannot explain intentionality, he does use it in his account of will and desire.

There is no doubt about his second point, which is that, as a matter of fact, nobody does have a special impression when he comes to believe something. He tries to reinforce this by arguing that there is in any case no need for such an impression, because his own theory that belief is a special property of the content-ideas renders it superfluous.[36] This is no real reinforcement, because a supporter of the theory of the special impression could equally well argue that *his* theory made Hume's alternative superfluous.

Hume's argument in this part of the Appendix would have been more persuasive if he had brought his own theory of the origin of the idea of necessity into the picture. According to that theory, a special impression of reflection *does* occur in the mind of a person forming a belief. But it is not a special impression of *belief*. It is the internal impression of constraint felt by him when he is being pushed along the associative track laid down by past observation towards belief in the content-idea.[37] If this theory of causal inference is right, there is no

---

[33] Hume's theory of the will is given in the *Treatise*, bk. II, pt. 3, §§ i–iii.
[34] Ibid. 625–6.
[35] Ibid. 625.
[36] Ibid.
[37] See above, pp. 12–15.

room for another impression in the sequence of mental occurrences. For how could the proposed special impression of belief fit into the sequence? If it did occur, it could not be *influenced* by the impression of necessitated transition which preceded it. It could only be a *new* experiential contribution, butting into the orderly sequence of causal inference described by Hume, and upsetting it rather than explaining it. So his suspicion that a special impression of belief would intervene inexplicably between beliefs and the evidence for them was correct, but the intervention is best presented in the context of his own theory of causal inference.

That might appear to conclude Hume's case for his theory that belief consists in the force and vivacity of its content-ideas. However, there is one more phase in his argumentation, a difficult one, concerned with the concept of *existence*. It will prove to be worth analysing, because it will throw light on his neglect of the composition of atomic judgements.[38]

Hume's argument for his theory of belief begins with some observations about existence:

> 'Tis evident, that all reasonings from causes or effects terminate in conclusions, concerning matters of fact; that is, concerning the existence of objects or their qualities. 'Tis also evident, that the idea of existence is nothing different from the idea of any object, and that when after the simple conception of anything we wou'd conceive it as existent, we in reality make no addition to or alteration on our first idea. Thus when we affirm, that God is existent, we simply form the idea of such a being, as he is represented to us; nor is the existence, which we attribute to him, conceiv'd by a particular idea, which we join to the idea of his other qualities, and can again separate and distinguish from them. But I go farther; and, not content with asserting, that the conception of the existence of any object is no addition to the simple conception of it, I likewise maintain, that the belief of the existence joins no new ideas to those, which compose the idea of the object. When I think of God, when I think of him as existent, and when I believe him to be existent, my idea of him neither encreases nor diminishes. But as 'tis certain there is a great difference betwixt the simple conception of the existence of an object, and the belief of it, and as this difference lies not in the parts or composition of the idea, which we conceive; it follows, that it must lie in the *manner*, in which we conceive it.[39]

This is an objection to a particular version of the thesis that belief consists in a special idea. The special idea proposed in this case is the

---

[38] See above, pp. 33–5.
[39] *Treatise*, pp. 94–5. Part of this passage was quoted above, p. 53.

idea of existence, and the objection to it is not that it would change the content of the belief by importing something extraneous into it. The objection is, rather, that existence is already included in the content in its own inconspicuous way, and that, therefore, there is no possibility of adding it as a distinct idea.

The objection is difficult to assess, because two different lines of thought have been combined in it. First, Hume is claiming that *existence* is not an idea like other ideas, and what he says here is very close to what other philosophers have meant when they claimed that 'existent' is not a predicate.[40] Secondly, he is arguing that, though the truth of any belief would consist in the existence of an impression which matched its content-idea, this is a general presupposition of belief, and there is no need to mark it by expressing every belief in the expanded form, 'There exists an impression which matches this . . . IMAGE'.

But how much connection is there really between these two points? And what effect does either of them have on the internal structure of atomic judgements? These are not easy questions to answer, and each of the two points will need careful scrutiny.

Let us look first at Hume's argument for his thesis that the idea of *existence* is not an idea like other ideas.

. . . since we never remember any idea or impression without attributing existence to it, the idea of existence must either be deriv'd from a distinct impression, conjoin'd with every perception or object of our thought, or must be the very same with the idea of the perception or object.

But

So far from there being any distinct impression, attending every impression and idea, that I do not think that there are any two distinct impressions, which are inseparably conjoin'd.

Therefore

. . . tho' every impression and idea we remember be consider'd as existent, the idea of existence is not deriv'd from any particular impression.

The idea of existence, then, is the very same with the idea of what we conceive to be existent. To reflect on any thing simply, and to reflect on it as existent, are nothing different from each another.[41]

---

[40] See above, pp. 34–5. [41] *Treatise*, pp. 66–7.

The general line taken by Hume in this passage is clear enough. To think about a thing is to think about it as it would be, if it existed. So if it is a complex thing, all that we have to do is to combine the ideas of its simple properties in our minds, and we will not find the idea of existence occurring as a separate item among them. Similarly, to perceive a thing is to perceive it as it is, in existence. So if it is a complex thing, we will get impressions of each of its properties, but we will not find an impression of existence occurring as a separate item among them. This is evidently the analogue in Hume's theory of ideas of the thesis that 'existent' is not a predicate.

However, the conclusion that he then goes on to draw from this is unconvincing:

> For *first*, 'tis far from being true, that in every judgment, which we form, we unite two different ideas; since in that proposition, *God is*, or indeed any other, which regards existence, the idea of existence is no distinct idea, which we unite with that of the object, and which is capable of forming a compound idea by the union. *Secondly*, As we can thus form a proposition, which contains only one idea . . . [42]

This is an unconvincing inference. Its linguistic counterpart would be the claim that, since 'existent' is not a predicate, the verb 'exists' can be eliminated from any sentence in which it occurs, leaving the other term standing alone. But that would be absurd. The sentence 'God exists' does have an internal structure even if it is not the same as the internal structure of the sentence 'God is merciful'. Similarly, Hume ought to have allowed that the thought that God exists does have an internal structure, because it does contain a second idea, the idea of existence, even though it is not the same as the internal structure of the thought that God is merciful, because the idea of existence is not an idea like other ideas.

It was pointed out in the previous chapter that Hume often shapes his theory of ideas under the guidance of language without stopping to look carefully at the way in which language works.[43] In the case which is now under scrutiny the trouble is worse. If he had examined existential sentences carefully, he would have found that he could not match them in his system without altering his fundamental axiom that ideas copy impressions. For, as he himself observes, the idea of existence does not conform to this axiom, and yet he cannot explain the

---

[42] Ibid. 96 n. 1.   [43] See above, pp. 32–3.

construction of existential thoughts without it. Later we shall see how he deals with the somewhat similar problem posed by the idea of causal necessity.[44]

He never faced the problem of the idea of existence squarely and he never seems to have realized that the only way to get the right kind of structure into existential thoughts would have been to abandon the axiom that ideas copy impressions. He sweeps the problem under the carpet, stoutly maintaining that the structure of complex ideas is the only kind of structure that need be recognized.

Whether we consider a single object, or several; whether we dwell on these objects, or run from them to others; and in whatever form or order we survey them, the act of the mind exceeds not a simple conception; and the only remarkable difference, which occurs on this occasion, is, when we join belief to the conception, and are perswaded of the truth of what we conceive.[45]

This is, unfortunately, an evasion, because it says nothing about considering possibilities.[46]

What still remains to be examined is the other line of argument which Hume weaves into his objection to the thesis that belief consists in a special idea, namely the idea of existence. A philosopher who supported this thesis would be restricting it to overtly existential beliefs. His thought would be that, if all singular beliefs are analysed in Hume's way, as complex ideas, then, at least, it will have to be admitted that they are covertly existential. For what a person is really assenting to in such a case is 'There exists an impression matching this . . . IMAGE'.

Hume does not meet this with a flat denial. He has two objections to it, both oblique. First, although this is, indeed, a presupposition of the truth of any belief, there is no need to mark it by giving the content of every belief this form.[47] Secondly, when they are given this form, they contain an idea which is not a copy of a distinct impression. So is it not preferable to eliminate that idea from the content, to reduce the complexity of judgement to the complexity of 'simple conception', and to deal with the shortfall by invoking the 'force and vivacity' of the remaining content-ideas?

---

[44] His solution to that problem was sketched above, pp. 12–15, but the details will be given in the next three chapters.

[45] *Treatise*, p. 97, continuation of p. 96 n. 1, quoted above, p. 57.

[46] See above, p. 13.

[47] See above, p. 56.

Although both Hume and his adversary seem to be mistaken, the dispute between them does reveal very clearly what has gone wrong. Their common error is to try to make do without any analogue of singular references in the system of ideas. The obvious alternative is to use the concept of existence instead. But the axiom of copying makes Hume refuse to allow that an existential analysis gives the real form of the content of a belief. His refusal is reinforced by his misguided treatment of overtly existential judgements. Thus he reaches his conclusion that belief can only consist in a property of the content-ideas.

PART II

THE APPLICATION OF THE THEORY OF MIND TO THREE PROBLEMS: CAUSATION, PERSONAL IDENTITY, AND PERCEPTION

5

Causation: The Evidence and its First Effect on Us

IN the last three chapters the emphasis has been on the shortcomings of Hume's theory of mind. Its failure to deal with the problem of meaning separately from the problem of truth and evidence, its excessive assimilation of thought to perception, and its consequent underestimation of the importance of activity were all serious faults. It emerged as a loosely constructed theory, based on an intuition of empiricism and worked out with insufficient care. However, when he applied it to the three problems, causation, personal identity, and perception, he turned its loose construction to advantage. His best ideas were not hampered by it, but were able to develop with a large measure of freedom in the open interstices.

His treatment of the first of the three problems, causation, is the centre-piece of the *Treatise*. This is not surprising given his convictions that all belief is inferential and that causal inference is the only kind that takes us beyond what we immediately perceive. There is also something else which contributes to the importance of causation: causal inference is itself a causal process. That is his answer to the question about the origin of belief that was posed at the beginning of the previous chapter.

The examination of his account of causation will occupy this chapter and the next two. It will contribute to answering two general questions about the position taken up by him in the *Treatise*. Is he a sceptic?[1] And which of his two theories carries the main burden of his argument about causation, his theory of meaning or his theory of belief?[2]

If the claims made in Chapter 1 are valid, he was not a simple

---

[1] See above, Preface, p. viii. [2] See above, pp. 3–10.

sceptic. But nor was he content with the reductive theory that causal statements about the physical world simply record the relations between our sense-impressions. If we have to give him a small label, it would be 'Cautious Naturalist'. That is the steady tendency of his work and he would not pick up any of the labels which philosophers engaged in similar controversies today would offer him. He is not a sceptic about causation, because the extra content of causal statements about which he might have been a sceptic is eliminated by his theory of meaning. This would suggest that he is a reductionist, but he is not that either, because he is well aware that causal statements, like any other statements about the physical world, have more content, albeit illegitimate content, than is covered by his account of the phenomeno-logical evidence for them.

A modern philosopher might say that he has to make a choice at this point. But he evades it by a sideways step from his theory of meaning to his theory of belief. The implication of this move is not that his theory of meaning is unacceptable, or that it is unimportant in this context because it cannot be used to solve the problem of causation. On the contrary, he thinks that it makes a dramatic contribution to its solution. The point of the side-step is simply that another equally important contribution will be made by his account of the evidence for the force of causal statements. What is constant in his philosophy is not that he reaches, or even marches towards, any single ontological theory, but the cautious naturalism that he shows both when he is developing his theory of meaning and when he is developing his theory of belief.

This chapter will start by examining his reasons for believing causal inference to be the only kind that takes us further than perception. It will then move on to his attempt to explain it as a causal process. Or, perhaps, it would be more accurate to say that what he attempts to do is to *describe* it as a causal process. He is, after all, a naturalist, and his task is primarily to observe and describe. If the description is found explanatory, that need not be because it shows that causal inference rests on an independent basis, outside what is described. It is impor-tant to read him without the *arrière pensée* that he must be looking for an independently based explanation of the phenomena, and without deciding to charge him with circularity if, in the end, he does not offer that kind of explanation.

Our first question is 'Why did he believe that causal inference is the only kind that takes us further than perception?' But what other kinds of inference might be credited with this function? There are two possibilities to be considered: inferences guaranteed a priori and inferences with a non-causal a posteriori basis.

It is easy to see why he denied that a priori inferences are capable of taking us beyond what is immediately given in perception. Someone who makes an inference of this kind exploits relations which

... depend entirely on the ideas, which we compare together ... 'Tis from the idea of a triangle, that we discover the relation of equality, which its three angles bear to two right ones; and this relation is invariable, so long as our idea remains the same.[3]

So, to continue with the example, if someone gets a sense-impression matching the idea of a triangle and infers that its angles add up to two right angles, his conclusion will be verifiable from the impression itself and could have been based on direct observation.

When Hume develops his own theory of causation, he deploys it against two distinct adversaries. One of them is the type of rationalism that gives causal inferences some sort of a priori basis. The simplest theory of this type would say that, because flames have the power to melt wax, we can infer the fate of this candle a priori from the fact that it is lit. Hume retorts that, if this connection really did hold a priori, we could not be sure that we really had a flame until the wax began to run.[4] After all, that is how we would deal with any shape that we took to be a triangle: because the connection really is a priori in that case, we would withdraw the perceptual claim that it was a triangle if we found that its angles did not add up to two right angles.[5]

Hume's other adversary would speak up at this point. He would say that the attribution of the power to the flame does not have to wait for a sequel linked to it either a priori or a posteriori. On the contrary, it is based on a separate impression of the power in the flame as soon as it is lit. Hume meets this suggestion with a challenge to his adversary to identify this separate impression of the power in the flame, backed up by the argument that, if he did succeed in identifying it, it would be unable to retain any a priori connection with the sequel.[6]

It will be useful to have names for Hume's two adversaries. The Rationalist is, of course, already well known under that name. The

---

[3] *A Treatise of Human Nature*, ed. P. H. Nidditch (Oxford: Clarendon Press, 1989), 69.
[4] See below, pp. 88–9.
[5] This argument needs a qualification. See below, p. 89.
[6] See below, pp. 89–90.

second adversary, who claims that we have a distinct sense-impression of causal power, may be called 'the Naïve Empiricist'. Perhaps the best name for Hume's own theory is 'Sophisticated Empiricism'. Anyway, these names will be used from now on, not only in the discussion of his treatment of causation, but also in the discussion of his treatment of personal identity. For there too we are going to find the same strategic situation, with Hume fighting on two separate fronts—a triangle of forces.

But to return to the main line of the argument, if a priori inferences fail to take us beyond immediate perception, are a posteriori inferences with a non-causal basis any more successful in this enterprise? This question will lead us into an area that has not yet been explored, Hume's theory of the association of ideas.

The first effect that the evidence for a causal inference has on an observer is to establish an associative track in his mind. The second effect, which occurs later, when he gets another sense-impression of the same kind of cause, is that he is pushed along this track to the associated idea of the effect.[7] Now that amounts to more than a mere movement of thought. For the idea of the effect is not only brought into his mind, but also receives from the sense-impression the force and vivacity that make it a belief. If the idea were merely brought into his mind without this revitalization, he would be considering the possibility that the effect might follow but not believing that it would do so. The idea would occur to him, but that would be all.

This difference, between mere consideration of the possibility of the effect and belief that it will actually happen, was mentioned towards the end of Chapter 1.[8] It now needs to be looked at again. For some associations are capable only of bringing an idea into a person's mind, and so, if others really do produce belief, as Hume claims that they do, there must be some difference between them which will explain the difference in their effects. In this area Hume aspires to do more than merely record the phenomena. He has a theory which is intended to explain them.[9] But how will it do that?

---

[7] See above, pp. 12–15.

[8] See above, p. 13.

[9] He repeats with approval Newton's remark: '*Hypotheses non fingo*' (General Scholium at the end of *Principia*), but he does not mean that his theory of ideas is *merely* descriptive. True, it is not required to identify hypothetical causes, like the movements of animal spirits which may explain the association of ideas (*Treatise*, pp. 60–1; see ch. 7 n. 12), but it is required to find a unified set of principles which will explain how the associations work within the mind.

There is also another way in which the second effect of the evidence amounts to more than a mere movement of thought. When the observer is pushed along the associative track, he is aware that he is being pushed, because he feels an internal impression of constraint. This is an essential part of Hume's account of causal inference. It is essential not merely because it is required by his theory of the derivation of ideas from impressions, but also because whoever makes a causal inference must not only not make it arbitrarily,[10] but also be *aware* that he is not making it arbitrarily. So the internal impression of necessitated transition is not just postulated by Hume to satisfy the demand made by his theory of the derivation of ideas. It makes the observer aware, in the only way that is allowable in Hume's system, that his inference is sensitive to the evidence, and puts him in a position to review it and assess it.[11] This point is missed by commentators who adopt the usual simplistic approach to Hume's subtle theory and hit it with the question 'Is the necessity objective, or is it only in the mind?'

However, the discussion of the second effect of the evidence for a causal inference will have to be deferred to Chapter 6. Here we are concerned only with the first effect, the establishment of an associative track in the observer's mind. Two questions have been raised about this part of Hume's theory, and they will have to be answered. One was the question why he believes that a posteriori inferences with a non-causal basis do not succeed in taking us beyond what we immediately perceive. The other was the question why, if he is right, some associations merely pull ideas into our minds, while others produce belief. It will soon become apparent that the two questions are closely connected with one another.

What we need first is a general view of his theory of the association of ideas, its importance, and its place in his system. He offered the theory as an answer to the question 'How do we think?' Or, to put the question in a way that brings out the purpose of thinking, 'How do our thoughts succeed in reflecting the world around us?' His answer was that, among all the relations which hold between things in the world, there are three to which our minds are attuned and with which we find a natural affinity. They are resemblance, contiguity in time or place,

---

[10] Cf. the discussion of his opposition to Descartes's theory, that belief depends on the will (see above, p. 53).

[11] Hume describes this assessment in the chapter on 'Rules by which to Judge of Causes and Effects', *Treatise*, pp. 173–6.

and causation.[12] These are the three relations that govern the working of our minds by controlling the way our ideas are put together.

If this answer is right, a scientific study of these three ways of associating ideas ought to show us how we achieve the true record of the world around us that we do, on the whole, succeed in achieving, and why our successes terminate at a certain point. These two philosophical results of the scientific study of the mind, the extent and limit of our knowledge, are equally important.[13] Until they have been established, it will be impossible to say who is a sceptic and who suffers from too much credulity.

We have to make a considerable effort of imagination today in order to understand Hume's high hopes of his theory of the association of ideas. We immediately think of the menial function of association, bringing ideas into the mind, or even of the free association used in Freudian therapy. But he gave it the grander task of shaping our beliefs, and so it is not surprising, or, at least, not so surprising, that he credited it with a role in the mind as important as Newton's gravitation in the physical world.

Here is a kind of ATTRACTION, which in the mental world will be found to have as extraordinary effects as in the natural, and to shew itself in as many and as various forms. Its effects are every where conspicuous; but as to its causes, they are mostly unknown, and must be resolv'd into *original* qualities of human nature, which I pretend not to explain.[14]

The unambitious positivism expressed in this passage is another thing that we are likely to find alien. The concept of evolution has given us a different standpoint. When Hume explains our intellectual achievements merely by pointing to the fact that the human mind is attuned to three of the many relations holding between things in the world, and so finds it natural to follow them in its own thought-processes, we are less likely to be satisfied. Is our preference for the three relations that give us the key to the universe just a lucky fact? Surely function and natural selection must have played a part?

Hume does not venture into these depths. It seems to him to be enough to establish the two claims that he does make for his theory: that we do in fact think along the lines laid down by the three chosen

---

[12] *Treatise*, p. 11.

[13] See above, n. 9, where the importance of the limitation was emphasized. The advantages to be gained in philosophy from the scientific study of the mind are explained in detail by Hume in the Introduction to the *Treatise* (pp. xiii–xix).

[14] *Treatise*, pp. 12–13.

relations, and that, together, they explain the extent and limits of our thought. But is it really enough?

At the beginning of his chapter 'Of the Connexion or Association of Ideas' he enumerates the three relations to which nature has attuned our minds:

> The qualities, from which this association [he is speaking generally about the association of ideas] arises, and by which the mind is after this manner convey'd from one idea to another, are three, *viz.* RESEMBLANCE, CONTIGUITY in time or place, and CAUSE and EFFECT.[15]

Later in the book we find him calling these relations 'natural relations'.[16] He means that they are relations with which the human mind has a natural affinity, so that it slides as a matter of course from one idea to another in a pair related in one of these three ways. Of course, the class of relations includes many more than these three, but these three are the natural ones. The term that he uses for the all-inclusive class is 'philosophical relations':

> The word RELATION is commonly used in two senses considerably different from each other. Either for that quality, by which two ideas are connected together in the imagination, and the one naturally introduces the other, after the manner above-explained; or for that particular circumstance, in which, even upon the arbitrary union of two ideas in the fancy, we may think proper to compare them. In common language the former is always the sense, in which we use the word, relation; and 'tis only in philosophy, that we extend it to mean any particular subject of comparison, without a connecting principle. Thus distance will be allowed by philosophers to be a true relation, because we acquire an idea of it by the comparing of objects: But in a common way we say, *that nothing can be more distant than such or such things from each other, nothing can have less relation*; as if distance and relation were incompatible.[17]

The task of establishing that the three natural relations do in fact determine our lines of thought is taken very easily by Hume:

> I believe it will not be very necessary to prove, that these qualities produce an association among ideas, and upon the appearance of one idea naturally introduce another. 'Tis plain, that in the course of our thinking, and in the constant revolution of our ideas, our imagination runs easily from one idea to any other that *resembles* it . . . [18]

---

[15] Ibid. 11.
[16] Ibid. 94.
[17] Ibid. 13–14.
[18] Ibid. 11.

He continues in the same vein, offering the same, rather facile argument for adding *contiguity* in time or place and *causation* to the list of natural relations.[19]

Perhaps this part of his task really is not very difficult to carry out. Certainly it is made easier by the fact that he has not yet begun to explain inference or belief. At this stage it may really be enough to list the commonest forms of associative thinking. If these are the ways in which ideas are pulled into the mind, it may be sufficient for him merely to record them. But later, when he goes on to develop an explanation of inference and belief, he will find himself on rougher ground. For the theory of the association of ideas will have to show why these three principles of association, and no more and no less, produce the patterns of a posteriori inference that we actually use. In particular, it will have to show why causal inference is the only kind that takes us beyond what we are given in immediate perception.

However, even at the earlier stage there are problems which he takes too lightly. Association by resemblance is supposed to explain why we group things together under general terms in the way that we do. But the long and varied history of philosophers' attempts to answer this question suggests that it may be harder than he thinks. Nevertheless, it is true that the really difficult problems do not start until he brings in contiguity and causation to explain our inferences and beliefs. For what these two relations are required to provide is an explanation of the way we map the space around us beyond the horizon of present perception and discover what time has in store for us. That is a much more complex achievement than merely explaining how ideas are brought into our minds.

Can such an explanation really be found in Hume's theory of the association of ideas? In the remainder of this chapter it will be argued that the explanation that he offers is not as complete as he claims that it is. The argument will turn mainly on his failure to give separate explanations of the two different functions of association, pulling ideas into the mind and generating belief. But his failure to appreciate the importance of reference will also play a role.

He is, of course, aware that, when the basis of an association is merely resemblance or contiguity, it can only serve to bring ideas into the mind and never to produce belief. In fact, one of his central points is that belief can be produced only by an association based on causa-

[19] *Treatise*, p. 11.

tion. But *why* is this? It is not enough for him just to state the fact: he must also explain it. Now it is true that he does offer some sort of explanation: he analyses causation and shows that it is a complex relation which involves the other two relations, resemblance and contiguity. However, that is still not enough. For we have yet to be told why this complex relation produces belief, while the other two are not capable of that function, when they are operating alone. Until we are told that, we shall not have an explanation tracing all the phenomena back to the association of ideas. To put the criticism in another way, if he cannot meet this demand, he will have to admit that his theory leaves the central fact unexplained and that, when he encounters this difficulty, he sits back and reverts to plain description of the phenomena.

We may start by asking why an association based on resemblance is incapable of producing belief? The first difficulty is to see what such a belief would be, if it were produced. When the white ball strikes the red one on the billiards table, contiguity fixes where the inferred movement must be located in space and time.[20] To put the point in another way, contiguity fixes the reference of the pronoun in the conclusion 'It will move'.[21] But if you saw a meteorite flash across the night sky and if, for some reason, you inferred that there must be others like it, where would you locate them in space and time? The reference in a causal inference is fixed by contiguity, and the lack of anything to play that role in an inference based on resemblance alone explains why we do not form inferential beliefs of this kind.

Suppose that we make things easier for resemblance by giving it contiguity as a partner. Then perhaps that would fix the location of whatever you inferred. But now there is another difficulty. What reason would you have to infer *anything*? Your only possible reason would be repeated observation in the past of contiguous couples linked by resemblance—for example, fossil shells and the negative imprints that they leave in the rock in which they are embedded. But that kind of reason, constant conjunction, has not been included in the example, and, if it were included, it would immediately become a special case of causal inference.

The two obstacles which prevent associations based on resemblance alone from producing beliefs are glaringly obvious. An inferential belief must have a definite reference, and it must be based on the

---

[20] See above, p. 34.   [21] See above, p. 48.

observation of repeated positive instances. Resemblance alone is unable to meet the first requirement, and, even when it is reinforced by contiguity, it still fails to meet the second requirement. Now Hume describes the basis of a causal inference in a way that makes it the only kind of inference that meets both requirements. That is why he maintains that it is the only kind of a posteriori inference which takes us beyond immediate perception. This thesis of his might be questioned on the ground that there are functional laws which meet both requirements but are not causal. But nobody would reject it on the ground that associations based on the other two natural relations are capable of producing belief. That would be absurd.

The point of analysing the reasons for the incapacity of the other two natural relations was not to demonstrate the absurdity, because it is only too obvious. It was to show that an explanation of our patterns of thought, which appeals to the association of ideas in the indiscriminate way that Hume does, remains incomplete.

In order to complete it, we need to answer the theoretical question why associations based on all three of his natural relations produce belief, while associations based on the other two alone are incapable of producing it. He only records the difference as a matter of fact. If we want to understand it, we must go further and determine to what extent it depends on the theory of the association of ideas and to what extent it depends on other considerations.

The direction in which further progress might be made is indicated by the ways in which resemblance and contiguity fail to qualify as producers of belief. Associations based on causation produce beliefs which are pinned on to the world at definite points and which are sensitive to evidence. Associations based on resemblance alone would fail on both scores and, if they did produce anything that could be called a pattern of thought, it would be one that had no contact whatsoever with reality. Associations based on both resemblance and contiguity would produce recognizable thoughts, pinned to the world at identifiable points, but without any sensitivity to evidence. Both would be symptoms of insanity. So maybe the explanation of the prevalence of beliefs produced by associations based on causation is natural selection. Certainly it is not deducible from the theory of association alone, because there is nothing in association, taken by itself, which will select which of its two very different functions it will perform, bringing ideas into the mind or producing belief.

This criticism cuts back the claim made by Hume for his theory of the association of ideas. It leaves his main point unscathed, because association really does play various roles in the production of beliefs that take us beyond what we immediately perceive. The basic role of classifying kinds of events is played by associations based on resemblance. Associations based on contiguity fix the reference of whatever inferential belief is formed. Finally, the extra feature which is required for causation, constant conjunction of the two kinds of events, actually produces the belief.

Hume might reply that he never quite aspired to imitate Newton's mechanics in his psychology. If the phenomena cannot be completely explained simply as direct consequences of the theory of association, then he will give up the task of explanation and fill the gap by merely recording the way nature has shaped our thoughts for us. At some point he will be forced to rest his case on mere description. Does it really matter where?

It does matter if, as he often implies, he is aiming at an explanation of all our thinking unified under a single theory. Judged against that programme, his achievement suffers from the indiscriminateness of his appeals to association. However, if he is not aiming so high, but merely using the theory of association in a piecemeal way against his two adversaries, the Rationalist and the Naïve Empiricist,[22] the defence which has just been put into his mouth may be acceptable.

There is no need for adjudication. The important thing is to appreciate the strategic situation. Hume's naturalism is not flatly descriptive, but partly theoretical. Now either the theory, taken by itself, yields deductions across the whole field, like Newton's theory, or it does not. The argument which demonstrates that it is not so powerful is not a trivial or a pedantic criticism. It is based on certain distinctions in the theory of meaning which show up the inadequacy of an indiscriminate appeal to association. Here, therefore, we have yet another example of psychology guided by language but incompletely guided and going astray, because language was not scrutinized with enough care.[23]

This criticism too may seem to be less than fair, because Hume can hardly be represented as *translating* linguistic expressions into the

---

[22] See above, pp. 65–6.

[23] See above, pp. 29–30 and 32–3. Of course, this is not the only point of view from which Hume's use of the association of ideas might be criticized. His 19th-cent. critics objected that human thought is not so mechanical. That is a different line of attack, and something will be said about it in the next chapter.

symbolism of ideas. His method, it may be said in his defence, is to use a kind of introspection which is direct and independent of language. True, that is how he describes his method, but do we have to take his description at face value? When he looks into his own mind in order to discover the structures of his thoughts, is it really likely that anything so intricate can be investigated in one mind independently of the language in which it would be passed from that mind to another one? The linguistic expression of a thought has to transmit it in its entirety and so it cannot afford to omit or blur anything that is essential to its structure. No doubt, you know what you are thinking without having to wait to hear yourself speaking, but the structure even of a simple thought does not reveal itself so readily to introspection. So when Hume looks for it in his own mind, he cannot help looking back over his shoulder at its linguistic expression. The criticism is that he exaggerates the perspicuity of the mind and then, when he finds himself forced to pay heed to language, he does little more than glance at it in an oblique and perfunctory way.

6

Causation: The Gap between Evidence and Belief

THE second effect of the evidence for a causal inference is the internal impression of constraint that occurs in us when we move along the associative track to its conclusion. That is a difficult topic, and it will be broached in the next chapter. There is another topic which must be taken first, the gap between evidence and belief.

We may begin with a brief recapitulation of the discussion of the first effect in the previous chapter. Hume's view of the evidence for a causal inference — for example, from the impact of the white ball to the movement of the red one — is that it consists merely in observations of similar pairs of events. They must be constantly conjoined and in each pair the cause-event must be contiguous with the effect-event in space and time and prior to it. In any normal observer this sequence of pairs of events will produce an association between the idea of the first event and the idea of the second one. This mental sequence has the same structure as the external sequence that produced it. It is a causal sequence in the mind produced by, and reflecting, a causal sequence outside the mind. The two sequences are like two cog-wheels: the external one sets the internal one spinning with a force sufficient to keep it in motion when they are no longer in gear.

Hume offers his view as an alternative to two distinct rival views. One is Rationalism, which claims that the connection between the idea of the cause and the idea of the effect is really a priori. The other rival, Naïve Empiricism, agrees with Hume that it is a posteriori, but disagrees with him about its basis. Instead of spreading its basis over many observations, as Hume does, this adversary tries to concentrate it in a sense-impression of a single type, an external impression of necessity. Hume, of course, allows that there is an impression of necessity, but only an internal one.[1]

---

[1] Although this is a correct way of contrasting the two views, it is potentially misleading because it suggests that the difference is only between an external and an internal

Taken as a whole, Hume's theory exhibits an ingenious structure. He describes two causal processes, one in the world outside us and the other in our minds, the latter brought into congruence with the former by a process which is itself causal. However, critics have found fault both with his account of what happens in the world and with his account of what happens in our minds. On both fronts, their battle-cry has been 'Scepticism!' So it would be as well to start with a general view of the various ways in which Hume's theory of causation might appear to be sceptical.

First, his account of what happens in the world keeps very close to the evidence that gets through to our minds. This is to be expected from an empiricist, but it is arguable that he leaves out something essential at this point. The usual criticism is the simple one, that he leaves out the necessity from his account of what happens in the world outside our minds. The constant conjunctions that he describes might be purely coincidental, because there is nothing in his description of them to exclude that possibility. If this were a valid criticism, Hume would be a sceptic. For, if, by the accepted standards of well-founded belief, the necessity, as specified by his adversaries,[2] were credible, then anyone too cautious to believe in it would be a sceptic.

Hume would retort that, on the contrary, it is his critics who encourage scepticism at this point, but in a different way. For the external necessity that they require is not something that could ever get through to our minds, and anyone who postulates something empirically inaccessible, though it may look as if he only runs the risk of excessive credulity rather than scepticism, is actually promoting scepticism. For when he tells people that they ought to believe in something which turns out to be empirically inaccessible, they find that the belief is beyond their powers and abandon it.[3]

We see here two different ways in which philosophers may come to accuse each other of scepticism. Hume's adversaries assume that their own standards of credibility are correct, and, judging him by those

impression of exactly the same kind, and it says nothing about the difference in meaning between the phrase 'of necessity' applied to the external impression and the same phrase applied to the internal impression. See below, pp. 105–9.

[2] We must not forget that there may be other ways of specifying it.

[3] They might also find the extra element unintelligible. See above, p. 64. That consequence of empirical inaccessibility is guaranteed by Hume's theory of meaning and it will be examined in ch. 7.

standards, they call him a 'sceptic'. He retorts that their standards actually promote scepticism by putting the necessity, in which people are asked to believe, beyond their reach.

This part of the controversy is like a political argument, in which the key-term of abuse is treated as if it had a single, agreed criterion, when really both sides are manipulating its criterion to suit themselves. The only way to keep the battle-lines clearly demarcated is to avoid reliance on the slippery concept of *scepticism*, and to ask two independent questions about Hume's theory. First, does he give an adequate account of what goes on in the world outside our minds? Secondly, does his account of what goes on inside our minds give us the access that we need to what goes on outside them, accurately described (i.e. with his *under-description* corrected, if he really does under-describe it)?

These two questions must be kept separate from one another. We must first ask whether he does under-describe external causal processes; and then, independently, we must ask whether our mental powers, as he describes them, give us the access that we need to what really goes on outside our minds. It can only cause confusion to run these two questions together and to judge the adequacy of his account of the internal processes by the standard set by his critics' account of the external processes, if, as may well be the case, their account is an over-description.

A conspicuous example of this confusion is a criticism of Hume which will be analysed later, but which ought to be mentioned now. Those who criticize him for omitting the necessity from his description of external causal processes are, of course, aware that, if he had added what they require, he, being an empiricist, would have had to find an impression to convey it into our minds. But the only impression of necessity actually found by him is the internal impression of the determination of the mind to move from the first to the second idea in an associated pair. Now he explicitly says that this impression is not an impression of the kind of necessity that they require, perversely transferred by him from external to internal causal processes.[4] But ignoring his disclaimer they criticize him for 'confining necessity to the mind', and they challenge him to explain the necessity of which he says that he has found the internal impression. But his point was not that the inevitability of a causal inference is stronger than the inevitability of the

---

[4] See *A Treatise of Human Nature*, ed. P. H. Nidditch (Oxford: Clarendon Press, 1989), 169, quoted below, pp. 105–6.

inferred effect, but only that we feel it because it is we who make the inference.[5]

Evidently, the best strategy would be to start by asking the first question, which is concerned with his account of causal processes outside our minds. Is it a sceptical account? For reasons already explained, we must take this question to be asking whether he gives an adequate description of external causal processes or under-describes them. To put it in a slightly different way, does he include as much as he ought to include in his description of external causal processes?

This is not an easy question to answer. On the one hand, with uncompromising austerity, he restricts the available *evidence* to the repetition of similar pairs of events, on each occasion in immediate contiguity with one another. On the other hand, he says that nature has so formed his mind that, confronted by the first member of such a pair, he cannot avoid *believing* that the second member will follow immediately. So should we take his view of the external processes to be completely expressed by his austere specification of the evidence, or should we include the tendency of that evidence to produce the belief which, according to him, it inevitably plants in his mind? There is, of course, a gap between the evidence and the belief, but, if the bridge that he uses to cross it is a shaky one—the habit of believing with which nature has endowed us—that will not affect our answer to the first question. For what it asks is simply whether his description of external causal processes comes up to the mark, and if he includes their tendency to produce the effect on our minds, maybe it does. The fact that the effect is a questionable belief is not a fault in his description of the external causal processes. If the habit of believing really is too weak to support the belief, that will influence our answer to the second question, but not our answer to the first one.

It is, of course, the gap between evidence and belief that makes the problem of causation a difficult one. A belief based on a singular causal inference is always audacious, or, as Goodman calls it, 'projective'.[6] That is to say, it is always a move from the known out into the unknown. This is the challenge which different philosophical theories meet in different ways. Naïve Empiricists try to mitigate the audacity of causal inferences by basing them on an external impression of necessity. When Hume rejects this theory, they charge him with scepticism. But he can retort that his belief in causal necessity is manifested in his

[5] See below, pp. 109–14.
[6] N. Goodman, *Fact, Fiction and Forecast* (London: Athlone Press, 1954), chs. 1 and 4.

readiness to make audacious causal inferences and in his approval of the same readiness in others. This is a new move, because it makes the criterion of belief what a person does,[7] rather than what the evidence makes it safe for him to do. Of course, the belief in necessity which is manifested in a readiness to make audacious causal inferences is pre-theoretical. It is an unanalysed belief, implanted in our minds by nature, and, if philosophical analysis then shows it to be audacious, the conclusion is not that we should abandon it, but only that it cannot be defended by reason. Where reason fails us, nature supports us. That is the message of Hume's naturalism.

This opens up a new way of assessing a philosopher's belief in causal necessity. The criterion of his belief is no longer the optimism of his philosophical analysis of our pre-theoretical patterns of thought about causation. The test that is now to be used is not whether he enhances the evidence in the way that Hume's adversaries hoped to be able to enhance it. The test is whether he is prepared to make auda-cious causal inferences. Perhaps it would be too paradoxical to say that the larger the gap between evidence and belief, the stronger the belief in causal necessity, but it is a paradox that shows up the point of Hume's naturalism.

How does his theory of causation fare, when it is assessed from this new point of view? In order to answer this question we must look more closely at the concept of *audacious inference*. We may start by examining an example of an inference which does *not* exhibit audacity, and then, to bring out the contrast, we will look at an inference which *does* exhibit it. If I know that all the coins in my pocket this morning were silver, then, noticing a copper coin on the floor, I can argue, without any audacity, that, if it had been one of the coins in my pocket this morn-ing, it would have been silver. This is an inference which does *not* take me beyond the evidence on which it was based. But if I argue that because a certain casino has always paid my winnings in silver coins, it will now do so again, that inference does show the audacity that poses the problem. Exactly the same is true of the parallel inference from an unrealized possibility made after I have lost: if I had won, I would have been paid in silver.

The causal inferences examined by Hume are a little more scientific in character, but they all exhibit this essential audacity. So when he speaks of the constant conjunction of pairs of similar events, we must

---

[7] This gives Hume a further reason for changing his official theory of belief by attaching it more closely to behaviour than to feeling. See above, pp. 50–1.

not interpret his words in a way that would eliminate it. The *evidence* can only be a limited set of observed conjunctions, and, when he says it must be constant, he is requiring that there be no exceptions *within* this set—no cases of the red ball being struck without moving, or moving without being struck on a level table, in a draught-free room. But if we ask what he thinks that the observer *means* when he claims to have found a constant conjunction, his answer must be that he means something audacious: he is claiming that the conjunction is constant for ever, and, therefore, includes the *further* case about which he is now drawing the conclusion 'It will move'. Hume is not making causal inferences safe by confining them to the limited set of observed conjunctions, like the inference about the copper coin found on the floor.

At this point two more questions may be raised, one about the adequacy of his account of the evidence for causal inferences, and the other about the scope of the causal inferences which his theory allows the observer to make. The second question will be taken first, because it is a question about meaning, and, like all such questions, ought to come before questions about evidence and truth.

The question about meaning is this: 'What, according to Hume, is the scope of the inferences which the observer of a limited set of conjunctions is prepared to make?' In other words, 'In what directions will his audacity take him beyond his evidence?' Now in the case of the silver coins, my first inference showed no audacity: 'If that coin had been one of the coins in my pocket this morning, it would have been silver.' This contains a contrary-to-fact antecedent, and is the kind of conditional sentence which is classified as 'counterfactual'. It is, therefore, a *non*-audacious counterfactual. The question is: 'Does Hume assume that his observers are prepared to make audacious counterfactual inferences?' He evidently assumes that they are prepared to make audacious inferences about open future cases—his discussion is full of examples of this kind—but does he think that they are also prepared to make audacious counterfactual inferences? And would he himself countenance such inferences? They would, of course, be unlike the inference requiring no audacity, and like the counterfactual inference made in the casino: 'If I had won, I would have been paid in silver.' Or, to use Hume's rather more scientific kind of example, 'If the red ball had been struck it would have moved.'

In the last forty years, this question about Hume's attitude to audacious counterfactual inferences has been debated by many commentators, who supposed that the answer to it would yield an answer to the first of the two main questions under examination in this chapter: 'Did he give an adequate account of external causal processes, or did he under-describe them?' The connection between the two questions, as these commentators see it, is close. For Hume has to cover the necessity of external causal processes, and they think that the way to test whether he succeeds in covering it is to ask whether he allows audacious counterfactual inferences. For if he only allowed audacious inferences about the open future, those would be inferences whose verification, if they did come true, could be attributed to chance rather than to necessity. Their idea is that even a conjunction that is constant for ever might be a coincidence, so that the real test of a philosopher's belief in the necessity of external causal processes is to inquire whether he allows audacious counterfactual inferences.

Before we try to see whether Hume did allow them, it might be worth questioning the weight that these commentators attach to the answer. It may not be such a momentous issue as they think. Let us see.

If I make an audacious causal inference about the future course of events, I am surely revealing a belief in the necessity of the causal process involved. Of course, the *analysis* of this belief remains open, and it can be debated by the Rationalist, the Naïve Empiricist, and Hume. But my inference shows that I *do* believe in the necessity, whatever its true nature, and shows it in the only way that really counts. For it is a feature of human life that we have two different concepts here, *inferring the future* and *guessing the future*, each associated with its own characteristic behaviour, and, while guessing does not reveal belief in necessity, inference does reveal belief in it. So when Hume allows for this kind of audacious inference and the behaviour that goes with it, he is already revealing his belief in the necessity of external causal processes.

His belief is, for reasons already explained, pre-theoretical rather than philosophical. It still has to be analysed, and when he does offer his own analysis, we know that his opponents are going to say that the evidence is so niggardly and the inferences so bold that our final verdict must be that he does *not* believe in the necessity of external causal processes. But it is wise to start without any assumptions about the correct analysis, and to mark the point that, when the belief in necessity is tested in an ordinary, pre-theoretical way, Hume shares it and approves it.

Now what we have to ask supporters of the opposite interpretation is, first of all, this: 'Why would someone who was prepared to make audacious *counterfactual* inferences be giving any *better* indication of his belief in the necessity of external causal processes? Would he not be giving just as good an indication if he were prepared to extend his audacious inferences into the open future?

It is hard to see what valid reason could be given for attaching so much weight to audacious counterfactual inferences. It takes no more to persuade me to infer that the red ball would have moved if it had been struck than it takes to persuade me that it will move if it is struck. So if I am prepared to make the second kind of inference, I will also be prepared to make the first kind. It follows that a philosopher's belief in the necessity of external causal processes (at the pre-theoretical level) is shown equally by his willingness to make either kind of audacious inference.

There are two possible objections to this, both, I think, invalid. One objection would be to argue that Hume does see a difference between commitment to audacious inferences about the future and commitment to audacious counterfactual inferences, because he never mentions the latter, whereas he explicitly countenances the former. The other objection would be that, whatever he thinks about the matter, his own account of the evidence makes it incapable of supporting audacious counterfactual inferences.

The second objection is evidently the more important one, and so it will be taken first. It is based on the idea that a constant conjunction—even one that is constant for ever—might merely be a massive coincidence and, therefore, belief in such a conjunction is no indication of belief in necessity. But this is hardly convincing. If such a conjunction were coincidental, that would be because none of the cases in which the sequence would have been broken ever became actual, and in that way it would be preserved by chance. But in an unlimited sequence the actual cases of the cause-event could not fail to be a fair sample of the set which also included the merely possible cases. Therefore, the idea of an unlimited coincidence of this kind is incoherent.

There is another idea standing in the shadows behind this second objection to treating the extension of audacious inferences into the open future as an indication of belief in the necessity of external causal processes. Hume's view is often tacitly assimilated to the modern view that law-like statements are merely universally quantified material implications of the form $(x)\,(\phi x) \supset (\psi x)$. This formula would be verified if nothing ever exhibited the property specified in its antecedent, and, therefore, it is argued, no counterfactual inference can be based on it. But the assimilation is mistaken. For Hume's account of constant conjunctions makes it perfectly clear that the evidence that he has in mind consists of actual cases of the cause-event followed by the effect-event.

But did he in fact allow for inferences from unrealized contingencies? The first of the two objections was that he did not, and that this was deliberate: he saw that counterfactual inferences were different and, perhaps, not allowable in the framework of his theory, and, therefore, he did not commit himself to them. Is that really so?

He certainly mentions hypothetical inferences,[8] but he does not single out the subclass of counterfactual inferences for special comment. However, this omission seems to be entirely unconnected with the idea that counterfactual inferences would not be supported by a description of what actually happens in the world. To make the point in a reflexive way, Hume's omission of the special case of counterfactual inferences is, from this point of view, coincidental. If it needs an explanation, one can be found in his concentration on inferences from actual cases, which steer us into the future—almost, one might say, animal inferences.[9] In any case, his lawlike generalizations are obviously not mere summaries of what has happened. His treatment of audacious inferences to future effects is enough to show that. Of course, we may say, if we like, that his lawlike generalizations are mere summaries of *what has, will, and would have, happened*. But then we must realize that, if the word 'summary' is used in this way, it loses its contrast with audacious inference.

So, to sum up this discussion, when Hume's belief in causal necessity is assessed by his readiness to make audacious causal inferences, the result of the test is positive. He did believe in it, but he attributed the belief to nature rather than to reason.

However, there is a problem about his treatment of hypothetical inferences. It is not the problem presented by the critics whose case against him has just been reviewed, but it might be helpful to identify it, because it really is raised by this part of his text. So let us now look at what he says about hypothetical inferences in his chapter on 'The Component Parts of our Reasonings concerning Causes and Effects'. He considers the case of someone reading an account of Julius

---

[8] See *Treatise*, p. 83.
[9] See ibid. 176–9, 'Of the Reason of Animals'.

Caesar's assassination in a history book and making an inference from it to the actual event:

> 'Tis obvious all this chain of argument or connexion of causes and effects, is at first founded on those characters or letters, which are seen or remember'd, and that without the authority either of the memory or senses our whole reasoning wou'd be chimerical and without foundation. Every link of the chain wou'd in that case hang upon another; but there wou'd not be anything fix'd to one end of it, capable of sustaining the whole; and consequently there wou'd be no belief nor evidence. And this actually is the case with all *hypothetical* arguments, or reasonings upon a supposition; there being in them neither any present impression, nor belief of a real existence.[10]

Yes, but what does he suppose goes on in the mind of a person making a hypothetical inference? The resources offered by his psychological system do not seem to be sufficient to supply him with an answer to this question. That is the problem which really does confront him in this part of the subject.

The fact is that a person can infer what will happen if the white ball strikes the red one with just as much conviction as he would feel if his inference started from the actual observed impact. But how will Hume's theory of inference deal with this fact? This problem has nothing to do with commitment to the necessity of external causal processes, because that commitment is sufficiently indicated by either of the two types of inference, categorical or hypothetical. It is only a problem about what goes on in the mind of a person making a hypo-thetical inference. The difficulty is that an inference of this kind is evidently made with the same degree of conviction that leads Hume to identify an internal impression of constraint when the inference is categorical, and so it would not be enough to attribute an *idea* of necessitated transition to a person reasoning hypothetically. For that attribution is appropriate to the quite different case, discussed in Chapter 1,[11] of a person who is merely considering the *possibility* that two events may be causally connected, whereas in a hypothetical inference the connection is taken to be actual and it is only the occur-rence of the cause-event that is put forward as a mere possibility.

So what can Hume suggest? If he does attribute an internal impression of necessitated transition to the reasoner, it will not be produced by a sense-impression of the cause-event. Consequently,

---

[10] *Treatise*, p. 83.   [11] See above, p. 13.

there will be no external source of the force and vivacity required for belief. In any case, it is not the idea of the effect-event that is due to get force and vivacity in this case, but the complex hypothetical idea of *movement of the red ball if hit by the white ball.*

Hume's psychological system just does not have the resources that would enable it to match the structure of a molecular sentence.[12] However, this is, perhaps, only a case of poverty of *expression*, and the connection embedded in the hypothetical idea is represented in his account of the *mechanism* of belief-formation. He can express the thought-process of someone using this mechanism in a categorical inference, but he cannot express the thought-process of someone rehearsing it without any current sensory input. One might almost say that he does not appreciate the autonomy of thinking. He concentrates on the basic kind of inference which steers us into the future and he neglects the free-wheeling exercises of hypothetical inference. It is also arguable that he pays insufficient attention to the thought-processes of a person who reviews a problematical inference and checks its reliability.[13]

Anyway, this problem, a real one for Hume, has nothing to do with commitment to belief in the necessity of external causal processes.[14] It may, therefore, be left at this point, so that the discussion of the other main question, posed above,[15] can be taken up: 'Does his account of what goes on inside our minds give us the access that we need to what goes on outside them?' This question raises three distinct issues. First, there is the possibility that his account of the evidence that gets through to our minds is too niggardly. The discussion of this possibility will occupy the remainder of this chapter. The other two issues will then be taken up in the next chapter. One is the question whether he makes what goes on in our minds too automatic and too insensitive to rational review. The other question is how, if at all, our apprehension of external causal sequences is helped by the internal impression of constraint when it moves to its conclusion.

So let us now ask whether his description of the evidence is

---

[12] It does not even have the resources that would enable it to match the structure of an atomic sentence. (See above, pp. 41–2.) But that is another, more basic deficiency.

[13] See below, pp. 96–7.

[14] However, it may help to explain why he does not mention the special case of counterfactual inferences. For they are even further out on the same line: when a hypothetical inference is open, there is no impression of the cause, but when it is counterfactual, there never will be an impression of the cause.

[15] See above, p. 77.

adequate. The point to remember is that we are not asking whether he fails to close the gap between evidence and belief—of course, he 'fails'—but whether, by omitting some important aspect of the evidence, he makes the gap appear bigger than it really is. Similarly, the question about his adversaries, the Rationalist and the Naïve Empiricist, is whether they make it appear smaller than it really is, by inventing unacceptable ways of reducing it.

There is a misunderstanding that needs to be identified and carefully avoided before we try to assess Hume's account of the available evidence. When we look back on his theory from our standpoint in this century, we are likely to see it as the reductive theory that a general causal statement only means that the relevant conjunction is constant. But this cannot be represented as his theory, unless the word 'constant' means 'constant for ever', and thus carries the implication of necessity. But the stipulation that the conjunction is constant for ever is not a specification of a collection of evidence that is ever going to be available. So though Hume puts a restriction on the type of evidence—it will be more and more instances of the same conjunction—he never reduces the content of the general causal belief to any finite sequence of instances. The belief is always audacious, and this is not a supplement hastily added to an originally reductive theory. It was an essential part of the theory right from the start.

The point is worth remembering, because his critics often represent him as eliminating the gap between belief and evidence, keeping the evidence meagre, and then giving an inadequate account of the content of the belief. But that is not what he does. It is the Rationalist and the Naïve Empiricist who try to eliminate the gap, and they, of course, try to do it by puffing up the evidence for the belief. *His* view is that the gap cannot be eliminated in their way or in any other way, and so, he concludes, all that a philosopher can do is to provide a naturalistic account of the origin of a belief which cannot be justified by the standards of either of the two kinds of non-audacious thought—a priori ratiocination and a posteriori reflection on a current sense-impression.

Everyone who reads Hume's account of the evidence for causal inference and belief is immediately struck by its superficiality. Constant conjunctions certainly do alert us to the existence of causal connections, but their discovery seldom brings an investigation to an end. It is usually followed by a careful analysis of the phenomena, designed to elicit what feature of the apparent cause is connected with what feature of the apparent effect, and to find out whether the causation really does flow directly from the former to the latter, rather than directly to both of them from some yet-to-be-discovered common cause. Hume greatly over-simplifies our sifting of the evidence when he assumes that we start with an accurate identification of the operative features of the apparent cause and the apparent effect, and that all that we then have to do is to find more events with the former feature and observe whether they are followed by further events with the latter one.

His favourite example, Newton's Laws, may be used to illustrate the point. Anyone who lives on the sea will notice that the tides are higher both when the moon is full, and when it is new. If the moon pulls the water up, why is its action stronger on those two occasions? Even when we have gone far beyond the original constant conjunction and have isolated an operative feature of the apparent cause—gravitational force, a function of mass and distance—we will still need an answer to the question about the periodicity of its operation. The answer that the moon's gravitational force is not working alone, but is helped by the gravitational force of the sun, was never obvious. And even that does not explain why especially high tides come when the moon is full, and so on the *opposite* side of the earth to the sun, as well as when it is new, and so on the *same* side. That needs a new piece of information. Earth and moon form a binary system which, by centrifugal force, raises the water on the side of the earth that faces away from the moon, and it is this effect of the moon which co-operates with the gravitational pull of the sun when the moon is full.

In this example, we start with two constant conjunctions between the states of the moon and the height of the tides. But we are not satisfied by the mere fact that they continue without any exceptions. We feel that we must go deeper and find the relevant features of the apparent causes and effects. In the course of this investigation, we also find that the causal pattern is more complex than at first appeared. For it depends not only on gravitational force but also on the centrifugal force of a binary system.

How much damage is done to Hume's account of the evidence for causal inference and belief by examples like this one? We may cast the answer in the form of an auction, starting with points which he will have to concede, and then raising the bidding and asking whether his critique of his two adversaries, the Rationalist and the Naïve Empiricist, will still retain any force.

He certainly has to concede that causal investigations have a depth that his theory greatly underestimates. The features of events that strike us first and send us off on an investigation very seldom turn out to be the ones that figure in the general statement which we eventually accept as lawlike. Of course, that might happen—an investigation might reach its conclusion in the simple, streamlined way that he describes—but we cannot expect to be so lucky. The concepts which we use to sort out phenomena in daily life will hardly ever be generalizable in his straightforward way.[16]

In any case, it is an over-simplification to suggest that the goal of causal investigations is merely the discovery of general statements based on sets of positive confirmatory instances or constant conjunctions. We also seek understanding, as the example of the moon and tides shows very clearly, and we get it in many different ways. It is probably true that experience has conditioned us to find certain kinds of explanation acceptable, but what we say to ourselves when we accept them is 'Now I see how it works', and not 'Now I see that this sequence will continue.'

There is also another, deeper point which Hume would probably have to concede, but it needs a certain amount of introduction. It is well known that he often emphasizes the independence of our descriptions of a cause and its effect. For example, he says,

... as the power, by which one object produces another, is never discoverable merely from their idea, 'tis evident *cause* and *effect* are relations, of which we receive information from experience, and not from any abstract reasoning or reflexion.[17]

Later, in his chapter 'Of The Idea of Necessary Connexion', he argues that 'we have really no idea of any real connexion between causes and effects', and in the Appendix to the *Treatise*, he recapitulates this part of his reasoning in an especially lucid and stark form:

Whatever is distinct is distinguishable; and whatever is distinguishable is separable by the thought and imagination. All perceptions are distinct. They are, therefore, distinguishable, and separable, and may be conceiv'd as separably existent, and may exist separately, without any contradiction or absurdity.[18]

This is his objection to Rationalism. But can he really sustain it in this

---

[16] Cf. D. Davidson, 'Causal Relations', *Journal of Philosophy*, 64 (1967), 691–703; repr. in Davidson, *Essays on Actions and Events* (Oxford: Clarendon Press, 1980).

[17] *Treatise*, p. 69.

[18] Ibid. 634.

extreme form? The distinctness of a cause from its effect depends on the way in which we conceive them and describe them, and it is arguable that our concepts and descriptions do not always pick them out in complete isolation from one another. Is it not more probable that our dissection of phenomena – the picking out of the specific features that we do pick out – can be explained by its success in yielding well-confirmed general statements? And, if that is so, will he not have to concede that, under these descriptions, cause and effect are not as distinct, distinguishable, and separable as he claims?

This is a much higher bid, and its impact on Hume's theory is controversial. He might concede the functional explanation of the evolution of our ordinary conceptual scheme. He might also allow the extension of this explanation to scientific terminology, which is often chosen for its yield of well-confirmed general statements. He might even concede that our descriptions (our general ideas) of things are affected by their connections and are not as distinct from one another as he claims, and even that they often carry causal implications. But he would certainly end his concessions at this point, and never agree with the Rationalist's analysis of causal connection.

His resistance would be based on the arguments that he uses in the text, but he would have to give them an extra twist. Instead of arguing that causal inferences are never a priori, he would have to argue that, when they are a priori, they are no longer audacious and, to that extent, fail as guides to the future. If the production of *that* effect is required a priori for the occurrence of *this* cause, then the inference will merely serve as a reminder that the description of the cause will have to be reviewed later in the light of what follows. But it would obviously be absurd to treat all causal inferences in this way, because the use that we make of them in our lives must often expose them to the risk of falsification. Scientific theories are under a similar constraint: however abstract they may be, and however rarefied the atmosphere in which they move, in the end they have to come down and face experiments which may falsify them.

It is much easier for him to deal with the criticism that his account of the evidence for causal inferences is inadequate, when it is made by his other adversary, the Naïve Empiricist. On this front, his strategy is simply to challenge his critic to point to a sense-impression of *power* or *efficacy*.[19] Not surprisingly, he is unable to comply. It would be like

---

[19] See e.g. ibid. 158–62.

trying to point to a sense-impression of *probability* when something probable happens.

There is a certain crudity in this part of Hume's argument, but it is entirely the fault of his adversary, and Hume's dismissal of him is not vitiated by the defects in his theory of the derivation of ideas from impressions.[20] For it is his adversary who is claiming that Hume overlooks the external impression of necessity in the account that he gives of the available evidence. So in this disagreement his adversary lays himself open to a very simple objection, whereas in his disagreement with the Rationalist a lot of preliminary work was needed before he could make his simple objection, and he left much of that work undone.

If his objection to the Naïve Empiricist has a fault, it is incompleteness. He argues that there is no external impression of necessity. But he could have gone further, and argued that, even if there were such an impression, it could not possibly get its description from its intrinsic character, but only from its place in the sequence of other impressions;[21] and that, even if it did get its description from its intrinsic character, it would immediately become necessary to explain its connection with its neighbours, the cause-impression and the effect-impression, and if that involved further impressions, each with their own intrinsic character, the process would continue to infinity. So, instead of arguing that we do not have an external impression of necessity, he ought to have argued that we could not possibly have such an impression, and one way of doing that would have been to argue by *reductio* that his adversary's thesis leads to an infinite regress. It is interesting that, when he is criticizing the Naïve Empiricist's account of personal identity, he does argue not only that we do not have an internal impression of the self, but also that we could not possibly have one.[22]

When Hume rejects the Naïve Empiricist's suggestion, it might be supposed that he is only rejecting his implausible view of the *evidence* for the underlying causal connexions between physical events, and leaving their *existence* unquestioned. He says, for example, that

. . . my intention never was to penetrate into the nature of bodies, or explain the secret causes of their operations. For besides that this belongs not to my present purpose, I am afraid, that such an enterprize is beyond the reach of

[20] See above, ch. 2.
[21] See above, pp. 50–1, for a similar criticism of Hume's account of ideas of belief.
[22] See below, pp. 126–9.

human understanding, and that we can never pretend to know body otherwise than by those external properties, which discover themselves to the senses.[23]

Later in the *Treatise* he looks back on his treatment of causation and endorses it:

It has been observ'd already, that in no single instance the ultimate connexion of any objects is discoverable, either by our senses or reason, and that we can never penetrate so far into the essence and construction of bodies, as to perceive the principle, on which their mutual influence depends. 'Tis their constant union alone, with which we are acquainted, and 'tis from the constant union the necessity arises.[24]

Here he may seem to be implying that there really is an aspect of causation in the physical world which is inaccessible not only to the senses but also to reason.

G. Strawson uses these and other, similar passages to support his view that Hume's naturalistic treatment of causation is restricted in its application to causation as far as we have any knowledge of it.[25] His interpretation then faces a difficulty: according to Hume, it is not only causal belief, but also the very idea of causal necessity that is derived from experience. Something more is needed to reconcile Strawson's Lockean interpretation of Hume's account of what we believe with his theory of meaning.

Strawson's suggestion is that we possess a relative idea of causation in the physical world.[26] Hume himself proposes this reconciliation when he is dealing with the gap between our idea of *external existence* and our available experience, which is, of course, restricted to sense-impressions:

The farthest we can go towards a conception of external objects, when suppos'd *specifically* different from our perceptions, is to form a relative idea of them, without pretending to comprehend the related objects. Generally speaking we do not suppose them specifically different; but only attribute to them different relations, connexions and durations. But of this more fully hereafter.[27]

---

[23] *Treatise*, p. 64.
[24] Ibid. 400.
[25] G. Strawson, *The Secret Connexion: Causation, Realism, and David Hume* (Oxford: Clarendon Press, 1989), 145–73.
[26] Ibid. 170.
[27] *Treatise*, p. 68. See below, p. 157. Hume's reference is to his later chapter 'Of Scepticism with regard to the Senses', discussed below, chs. 10 and 11.

This looks like a substantial relaxation of his theory of meaning. Instead of requiring the complex idea of a physical object to be completely specific, he is prepared to leave a gap at the point where we might expect an intrinsic specification. Russell made the same move when he allowed that physical objects are not known by acquaintance but only by description, and yet the phrase 'physical object' is meaningful.[28] If empiricists, like Russell and Hume, can relax their theories of meaning to accommodate the idea of physical existence, why should they not also relax them to accommodate the idea of physical causation? The passages from the *Treatise* quoted above[29] suggest that that is precisely what he does.

It will be shown later[30] that in the case of the existence of physical objects Hume does not exploit this relaxation in his theory of meaning, and the reason why he does not exploit it will be explained. Briefly, it is that, on his view of perception, it is theoretically necessary that our lack of knowledge of physical objects should always be total.

But let us now imagine that this obstacle had been removed, and that Hume had allowed that we have direct perceptual access to physical objects. Would the Russellian relaxation of his theory of meaning supply a content for the split theory of causation which Strawson ascribes to him — causation as far as we know it, and causation as it is in nature?[31]

On paper it would supply the required content. It is no good objecting that, when Hume speaks of causation as it is in nature, he is speaking ironically. He is using plain language and he is offering the only plausible explanation of its meaningfulness that is allowed by his theory of meaning. But the trouble is that at this point a second, more formidable obstacle blocks the way ahead: it is theoretically necessary that our lack of further knowledge of causation as it is in nature should always be total.

We can, of course, describe scientific discoveries, which make Hume's constant conjunctions intelligible, as Newton's theory made seafarers' tide-tables intelligible.[32] But we cannot imagine a discovery

---

[28] See below p. 195.

[29] See above, pp. 90–1.

[30] In ch. 11.

[31] It is a mistake to restrict the 'secret connexion' to the physical world. Anything that made physical causal sequences opaque would also make mental causal sequences opaque (*Treatise*, p. 169; quoted below, pp. 105–6). The 'secrecy' is not broken by the internal impression of the determination of the mind which occurs when someone makes a causal inference. See below, pp. 108–17.

[32] See above, p. 87.

that would make us say that the Naïve Empiricist was right after all. His picture of natural necessity is more than contingently inapplicable—it generates an infinite regress.[33] So if that is what our further knowledge of causation as it is in nature would have to be like, it is theoretically flawed and necessarily unattainable. This obstacle is more formidable than the one which, according to Hume, blocks the road to further knowledge of physical objects. For the theory which produces that obstacle—the theory that our impressions are our only objects—can be challenged, but the theory which produces this obstacle is unchallengeable. Certainly, there is more evidence for necessity in the physical world than Hume describes, but anyone who looks for evidence that would have to be described in a completely different way has been misled by a false analogy between ordinary impressions and impressions of modalities.[34]

[33] See above, p. 90.   [34] See above, pp. 89–90.

7

Causation: The Second Effect of the Evidence

THE second effect produced on us by the evidence for a causal inference must now be examined in greater depth. The first effect was the laying down of the associative track in the observer's mind, and the second one is the internal impression of constraint or inevitability that he feels when on some later occasion he moves along this track from the premiss to the conclusion of a causal inference:

For after a frequent repetition, I find, that upon the appearance of one of the objects, the mind is *determin'd* by custom to consider its usual attendant, and to consider it in a stronger light upon account of its relation to the first object.[1]

This determination is passive. Hume does not mean that, after frequent repetition, we make up our minds to consider the second object in the pair in a stronger light: he means that the repetition makes our minds work in this way, and that we feel it happening to us:[2]

Tho' the several resembling instances, which give rise to the idea of power, have no influence on each other, and can never produce any new quality *in the object*, which can be the model of that idea, yet the *observation* of this resemblance produces a new impression *in the mind*, which is its real model. For after we have observ'd the resemblance in a sufficient number of instances, we immediately feel a determination of the mind to pass from one object to its usual attendant, and to conceive it in a stronger light upon account of that relation. This determination is the only effect of the resemblance; and therefore must be the same with power or efficacy, whose idea is deriv'd from the resemblance. The several instances of resembling conjunctions lead us into the notion of power and necessity. These instances are in themselves totally

---

[1] *A Treatise of Human Nature*, ed. P. H. Nidditch (Oxford: Clarendon Press, 1989), 156.

[2] As usual, he rejects Descartes's idea that belief is a function of the will. See above, p. 53.

distinct from each other, and have no union but in the mind, which observes them, and collects their ideas. Necessity, then, is the effect of this observation, and is nothing but an internal impression of the mind, or a determination to carry our thoughts from one object to another.[3] Without considering it in this view, we can never arrive at the most distant notion of it, or be able to attribute it either to external or internal objects, to spirit or body, to causes or effects.[4]

The final sentence draws out the consequence of his theory of the derivation of ideas from impressions: if we did not have this internal impression of constraint or inevitability, we would have no genuine idea of necessity and we would not be able to make (or understand) any attributions of it to anything. Without meaning, there is no question of truth.

Commentators on this part of the *Treatise* usually find themselves locked into a controversy about the *status* of the necessity which has this internal impression as its origin. It is obviously not objective in the way in which someone thinking about it at the pre-theoretical stage might expect it to be. So is Hume's theory subjectivist? Or perhaps it would be more accurate to call it 'projectivist', because, as he himself says, 'the mind has a great propensity to spread itself on external objects'.[5] Preoccupation with this question, an interesting one, has put Hume's main enterprise, which is at least as interesting, out of focus. So the strategy that will be adopted now is to concentrate first on the major insight which Hume is trying to present in the rather primitive terminology of his system. The other questions will be taken up later.

The argument of the previous chapter shows that Hume's belief in the necessity[6] of external causal processes is sufficient to exonerate

---

[3] Notice the argument: it is the *repetition* of pairs of suitably related events which produces the impression of necessity, but nobody would ever suggest locating the necessity *between the pairs*. That would not be a plausible external location for it. The only conceivable external location would be between the members of each pair. But that is not the location which he discovers it to have.

[4] *Treatise*, pp. 164–5.

[5] Ibid. 167, quoted above, ch. 1 n. 22.

[6] It is important to resist, from the start, the temptation to put inverted commas around this word. For if we do that, we will be presenting his theory in a way that presupposes the truth of one of the theories held by his adversaries, Rationalism or Naïve Empiricism. Our pre-theoretical reflections on causal necessity may lead us to *expect* a theory which plants it in the external world in a simpler way than Hume's theory does. But we must not present his theory in a way that presupposes the *truth* of one of his adversaries' theories, merely because what they tell us is more in line with what we expect. Hume is right when he calls his theory 'a paradox' (*Treatise*, p. 166), but his readers are misled if they think that that word carries any deeper meaning than 'contrary to our expectations'. Anyone who argues that this in itself entails falsehood is forgetting

him from scepticism about what goes on outside our minds. On the other hand, his account of the evidence that reaches our minds, and of the effect that it produces there, is certainly austere. However, even if it is too austere, no legitimate enrichment of it can possibly close the gap between evidence and belief. Certainly Hume did not think that it could be closed, and he took a very different view of his task as a philosopher. His business, he believed, was not to shore up our uncritical pre-theoretical expectations with shaky philosophical dogmas, but to give a cool, naturalistic account of the way in which our beliefs are flung across the gap in everyday life. That was how he saw his main enterprise.

Of course, when he sums up this account, he does not always write coolly. Here is a notorious, provocative presentation of his view:

> Thus all probable reasoning is nothing but a species of sensation. 'Tis not solely in poetry and music we must follow our taste and sentiment, but likewise in philosophy.[7] When I am convinc'd of any principle, 'tis only an idea, which strikes more strongly upon me. When I give the preference to one set of arguments above another, I do nothing but decide from my feeling about the superiority of their influence. Objects have no discoverable connection together; nor is it from any other principle but custom operating on the imagination, that we can draw any inference from the appearance of one to the existence of another.[8]

This is one of many passages in which he presents his theory on a popular stage in paint and powder.

One question left unanswered in the previous chapter was whether he pays insufficient attention to the thought-processes of a person who reviews a problematical inference and checks its reliability.[9] This passage seems to supply us with an answer, and it is a surprising one: 'When I give the preference to one set of arguments above another, I do nothing but decide from my feeling about the superiority of their influence.' Can he really mean this?

If we read his later chapter, 'Rules by which to Judge of Causes and Effects',[10] we find what seems to be the different view that, when we assess evidence, we follow rules. An effect which is not constantly conjoined with a proposed cause cannot be the effect of that cause

that in a philosophical investigation of this kind the truth, when it is found, may be very surprising.

[7] As usual, 'philosophy' includes science.
[8] *Treatise*, p. 103.
[9] See above, p. 85.   [10] See above, pp. 87–8.

alone. An effect which is not contiguous with a proposed cause cannot even be partly caused by it. Other similar rules are given, and there is no suggestion that any credence should be put in the observer's feeling when it goes against them.

The two passages can be reconciled with one another, but only at a price. We can take his view to be that, when there is a conflict between evidence and feeling, the evidence should win. For he would hardly vote for a superstition, however passionately held. But that presupposes that the evidence points clearly in one direction or another. Suppose, then, that the evidence is exactly balanced. Then feeling will be autonomous, but in all other cases it will be subservient to evidence.

However, this is not a reconciliation which lends any support to the paradox that 'I do nothing but decide from my feeling about the superiority of their influence'. For if the evidence really is exactly balanced, Hume can only be guessing, and he was supposed to be telling us how inference works.

So we must conclude that he was carried away by his own rhetoric in the provocative passage that has just been quoted. He ought not to have implied that causal inference is ever a response to autonomous feeling. That is an excess which spoils his real point, that, though it is a response to evidence, it is mediated by the non-rational part of our nature. This is a powerful and, to some extent, original[11] application of naturalism. When other philosophers ask for a justification of causal inferences and make it clear that what they want is to see the gap between evidence and belief closed in some way, he replies that there is no such justification to be had. For this is a point at which justifications run out, and all that a philosopher can do is to observe that nature covers the gap, without closing it, by giving us minds which extrapolate constant conjunctions automatically, and, in uncomplicated cases, inevitably. There is a profound, and, for most people, disarming simplicity about this thesis. Is it not obvious that justifications are always offered within an agreed framework, so that, when that framework is questioned, a different kind of reassurance will be needed? So a wise philosopher will be one who recognizes when that point has been reached, and turns the request for justification by observing that we just find it natural to go on in the way that is being questioned—in this case, we just find it natural to make causal inferences in line with the associations of ideas that experience has established in our minds.

---

[11] Not entirely original, because it can be found in the writings of Sextus Empiricus.

This version of naturalism reappears two centuries later in the philosophy of Wittgenstein, but in the context of a discussion of a different set of problems. Wittgenstein is concerned with the question, 'What makes a certain way of continuing a mathematical series correct, when other ways are possible?', and also with the question, 'What makes our way of extending the application of a certain descriptive word to new cases correct, when it is not the only possible way?' His answer is that these are the ways in which people who have been trained find it natural to go on, and he gives the same answer to anyone who questions a logical or mathematical inference. Like Hume, he intends to make this move only when justifications within the accepted framework really have run out, and yet the questioner remains dissatisfied.

There are, of course, many differences between Hume's appeal to this kind of naturalism and Wittgenstein's, and perhaps the two main ones should be mentioned. One is that Hume appeals to it when he reaches bedrock in the exploration of the basis of causal inferences, whereas Wittgenstein appeals to it at the same point in the investigation of logical and mathematical inference and of the foundations of descriptive language.

The second difference lies in the two philosophers' views of what they were doing. Hume made it clear that, if he had been able to take the exploration any deeper, he would have done so, but, lacking the necessary scientific knowledge, he refuses to speculate.[12] He drew no distinction between philosophy and science, and he thought of his investigation as a single, continuous one which could be given either of the two titles. But Wittgenstein saw his investigation in an entirely different way. He drew a sharp distinction between philosophy and science: philosophy examines language from the point of view of its users, observes their practices, and argues that they must contribute to the standard of correctness to which they conform. The scientific question how they came to have the practices that they do have is one that he treats as irrelevant to his philosophical inquiry. So he denies the relevance of evolutionary theory to philosophy, whereas Hume would have included it in the same seamless pattern, if he had known about it.

Hume's naturalism receives its clearest expression at the beginning

---

[12] There is one exception to this abstinence and that is his speculation about the dependence of associations of ideas on movements of the animal spirits in the brain. See *Treatise*, p. 60.

of his examination of the third, difficult problem that he tackles in Book I of the *Treatise*, our perception of the world around us:

Thus the sceptic still continues to reason and believe, even tho' he asserts, that he cannot defend his reason by reason; and by the same rule he must assent to the principle concerning the existence of body, tho' he cannot pretend by any arguments of philosophy to maintain its veracity. Nature has not left this to his choice, and has doubtless esteem'd it an affair of too great importance to be trusted to our uncertain reasonings and speculations. We may well ask, *What causes induce us to believe in the existence of body?* but 'tis vain to ask, *Whether there be body or not?* That is a point, which we must take for granted in all our reasonings.[13]

Reason cannot defend the principles which we need to steer us through our lives, and so nature takes over and engraves them on our minds. When rational justifications run out, we just go on in the way that we find natural.

However, when Hume applies this naturalism to the problem of causal inference, he complicates its effect by introducing the internal impression of being forced to a causal conclusion. So he is recording not only what we naturally *do*, like Wittgenstein later, but also what we *feel* when nature shapes our inferences. That raises several questions about the internal impression that he claims to have found. There is, first, the phenomenological question, 'What is it like?' Then there is a question posed in the previous chapter about its function in his system, 'Does it help us to gain access to causal sequences outside our minds? Or is it postulated merely to satisfy his theory of the derivation of ideas?'[14] These questions will be taken first, and after that the discussion will range more widely over the controversy about the philosophical classification of his theory of causal necessity, 'Is it objectivist, subjectivist, or projectivist?'

The phenomenological question about the internal impression of necessitated transition is an interesting one. At first sight, it looks like another case of a 'special experience' invented to explain something which really needs an explanation of a different kind. Hume's treatment of belief was a clear example of that mistake, and it was criticized on the ground that there is, in fact, no common feeling-tone for belief, so that the only way to preserve his theory would be to define the

---

[13] Ibid. 187. [14] See above, pp. 13 and 77–8.

belief-feeling as 'whatever feeling leads to actions in line with the belief'. But that would drain his theory of its content.[15]

However, if we look closely at what he actually says about the internal impression of being forced to a causal conclusion, we will find it more interesting than what he says about the belief-feeling. First of all, it is not a piece of mythology, like the belief-feeling, because we really do feel impelled to follow the tracks of certain associations of ideas. As Wittgenstein would say, 'We do it as a matter of course.'[16] Hume puts it differently: 'We feel forced to go that way.' This, of course, is a third difference between the two philosophers' views of the transitions that we make in our minds, and it is a very important one. But it would be a mistake to describe this difference by saying that Hume recognizes the existence of a feeling of irresistible guidance, whereas Wittgenstein does not recognize it. The difference is more subtle, and it turns on the general implications of the word 'feeling' in this context, and on the specific description of the feeling that is supposed to be involved in this particular case.

The crucial question is this: 'How did Hume think that the internal impression of being forced to a causal conclusion ever acquired that description? There were two ways in which he might have answered this question. First, he might have thought that the impression exhibited an intrinsic property of forcefulness, which would be immediately recognizable, whatever the setting in which it occurred. Secondly, he might have thought that the property of the impression was relational, and that you recognized it as the feeling of being pushed along an associational track.[17] If the first view were correct, you might start by learning to recognize the impression by its intrinsic property, and not notice until later that it always occurred when you were making a mental transition under the constraint of an association of ideas. This might well be taken as a *reductio ad absurdum* of the first view. The second view is less implausible, because, according to it, you would learn to identify, and, later, reidentify, the impression simply as the feeling of being subjected to this kind of constraint.

If the suggestion that the impression of necessitated transition is recognized by some intrinsic property verges on absurdity, it might

[15] See above, pp. 50–1.

[16] See Wittgenstein, *Philosophical Investigations*, pt. 1, § 238.

[17] There is also a third possibility, which would never have occurred to him. As Wittgenstein sometimes suggests, there might be no feeling at all, except in this sense: you feel *that* you are moving under constraint.

seem to be not worth considering. However, its interest lies not in any claim that it might make to plausibility, but in the light that it throws on this part of Hume's philosophy of mind. In a system like his it is very easy to mistake the relational properties of impressions for intrinsic properties. Given his conception of phenomenological analysis, it was a mistake that he was likely to make without even being aware that he had made any move. For it was his unquestioned assumption that the analysis of complex ideas would always be guided by conjunctive definitions giving the intrinsic features of the things whose ideas were being analysed, and that this process could come to an end only when it reached simple ideas of things in which no further intrinsic features could be discerned. So it might end with the simple idea of a specific shade of blue which could only be derived from an impression exemplifying that shade. It just would not occur to him that what he took to be an intrinsic property of an impression might really be relational. That would have been inconsistent with the fundamental assumptions of his atomism.[18]

Hume's atomism made him especially likely to mistake a relational property of an impression for an intrinsic property. But the tendency to fall into this error is not confined to atomists. For there is also another, more general explanation of the error. Consider some physical analogues of Hume's internal impression of necessitated transition. Suppose that, instead of being pushed along an associational track in your mind, you are pushed forwards in space by an accelerating car or plane. In that kind of case you would have the sense that you were moving forwards even if your eyes were shut, and you would also have certain clearly identifiable bodily sensations, like the sensation of the pressure exerted by the back of your seat, or the sensation of the pressure exerted by the back of your rib-cage on your internal organs. But it is also important to notice that there is another kind of physical case, in which you have the sense—for example, that you are not in an upright position—without any definite bodily sensations. It is easy to forget that there are examples of this second kind, and to assume that the sense of being tilted is itself a sensation recognizable by some intrinsic property which we could learn to name independently of its setting. We may then forget that even in the other kind of case, where there are independently identifiable sensations, the sense that you are moving forwards is not one of them.

---

[18] See above, pp. 20–1 and 26–7.

These physical examples, or others like them, must have served as models for Hume's internal impression of constraint. For he construed causal inference as a passive process to be explained in a way that would approximate as closely as possible to Newton's explanation of the movement of stars in space.[19] But this way of treating our thought-processes immediately runs into difficulties. For when you make a causal inference, you will know that you are making it and you may also feel that your conclusion is inevitable, but what is there in your mind that could possibly be analogous to a definite, identifiable, physical sensation? Maybe there is something analogous to the sense of tilted posture or of forced acceleration—we shall see—but there could hardly be anything analogous to sensations of external or internal pressure. What could the intrinsic property of such an internal impression possibly be?

Barry Stroud points out that Hume is strongly inclined to treat the internal impression of necessity as a simple impression.[20] For his search for it was inspired by the assumption that the idea of necessity cannot be compounded from simpler elements but must be derived directly from its own corresponding impression. But, as Stroud observes, this raises a question that is difficult for Hume to answer: 'How does he know that the internal impression that he eventually finds really is an impression of necessity?'[21]

Although this is a difficult question for Hume, it is not an impossible one. The trouble is that the price that he has to pay for the answer is so high. He must abandon the disastrous analogy with bodily sensations of pressure and visual impressions of shades of colour, at least when they are conceived in his way. There seem to be two moves away from this analogy[22] that he has to make.

First, he must reject the notion that the property of the internal impression, *of necessity*, is intrinsic to it. Now his conception of typical properties of sensations or impressions is that they are recognized in complete independence of their physical settings. This is a questionable conception of them, but it will not be questioned here.[23] They are, at least, definite, identifiable properties and, in that sense, intrinsic to

---

[19] See *Treatise*, pp. 12–13, quoted above, p. 68.

[20] *Hume* (London: Routledge and Kegan Paul, 1977), 85.

[21] Ibid. 86–7.

[22] There is also a third fault in the analogy: the sense in which we 'project necessity on to the world' is not the sense in which we 'project colours on to the world'. See below, pp. 108–16.

[23] It is challenged by Wittgenstein's Private Language Argument.

sensations and impressions. But in this particular case there is nothing in the mind to correspond to the familiar ranges of sensory properties and so he must admit that the property of the internal impression, *of necessity*, is purely relational. However, that is a high price to pay for an acceptable answer to the question, because it goes against one of the fundamental assumptions of his atomism.

It is arguable that he also has to make another move away from the disastrous analogy with bodily sensations of pressure. For it may well be that the best analogy for someone holding a passive theory of mind, as he does, would have been the *sense* that your posture is tilted, or—a closer example—the *sense* that you are accelerating rapidly. Certainly you could not be said to have the sensation of inferring rather than guessing, but it would not be so outlandish to say that you had the sense that you were inferring rather than guessing. Indeed, in certain cases it might be an accurate description of your situation.

This second move away from the disastrous analogy will not be explored here. It is connected with three topics which have already been introduced and discussed. First, it is a move which involves propositions expressed in substantival clauses: you feel *that* you are being pushed along an associational track. That would confront Hume once again with a problem which he never tackled, the problem of intentionality.[24] Secondly, it is in any case arguable that his whole theory of mind is too passive,[25] and that inference, above all, should be treated as an activity. In that case, the internal impression of necessity would serve as the basis of an agent's knowledge of what he is doing. But is that really the right account of this very special kind of knowledge?[26]

These questions will not be pursued any further for the moment, and the discussion of the phenomenology of the internal impression of necessity will be broken off at this point and resumed later in this chapter. Meanwhile, something must be said about the function of this impression in Hume's system. In particular, does it help us to gain access to causal sequences outside our minds?

When this question was posed in Chapter 5, it was given a quick answer: the internal impression of necessitated transition not only meets the requirements of Hume's theory of the derivation of ideas, but also provides us with an immediate way of knowing that we are

---

[24] See above, pp. 52–4. [25] See above, pp. 12 and 31–2.
[26] See above, p. 29.

making causal inferences rather than just guessing.[27] We can now add that it is not the right account of our knowledge of what we are doing, but it is the only kind of account that he could give without radically altering his system.

There are several further points that now need to be added to this quick answer. First—an obvious point—it is essential that a thinker should know immediately which of the two things he is doing, inferring or guessing. Suppose that we had no such internal impression (and no other way of knowing what we were doing). Then we would not be able to choose between saying what the ball *must* do and what the ball *will* do—between what we would say about events on a billiards table and events on a roulette wheel.

This is not merely a point about the correct expression of our thoughts, but a point about the trust that we would want to put in them. There is also something further to be learned from the occurrence of the internal impression of necessity. It connects the conclusion with the premiss and so puts us in a position to review the evidence for the inference.[28] This is an important function of the internal impression, because the mere fact that you believe the conclusion is not enough to assure you that your belief is well grounded, still less to indicate to you what its grounds are. If it were not for this function, the internal impression of necessitated transition could be criticized for redundancy, because the strength and liveliness of the idea of the conclusion would be enough. In fact, it is evidently not enough, because it marks the destination but not the route to it.

These are important functions and they are overlooked by those critics who say that Hume merely postulates the internal impression of necessity to meet the requirements of his theory of the derivation of ideas. It is, of course, true that the theory does require an impression to generate the idea of necessity. For Hume *never* suggested that it is a spurious idea or that there is no real difference between guessing and inferring. But it is not true that he merely postulated the internal impression to meet the requirements of his theory. He did not postulate it but found it and even tried to describe it. No doubt his description is faulty, but it does pick out something essential to the experience of making causal inference, the feeling of inevitability. If it picks it out in the wrong way, that is entirely different from fabricating it.

---

[27] See above, p. 67.
[28] See *Treatise*, pp. 173–6 (the chapter on 'Rules by which to Judge of Causes and Effects'), discussed above, pp. 96–7.

There is one more question that must be asked about the function of Hume's internal impression of necessity: 'An impression of necessity is an indication of necessity, but where is the necessity that it indicates?' The question is a trap, because it invites the answer 'Not in external causal sequences, but in our minds.' But if this is meant in any simple way, it is wrong, and it is important to see just how wrong it is.

It is, of course, true that the impression of necessity is, like any other impression, in our minds. But if the word 'of' is cognitive, is the necessity there too? Certainly it is not outside our minds, like the necessity of which, according to the Naïve Empiricist, we receive an external or sensory impression. For an internal impression is an impression provided by inner sense and so if it were of something existing apart from itself, an object set up for its scrutiny, it would be an object within the mind—in this case, mental necessity.

However, Hume did not interpret the feeling of mental constraint in this way. He was not a Naïve Empiricist of inner sense. What is more, if someone reflected on his own thought-processes and predicted that he was going to feel constrained to make the inference that the red ball would move, Hume's view was that this higher-order inference would work in exactly the same way as the basic inference about the physical events on the billiards table. Since the events would now be mental, the associated ideas would be *ideas of impressions and ideas*, the inference would be made with *another* feeling of constraint, and, if it came true, the idea of the basic impression of constraint would be matched by an actual basic impression of constraint. But inner sense would not catch necessity at work within his mind on either of the two levels, any more than it would catch it at work in the physical world if the predicted basic inference came true.

No doubt, we are tempted to take the word 'of' to be introducing an independent object of inner sense, just as the Naïve Empiricist takes it to introduce an independent object of outer sense. But we must resist the temptation, because we would be attributing to Hume something borrowed from his opponent's theory and entirely out of place in the theory that he is developing in this part of the *Treatise*. He dissociates himself from this line of thought in a very forceful passage:

When any object is presented to us, it immediately conveys to the mind a lively idea of that object, which is usually found to attend it; and this determination of the mind forms the necessary connexion of these objects. But when we change the point of view, from the objects to the perceptions, in that case the impression is to be considered as the cause, and the lively idea as the effect;

and their necessary connexion is that new determination, which we feel to pass from the idea of the one to that of the other. The uniting principle among our internal perceptions is as unintelligible as that among external objects, and is not known to us any other way than by experience. Now, the nature and effects of experience have already been sufficiently examin'd and explain'd. It never gives us any insight into the internal structure or operating principle of objects, but only accustoms the mind to pass from one to another.[29]

There is a difficulty in this passage which will have to be examined in a moment.[30] Why does he say that, when someone makes the basic inference, 'the determination of the mind forms the necessary connexion of these objects [sc. the physical objects]', and that, when he makes the higher-order inference, 'their necessary connexion [sc. of the ideas, or mental objects] is that new determination'? But this difficulty does not obscure his main point, which is that inner sense is no more successful at apprehending necessity directly than outer sense.

Then what does justify his description of the internal impression that he finds as 'an impression of necessity'? Stroud poses this question in his discussion of this part of Hume's theory,[31] and it ought to be taken first. If we do not know why Hume calls it 'an impression of necessity', we do not know what he means when he describes it in that way and we have not understood what is going on at the heart of this theory. So we may now take up the question of the description of Hume's internal impression of necessity at the point where we left it.[32] *Why* does he describe it in this way?

It was argued in the earlier part of this discussion that his reason for describing it in this way ought to have been that it occurs in the setting of a causal inference which you make because you find·it irresistible. However, his atomism misled him at this point and he assumed that, or, at least, wrote as if, this irresistibility were a purely intrinsic property of the impression, and that does not even seem to make sense.

If this argument convinces us that the right reason for calling Hume's internal impression an impression of necessity is that it occurs in the appropriate setting, must we conclude that it is an impression whose intrinsic properties simply do not matter? And if we take that step, must we go further and say that the whole idea of a

[29] *Treatise*, p. 169.   [30] See below, pp. 112–14.
[31] *Hume*, pp. 77–92.   [32] See above, p. 103.

phenomenology of causal inference is a mistake? And then must we take a third step and say that feeling is irrelevant unless it is an attitude to propositions—i.e. unless the point is that you make the inference because you feel *that*, in the light of the evidence, there is nothing else that you can do.

These are difficult questions, and we may start by looking at Stroud's analysis of the predicament of anyone trying to interpret this part of Hume's theory:

> If we ask why the idea of necessity comes into the mind, Hume's answer is that it is caused by a certain impression. Even if we grant that there is an impression that gives rise to that idea, we are still faced by the question why that impression produces the idea of *necessity*. That, after all, was what was to have been explained. Hume's answer again is that that impression produces the idea as opposed to some other idea (say, the idea of -1, or the idea of a golden mountain), because it is an impression *of* necessity or determination. But it looks as if he can say that only because he knows that impression is in fact the one that produces the idea of necessity.
>
> In general, Hume says nothing about the causes of our impressions—his theory of the mind simply starts with them. So in general he ignores the question of why some particular impression is said to be an impression of X. But in the case of necessity he does not simply ignore the question, he is precluded from answering it, since he cannot say that its being an impression of necessity consists in its being an impression derived from an instance in which necessity is exhibited. There are no such instances. So the impression and the idea of necessity simply live off each other. The idea is known to be an idea of necessity only because it is derived from an impression of necessity, and the impression is known to be an impression of necessity only because it gives rise to the idea of necessity.[33]

The predicament of Hume's interpreter at this point simply reflects Hume's predicament: given that necessity never lies in the evidence, but only in the mind's reaction to it, the word 'of' cannot have its usual meaning in the phrase 'impression of necessity'.

But does it follow, as Stroud implies, that it cannot have *any* meaning? For that would be the stark consequence if Hume's only response to a request for an explanation of its meaning was to refer the questioner from the impression to the idea, and then back to the impression again, in an endless, frustrating oscillation.

However, Hume's predicament may not be quite as bad as that. He can remind us of a very important fact, which is not mentioned by

[33] *Hume*, p. 88.

Stroud. When someone makes a causal inference which is based on strong evidence, he really does feel that the conclusion is unavoidable. Now a critic who takes Stroud's line will not deny that. He will argue, instead, that Hume cannot make any use of this important fact, because he cannot accommodate it in his system. If that is so, Hume really is in a bad predicament. But is it really so? We must take a closer look at his reason for describing the internal impression as an impression of necessity and at the meaning of that description.

We may start by picking up a point from the earlier part of the discussion of this question. A visual impression of a particular shade of blue is, according to Hume, a perfect example of an external impression with a simple, intrinsic property. It has already been argued that if there is an internal impression of necessity it must be an impression with a relational property rather than an intrinsic one. We can now add that it could hardly be a simple property, given the nature of the concept of inevitability. So the differences between Hume's internal impression and the visual impression can already be seen to be considerable, even before it occurs to us that this case really involves propositions and our attitudes to them.

It is worth observing that these differences are going to affect Hume's claim 'that the mind has a great propensity to spread itself on external objects'.[34] Perhaps we can understand the suggestion that a secondary property, like a colour, really belongs to our visual impressions and is mistakenly projected by us on to external objects. But, to put it in Stroud's way, what property of impressions does Hume think that we project on to external objects when we make causal inferences? That is much more difficult to understand, and yet there is no doubt that Hume thought he saw a similarity between the two cases:

This contrary biass [against Hume's theory of causation] is easily accounted for. 'Tis a common observation, that the mind has a great propensity to spread itself on external objects, and to conjoin with them any internal impressions, which they occasion, and which always make their appearance at the same time that these objects discover themselves to the senses. Thus, as certain sounds and smells are always found to attend certain visible objects, we naturally imagine a conjunction, even in place, betwixt the objects and qualities, tho' the qualities be of such a nature as to admit of no such conjunction, and really exist no where. But of this more fully hereafter. Mean while, 'tis sufficient to observe, that the same propensity is the reason, why we suppose necessity and

[34] *Treatise*, p. 167, quoted at length below. See p. 95.

power to lie in the objects we consider, not in our mind, that considers them; notwithstanding it is not possible for us to form the most distant idea of that quality, when it is not taken for the determination of the mind, to pass from the idea of an object to that of its usual attendant.[35]

If the internal impression of necessity is an impression of something which is neither intrinsic nor simple, our projection of it on to external objects is not going to be so easy to understand as our projection of a secondary property like a colour. At least, necessity, unlike the colour blue, cannot be regarded as a film which we just peel off our impressions and attach to their causes. (Nor can probability be regarded in this way.)

But, however difficult it may be to understand this part of Hume's theory, his predicament is not so bad as Stroud represents it as being. It is true that the internal impression of necessity 'is not derived from an instance in which necessity is exhibited' — not even from an internal instance. But it does not follow, nor is it true, that Hume has no way of justifying his description of it as an 'impression of necessity', and, therefore, can only refer his readers to the idea that it generates, and then, when that produces no satisfaction, is reduced to referring him back again to the impression from which the idea is derived. For he can explain why he calls it an 'impression of necessity' without treating the necessity as something existing apart from the impression, an independent object set up for scrutiny within the mind.

The explanation is not going to be an easy achievement. He has to give the internal impression a content which people will recognize and say, 'Yes, of course, that is just how it is when I catch myself making a causal inference.' At the same time, he has to avoid describing it in a way that implies that it is sensitive to any *real* necessity in the mind. This is a difficult feat and his performance of it, though it is not flawless, is the most brilliant and original, but, perhaps, not the best-understood, feature of this part of the *Treatise*.

He was familiar with the theory that the idea of causal power is derived from our experience of the effectiveness of our wills. This is a suggestion which many philosophers have found attractive since his day. Here is his version of it:

Some have asserted, that we feel an energy, or power, in our own mind; and that having in this manner acquir'd the idea of power, we transfer that quality to matter, where we are not able immediately to discover it. The motions of

[35] *Treatise*, p. 167.

our body, and the thoughts and sentiments of our mind, (say they) obey the will; nor do we seek any farther to acquire a just notion of force or power.[36]

Not surprisingly, he rejected this suggestion:

But to convince us how fallacious this reasoning is, we need only consider, that the will being here consider'd as a cause, has no more a discoverable connexion with its effects, than any material cause has with its proper effect.[37]

But what if, instead of appealing to the power of the will, he appealed to its powerlessness? When this inversion of the familiar philosophical suggestion was added to the theory that the idea of necessity does not originate in the mere perception of a causal process but only in its subsequent reflection in the mind, the jigsaw was complete.

It may be that Hume found the last piece which completed it in Berkeley's philosophy. For he too had used the felt powerlessness of the will, but for another purpose — to explain the difference between thinking and perceiving. Hume rejected this use of it in his theory of perception,[38] but it may well have struck him that it could be used more appropriately within the mind to distinguish inferring from guessing. If this was the origin of his final solution to the problem of necessity, it would have led, by a very natural transition, to his repudiation of Descartes's theory of belief.[39] For it would have seemed to him that the fault in that theory was that it made belief based on evidence too like guessing.

If a person who makes a causal inference feels the inevitability of the conclusion, what is gained by saying that he feels the powerlessness of his will? Is this not just another way of saying the same thing? It is, but it is also, from a certain point of view, a better way of saying it. For it traces the idea of necessity back to a very familiar experience which is not the apprehension of an object existing apart from the experience either in the physical world or within the mind. The will has its well-known limitations, and, when we run up against them, we do not immediately start speculating about their hidden causes, as we do when we think about the power of a physical cause to produce its effect.

Naturally, Hume's appeal to powerlessness could not close the matter. For how could powerlessness be any easier to *understand* than

---

[36] *Treatise*, p. 632.
[37] Ibid. Cf. ibid. 169, quoted above, pp. 105–6.
[38] See below, p. 173.
[39] See above, p. 53.

power? But it does have a conspicuous advantage in his system: it allows him to exploit an impression of necessity without having to treat the necessity as something existing 'objectively' apart from the impression, either in the physical world or in the mind. If someone objected that there is no need to feel the powerlessness of the will when you are only up against a constant conjunction and not up against any 'real necessity', I think you would answer, 'That is quite enough for me.' In short, this is another case where Hume appeals to the common experience of mankind rather than to an abstruse theory.

When Hume's description, 'impression of necessity', is interpreted in this way, it is possible to explain what he says about projection, or, as he puts it, about the mind's 'propensity to spread itself on external objects'. When this problem was introduced, it was pointed out that, though it is easy to understand his suggestion that a simple intrinsic property, like a colour, is projected on to the world, it is less easy to understand the same suggestion when it is made about necessity.[40] But we are now in a position to unravel this difficulty.

We need to distinguish two ways in which necessity might be projected on to the world. The first is the method of projection used by Hume's adversary, the Naïve Empiricist, who really makes two mistakes at this point. He takes the necessity of which we have an impression to be something independent of the impression existing somewhere 'objectively'; and then he takes its location to be the physical world, so that the impression has to be a sense-impression. It was pointed out in the earlier discussion that, since necessity is not a simple, intrinsic property of an impression, this way of projecting it is scarcely intelligible. However, that is not Hume's problem, but his adversary's. So the account of projection quoted above ends with these words:

... notwithstanding it is not possible for us to form the most distant idea of that quality [sc. necessity and power], when it is not taken for the determination of the mind, to pass from the idea of an object to that of its usual attendant.[41]

Hume is not obliged to show that his adversary's mistaken view is intelligible.

But the main implication of this passage is that it is not only the philosopher but also the plain man who projects necessity on to the

---

[40] See above, pp. 108–9.
[41] *Treatise*, p. 167, quoted above, pp. 108–9.

world. So we must face the question whether Hume is really content to attribute this tissue of absurdities to those of us who are not influenced by philosophy. His treatment of our pre-theoretical assumptions in another case, perception, suggests that he would prefer to be able to show that they are not absurd.[42] However, he does not explain in this case how they could avoid absurdity, and we can only guess the line that he would have taken.

Perhaps he would have suggested a second, quite different method of projection. The internal impression is an impression of the powerlessness of the will when the causal inference is made. If this powerlessness is going to be projected on to the world it must be attributed to the object in which the effect is produced — in Hume's example, the red billiards ball. For if the red ball was conscious, it would feel the powerlessness of its will to inhibit its own movement. This is the exact opposite of Spinoza's view that, if a falling stone were conscious, it would feel that it was falling freely.

Naturally, Hume would have regarded this kind of projection as a mistake. The red ball is not conscious. However, this projection is an improvement on the Naïve Empiricist's projection in two distinct ways. First, what is projected is now the appropriate property, powerlessness, recognized as what it is, neither simple nor intrinsic. Secondly, the suggested projection is perfectly intelligible: it is like saying 'I think that your croquet ball is like one of Alice's rolled-up hedgehogs.'

Hume evidently found it very difficult to explain how his internal impression could be an impression of necessity without treating the necessity as something existing in the mind independently of the impression. For in the first paragraph of his chapter 'Of the Idea of Necessary Connexion' he is reduced to saying something which is scarcely intelligible:

For after a frequent repetition, I find that, upon the appearance of one of the objects, the mind is *determin'd* by custom to consider its usual attendant, and to consider it in a stronger light upon account of its relation to the first object. 'Tis this impression, then, or *determination*, which affords me the idea of necessity.[43]

But, as Stroud points out,[44] it is impossible to understand how the internal impression can actually *be* the determination of the mind.

[42] See below, p. 183.
[43] *Treatise*, p. 156, quoted above, p. 94.
[44] *Hume*, p. 80.

He makes the same point about another of Hume's baffling identifications:

Necessity, then, is the effect of this observation [of a continued conjunction], and is nothing but an internal impression of the mind, or a determination to carry our thoughts from one object to another.[45]

But how can necessity *be* an internal impression?

It might be thought that Hume knew what he wanted to say at this crucial point, but was hampered by a difficulty of expression. However, his trouble went deeper than that. He knew what he wanted to avoid saying: he must not on any account say that the necessity existed independently within the mind and was apprehended through the internal impression. But what he ought to have said instead was far less clear to him, and that is why he offered these strictly unintelligible identifications: both necessity and the determination of the mind *are* the internal impression. These identifications make it clear that the necessity has no independent existence even within the mind, but they do not convey any positive message which can be understood.

Hume's difficulty at this point is really conceptual. The resources of his theory of mind do not allow him to steer a middle course between identifying the necessity with our internal impressions of it and conceding it independent existence. He wants to be able to say that, when people realize that they have observed a constant conjunction which provides overwhelming support for a causal inference, they feel that they cannot help making it. However, in his system, their feeling has to take the form of an impression *of* inevitability, and so it looks as if a place must be found for this inevitability, if only within the mind. But even placing it there would give it the objectivity which his whole endeavour has been to withhold from it. So he falls back on an unintelligible identification: the necessity *is* the impression.

What he needed was a theory which would explain how, after many repetitions, we can experience a conjunction *as* inevitable, without ever having any direct experience of inevitability.[46] If he had had such a theory, he would not have needed to make any special use of causal sequences in the mind, because the theory would have provided a direct explanation of our view of all causal sequences, physical or mental. However, no such theory could possibly be reconciled with his account of the derivation of ideas from impressions. He, therefore, felt

[45] *Treatise*, p. 165, quoted above, pp. 94–5.
[46] The explanation would involve intentionality. See above, pp. 53–4 and 103.

obliged to base his theory of causation on an internal impression which comes very close to being a direct experience of inevitability. But, of course, in his system it cannot quite be that. That is why he is reduced to saying things about it which are scarcely intelligible.

His system has another deficiency which may add to the difficulty of his predicament at this point. His theory of mind is mainly a theory of passivity,[47] and he does not sufficiently allow for the fact that inferring is something that people do, even if, given a certain amount of evidence, they do it inevitably. Now when a person does something intentionally, he often knows what he is doing through his intention without the help of any impressions.[48] It may be that, when he knows that he is powerless to avoid a foregone causal conclusion, that knowledge too is of the same immediate kind. If that is so, Hume need not have run himself into quite such an impasse when he used this special case of known powerlessness as the source of the idea of necessity. Of course, if you know that you cannot do something, it follows that you cannot do it. But perhaps, if Hume had not assumed that your knowledge comes to you in the form of an impression of impossibility, he would not have had to face the problem of the independent existence of the impossibility.[49]

That is speculative. What is certain is that, though he relies on the setting in which the internal impression of necessity occurs, he fails to see that his reliance on it is incompatible with his official atomism. So he continues to write as if he accepted the disastrous analogy between the impression of necessity and an impression of colour.[50] This refusal to admit what is really going on in his system then produces an unfortunate effect. People suppose that much of the weight is carried by a very mysterious internal impression of necessity identified by this simple, intrinsic property. But that is not how things really are in his system. The truth is that this impression owes its identity to the setting in which it occurs, and from that it follows that the weight is really carried by that setting. Now the setting that is essential to the description of the impression is the move made under the constraint of the evidence from the impression of the cause to the idea of the effect. But

---

[47] See above, pp. 29–30.

[48] See above, p. 42.

[49] i.e. of the necessity of your failing to avoid the conclusion.

[50] Not, of course, as if he accepted Naïve Empiricism. The impression of a colour is an impression of sensation while the impression of necessity is an impression of reflection. The analogy that he seems to accept is that both are impressions of something simple and intrinsic. See above, pp. 105–6.

the habit of making such moves is simply accepted by Hume as a fundamental feature of human nature. So the true foundation of this part of his system is its naturalism, and the atomism is merely an inappropriate piece of decoration.

The arguments that lead to this conclusion about Hume's internal impression of necessity were set out earlier in this chapter.[51] From the point that we have now reached we can appreciate the strength of the last argument, which was only sketched very lightly in the earlier discussion.[52] All the emphasis was on the analogy between the internal impression of necessity and the sense, but *not* the sensation, of being moved forwards. The last argument was that, perhaps, the truest analogy was with a person's feeling *that* he is moving under constraint—a cognitive attitude with a propositional content. It can now be seen that that suggestion was the right one. For when we talk about a person's impression of the inevitability of a causal inference, or about his impression of the powerlessness of his will to resist it, these noun-phrases are substitutes for substantival clauses. What we really mean is that he has the impression *that it is inevitable*, and the impression *that he cannot resist it*. This then is a case of the awareness that accompanies action and Hume's attempt to force it into the mould of sensory awareness cannot possibly succeed.

Here we have a conclusion about the internal impression of necessity which has far-reaching consequences for the interpretation of this part of Hume's system. If we take his official atomistic account of the impression at face value, it may strike us that it would have been possible for us to make all the causal inferences that we do make, but without any internal impression of necessity.[53] But if we then reflect that this type of impression cannot be identified merely by some intrinsic property, but must owe its identity largely to its relation to the setting in which it occurs, it will not seem so obvious to us that we might have made all the causal inferences that we do make without it. And if we reflect further that the function of this impression is to indicate to us what we are doing when we make those inferences, it will no longer seem so easily dispensable. Some animals may lack it, but it

---

[51] See above, pp. 99–103.

[52] See above, pp. 102–3.

[53] Stroud develops this speculation: 'Since it is a contingent fact that we get the idea of necessity in the way we do, or that we get it at all, Hume's account of the origin of the idea leaves open the possibility of there being people with minds very like ours, who do not have the idea of necessity at all [sc. because they do not have the internal impression]' (*Hume*, p. 90).

cannot fail to make an appearance when they achieve the ability to consider competing future courses of events.

We must, of course, avoid crediting Hume's internal impression of necessity with all the features that it would have to possess in order to perform its function properly. He himself certainly did not understand those features. But, on the other hand, we must not ignore the function which it was supposed to perform, monitoring our inferences. Above all, we must avoid treating it as the independent source of the idea of necessity in his system. It *is* the source of that idea, but its essential connection with the setting in which it occurs shows that it is not its *independent* source.

It was pointed out in the previous chapter that a person's tendency to extrapolate observed constant conjunctions is a sufficient indication of his belief in causal necessity.[54] We can now add that, if he extrapolates them, he, being an animal who has reached the requisite level of self-consciousness, cannot fail to get an internal impression of necessity. True, he himself may not realize the importance of this impression, and Hume's idea, that it is the original source of the idea of necessity, may never have occurred to him. Nevertheless, he will get it. Even if inexplicably, or, perhaps, *per impossibile*, he did not get it, he would still be in a position to get it and would get it, as soon as he reflected on what he was doing. Hume may give an erroneous description of this internal impression of necessity, but we must not forget that what he is describing is a familiar and essential part of our lives.

If this is right, it is important. For it follows immediately that it is a mistake to maintain that this part of Hume's system falls into two independent, and, perhaps, incompatible parts. For example, when Stroud develops his speculation about the people who happen to lack the internal impression of necessity, he takes the strong line that they will lack the idea of necessity too.[55] So if they, nevertheless, make all the causal inferences that we make,[56] they will express them by saying that the effect *will* follow, rather than that it *must* follow. But this line of thought underestimates the interconnections between the various parts of Hume's theory of causation.

---

[54] See above, pp. 78–9.

[55] *Hume*, pp. 226–32.

[56] Stroud makes an exception of counterfactual inferences. But if the argument developed in the previous chapter is valid, these people would make counterfactual inferences too. See above, pp. 81–3.

It is true that he says that the idea of necessity must be derived from an impression. So if someone seemed to make causal inferences without the internal impression of necessity, Stroud is right to claim that Hume would be in something of a quandary. However, the strong criticism, that he would have to admit that this person lacked the idea of necessity, is too simple. He could use the argument sketched above, that it would be impossible for a person with the habit of making causal inferences to lack the internal impression of necessity, though, of course, he might fail to see its importance. This part of Hume's system is more cleverly constructed than the strong criticism allows. It is a seamless garment rather than an ill-matched two-piece suit.

If we look back on Hume's theory of causation from the point of view of the analytic philosophy of this century, it is easy to get the illusion that it splits into two quite different, and apparently uncombinable, theories.[57] One is the cautious, almost niggardly theory of the evidence for a causal inference and its first effect on our minds, the association of the two ideas. This is often read today as a reductive theory of causal necessity. However, the interpretation continues, Hume seems to think that he has gone too far and altogether eliminated necessity, and so he offers another theory which brings it back on the scene, but only on the mental scene, because that is the best that he can do for it. True, he does say that we project it on to the physical world, but that is just our fiction, like the fiction that the sky is really blue.

It is partly Hume's own fault that he is read in this way. For he often makes remarks which seem to imply that he would have been happier if he had been able to plant necessity in the physical world instead of in the mind. But that is only the rhetoric of an intellectual revolution. His main point is that his two adversaries, who do plant it in the physical world, the Naïve Empiricist and the Rationalist, are completely mistaken. So what is it that he would have wanted to be able to say?

He is, of course, genuinely worried by the gap between the available evidence and our audacious beliefs. Watching the white ball hit the red, we believe that it *must* move. He would gain nothing by suggesting that we only believe that it *will* move, because the first of these two beliefs contains the only possible reason for the second one. So he leaves our pre-theoretical ideas unrevised, and treats the gap between evidence and belief as a fact to be explained rather than denied.

[57] This view is taken by T. Beauchamp and A. Rosenberg in their book *Hume and the Problem of Causation* (Oxford: Clarendon Press, 1981).

Even if he had wished he had been able to close the gap, he could hardly have hoped to do so by pointing to an impression of necessity in our minds. His motivation at this point must have been different. His atomistic theory of meaning forced him to hunt down a simple impression of necessity, and that was his real mistake. But he also had two further aims. One, which has been emphasized here, was to explain our immediate monitoring of our own causal inferences. The other was to show that the gap between belief and evidence, though large, is not as large as it appears to be to those who are fooled by the projection.

The evidence most commonly cited for the 'split interpretation' of Hume's theory of causal necessity is the fact that he formulates two different definitions of *cause*: first, as

> . . . *an object precedent and contiguous to another, and where all the objects resembling the former are plac'd in a like relation of priority and contiguity to those objects, that resemble the latter;*

and then as

> *An object precedent and contiguous to another, and so united with it in the imagination, that the idea of the one determines the mind to form the idea of the other, and the impression of the one to form a more lively idea of the other.*[58]

The first of these two definitions would be satisfied by an unobserved constant conjunction, but the second one seems to require an observer to associate the two ideas, make the forced transition, and feel the internal impression of necessity. So here it seems to come out into the open that Hume really has two quite different theories. Or so it is argued.

The argument is weakened if we take the consecutive clause in the second definition to *specify the way in which the two objects need to be united* in the imagination, rather than to require that the observer *should actually make the causal inference*. However, it may still be objected that Hume does not say that the objects *are related in a way that would lead to their being united in the imagination*: he says that they *are united* in the imagination. So this definition still formally requires the actual presence of an observer.

Against this, it is sufficient to observe that in this passage he is really trying to draw attention to two aspects of his theory: first, there is what

[58] *Treatise*, p. 172.

happens in the world, whether it is observed or not, and then there is what happens in the mind of an observer, if there is one around. The suggestion that the second sequence of events makes a *real* addition to the first one, without which the first one would not be a causal sequence, is absurd and should not be imputed so hastily to Hume. He is, as so often, writing with oracular imprecision. Either he should have avoided calling his two formulae 'definitions', or else he should have inserted in the second one the condition 'if there is an observer around'. But it is naïve to infer from this text that he really has two theories of causation, one requiring, and the other not requiring, an observer. In fact, he himself explicitly rejects the suggestion that his account of what goes on in the observer's mind rules out unobserved causal sequences:

As to what may be said, that the operations of nature are independent of our thought and reasoning, I allow it; and accordingly have observ'd, that objects bear to each other the relations of contiguity and succession; that like objects may be observ'd in several instances to have like relations: and that all this is independent of, and antecedent to our understanding. But if we go any farther, and ascribe a power of necessary connexion to these objects; this is what we can never observe in them, but must draw the idea of it from what we feel internally in contemplating them. And this I carry so far, that I am ready to convert my present reasoning into an instance of it, by a subtility, which it will not be difficult to comprehend.[59]

Against this, how much weight can be attached to the carelessly formulated second 'definition'?

[59] Ibid. 168–9. The immediate sequel to this passage was quoted above, pp. 105–6.

8

Personal Identity: The Problem and Hume's Rejection of Current Solutions

I N Book I of the *Treatise* Hume applies his theory of the derivation of ideas to three difficult problems, causation, personal identity, and our perception of the world around us. Personal identity may well be the most difficult of the three. Certainly, it produces a starker situation, in which there is less room for compromise than there was in the case of causation. For Hume's solution to the problem of causation does at least gesture in the direction of his adversaries' aspirations, because his naturalistic account of belief in causal necessity does not reduce the content of the belief to the evidence available for it at the time when it is formed. But he makes no such concession when he is dealing with personal identity.

As a matter of fact he was not satisfied with the solution to the problem of personal identity offered in the main text of the *Treatise*,[1] and in the Appendix[2] he retracts it, without, he admits, being able to replace it with anything better. The completeness and candour of this retraction are seldom found in the writings of philosophers, who usually have to leave such radical criticisms to be made by others.

Why, we may wonder, was he dissatisfied with his account of personal identity, but not with his account of causation? They were both the results of applying the same principles in much the same way. In fact, both are examples of the kind of theory which was given the name 'Sophisticated Empiricism' in Chapter 5.[3] In the case of personal identity, the 'Naïve Empiricism' that was rejected was the theory that we have an internal impression of the self as something apart from all our ordinary impressions and ideas, something which owns them and

[1] *A Treatise of Human Understanding*, ed. P. H. Nidditch (Oxford: Clarendon Press, 1989), 251–63.
[2] Ibid. 623–6.
[3] See above, pp. 66–7.

is aware of them. The 'Sophisticated Empiricism' which Hume proposes in its place is the theory that a person is nothing more than a particular sequence of ordinary impressions and ideas related to one another in certain ways, which he then goes on to specify.[4] It is this theory that he retracts in the Appendix, and we need to know why his reasons for retracting it did not also produce a retraction of his theory of causation. Was it simply too stark and uncompromising a theory or was there a deeper reason?

The explanation ought to lie in some difference, or differences, between the two problems. It may, therefore, be useful to start with a brief analysis of the problem of personal identity, which will show how it differs from the problem of causation. Naturally, this will not provide an instant explanation of Hume's selective recantation. That will have to wait until his theory has been set out in detail. But a preliminary analysis of the problem will provide the essential background.

Most modern discussions of personal identity concentrate on the criteria for identifying a person across an interval of time. 'Is he the person who witnessed the assault?' 'Am I the father of that child?' These questions are typical examples of their kind, and they draw attention to two important points. First, both of them show very clearly that a question of identity spanning time needs a reference both at the beginning and at the end of the interval. The question is whether the person picked out by the contemporary reference is the same person as the one picked out by the earlier reference. The second example also shows that someone may be unable to answer a question of identity about himself. This is easily overlooked, because it is apt to be confused with something else, a person's inability to give his own identity in his own way when asked for it, which is rare. Both these points have a further consequence, the need to make some use of the body. For how could you tell that there really had been a witness of the assault, unless you found his footprints on the wet pavement, or some such physical effect? And how could any purely personal memory, without any physical verification, settle a question of paternity?

Hume shows little direct interest in the criteria for identifying a person across an interval of time. His concern is mainly with the unity

---

[4] This is really a theory of the identity of a person's mind rather than of the identity of a complete person, mind and body. Of course, Hume is not denying that a person has a body, but only trying to give an account of his identity without making any use of his body. The impossibility of this undertaking will seem obvious to most of us. What is not so obvious is that it may not even be possible to give an account of the identity of a person's mind without making any use of his body. See below, p. 129.

of a person, and, of course, given the narrow focus of his inquiry, with the *psychological* unity of a person. Is a suitably related sequence of impressions and ideas really sufficiently unified to count as a single thing? To put the problem in his way, are we not really feigning identity in this case, instead of finding it?

There are really two distinct problems at this point. First, there is the possibility that the psychological integration of a person may be paradoxically loose, like a group of buildings around a farmyard. Secondly, there is the more perplexing possibility that it may be so loose that sometimes we shall not know where one person's mental territory ends and another's begins, like a row of houses with unfenced gardens on a street. Hume is very much concerned with the first of these two problems, but he says nothing about the second one.

Now the second problem may seem to be one which could never arise for persons. For though you can identify an outbuilding without knowing to which house it belongs, you cannot possibly identify a mental thing, like an impression or idea, without knowing whether it belongs to you or not, and when it does not belong to you, you will seldom be able to identify it without knowing to whom it does belong. However, Hume never says anything about the ways in which we ascribe impressions and ideas to ourselves and others, and, though he may have taken for granted that we do it successfully, there is nothing in his theory to explain how the success is achieved when the owner is another person. This is not surprising, because it can only be done through the other person's body. However, it does produce a strange effect. It makes it look as if he believed that all the impressions and ideas that are known to us, in ourselves and others, are first taken indiscriminately, and then divided up into different packets, just as we first see all the stars above us and then divide them up into constellations. But nobody could believe that.

So, to sum up this introduction to personal identity, the problem really has three distinguishable aspects. There is the question how we identify the owner of an experience at the time when it is had: then there is the question how unified or integrated the mental life of a single person is; and, finally, there is the much discussed question of the criteria for the identity of a person over time.

Causation presents a problem of a different kind. For it is a relation between two distinct events, whereas the aspect of personal identity which concerned Hume most was the unity of a person's mind, a single thing, if, indeed, a person's mind does really count as a single thing. It is, therefore, understandable that the resources offered by his theory of the derivation of ideas might enable him to solve the first of these two problems to his own satisfaction, but not the second one. For, to put the difference very roughly, the first problem did not seem to him to demand as close a bond between cause and effect as the second problem seemed to him to demand between the various elements in the mental life of a single person.[5] In fact, one of the relations that he required between these elements *was* causation, but in the Appendix he admitted that it did not provide an adequate bond. He went on to explain that that would not have mattered if the self had figured as a separate, unifying element within the mind. But, unfortunately, it did not, and so he was left unable to explain the mental unity of a person.

This sketch of the background to Hume's theory of personal identity should make it easier to understand it. For it puts us in a position to distinguish his different reactions to the various facets of the problem. He seems to have taken some aspects of our predicament as persons for granted and not to have made any attempt to explain them. But there are other parts of the problem that he did try to solve, with varying success.

His treatment of the whole topic falls into three parts. First, he argues against the suggestion that the unity of a person's mind can be explained by the persistence of a self. This self, according to his adversaries, would be a permanent mental nucleus around which the person's ever-changing impressions and ideas would cluster. It would, therefore, be an individual substance, but one with a special role, because it would be the subject which viewed the whole sequence of impressions and ideas presented to it as objects. Against this suggestion he argues that we do not, and could not possibly, have an internal impression of such a self. At this point he is attacking Naïve Empiricism of inner sense.

He then observes that there is another way in which a person's mind might have achieved the kind of unity that it would need in order to meet his high standard of genuine identity. Its composition might have remained unchanged over time, like the composition of a lump of iron with no particle added to it or subtracted from it. However, this route to genuine identity is obviously not open to a mind, because its impressions and ideas are, and must be, in constant flux.

---

[5] And yet he cannot use the Rationalist's notion that there may be a real connection between the distinct impressions and ideas of a single person. See *Treatise*, pp. 259–60.

These two arguments, supported by many interesting observations, which will be examined below, take up most of the negative part of his treatment of personal identity.[6] Its second, constructive, part tries to make the best of a difficult situation. All that is now left of a person, or, more accurately, of his mind, is a sequence of ever-changing impressions and ideas. So the only way in which Hume can explain the unity of such a sequence is to point to certain relations holding between the items in it. It is very important to appreciate that, when he does this, he is concerned with the unity of a single mind rather than with the line dividing one mind from another. He merely assumes that what he is considering is a single mind, and all that interests him is its internal structure. The question of demarcation, 'Is this where one mind ends and another one begins?', is never raised by him.

The third part of his treatment of personal identity is, of course, his recantation in the Appendix. His reasons for recanting are obscure and they will be explained later. However, one thing is quite clear: he is dissatisfied with his explanation of the unity of a single mind, because his account of its internal structure is, he now thinks, inadequate.

The remainder of this chapter will be concerned with the first of the three parts of his treatment of personal identity. In the exposition and discussion of his critique of our pre-theoretical concept and of philosophical theories about it three points will be conspicuous. The first one is his assumption that the identity of a mind can be investigated independently of its body. The second one is his uncritical application to the mind and its components of the same treatment that he had given to material objects and their parts. The third remarkable feature of this part of his discussion is his concentration on the problem of the internal unity of a person's mind, taken as given, and his neglect of the line of demarcation between one mind and another. This neglect affects not only his treatment of the individuation of contemporary minds (like the problem of the row of houses), but also his treatment of the identity or non-identity of minds at different points of time (his analogy is the rebuilt church).[7]

The leading idea which guides his treatment of the identity of a material object is a simple one: something must remain unchanged. So if there is any change in the component parts, they must belong to an unchanging individual substance. If that condition too is violated, then we do not have a case of genuine identity. Now an individual substance

---

[6] There is also a brief rejection of the Rationalist's solution. See n. 5 above.
[7] *Treatise*, p. 258.

is not something extra, which is empirically discoverable, like the grain of sand at the centre of a growing pearl, but, rather, the thing itself. However, Hume assumes that, if the thing is more than the sum of its perceptible parts, the substance must really be something extra, and in that case we ought to have a separate impression of it. But, he argues, we have no such impression. Therefore, there is really only one way left for a material object to achieve genuine identity, and that is by undergoing no change in its composition. This condition is met by a lump of matter which has no particle added to it or subtracted from it,[8] but not by a ship, a building, a tree, or an animal, all of which can, therefore, only achieve a fictitious, second-best substitute for genuine identity.

Hume's intolerant downgrading of the identities of most material objects is obviously questionable and it has been criticized by many commentators. How can what we *count* as identity possibly fail to *be* identity? Why not allow more importance to structure, function, and the mutual co-operation of parts? But when he transfers the same intolerant treatment to the mind, there are other, more serious causes for complaint. For even if he had attached due weight to the structure, development, and internal working of a mind, that would not have helped him much with its identity or individuation.

However, before we inquire why these things are so much help in the case of a material object but so little help in the case of a mind, we need to appreciate the effect of his uncritical transference of his treatment of the identity of material objects to the identity of minds. The trouble starts right at the beginning of his chapter 'Of Personal Identity'. It is obvious that one of his two routes to genuine identity, unchanging composition, is not open to a mind, because it would be incompatible with the essential mutability of perception and thought. So he immediately focuses on to the other possibility, that the self is an individual mental substance. He assumes, as he did in the case of material objects, that, if a mind did achieve genuine identity in this way, the substance would be something extra — something additional to the ordinary impressions and ideas that clustered around it — and that, therefore, it ought to be empirically detectable. But, he argues, it is not empirically detectable, because nobody has an internal impression of such a self. The parallelism with his critique of individual physical substances is close. They would require external impressions and

---

[8] Ibid. 255–6.

individual mental substances would require internal impressions, but in neither case are the requisite impressions available.

Here is his argument:

. . . nor have we any idea of *self*, after the manner it is here explain'd. For from what impression cou'd this idea be deriv'd? This question 'tis impossible to answer without a manifest contradiction and absurdity; and yet 'tis a question, which must necessarily be answer'd, if we wou'd have the idea of self pass for clear and intelligible. It must be some one impression, that gives rise to every real idea. But self or person is not any one impression, but that to which our several impressions and ideas are suppos'd to have a reference. If any impression gives rise to the idea of self, that impression must continue invariably the same, thro' the whole course of our lives; since self is suppos'd to exist after that manner. But there is no impression constant and invariable. Pain and pleasure, grief and joy, passions and sensations succeed each other, and never all exist at the same time. It cannot, therefore, be from any of these impressions, or from any other, that the idea of self is deriv'd; and consequently there is no such idea.[9]

There is a looseness in the writing of this passage which is a sign of trouble. Is it just that we *do* not have any separate impression of the self? Or is it, rather, that we *could* not have one? And, if his claim is the stronger one, that we *could* not have such an impression, what is his argument for that? And what does he mean when he says that 'self or person is . . . that to which our several impressions and ideas are suppos'd to have a reference'? Does he mean merely that they are supposed to belong to the self, or does he mean that they are supposed to belong to it *as objects of its awareness*? The paragraphs that follow this passage suggest that he means the latter, because he goes on to argue for subjectivity without a subject: your ordinary impressions and ideas parade on the stage of your mind like actors, but without any distinct spectator, and, to make the analogy even more limited, without any distinct stage or theatre.[10]

It is not immediately obvious why Hume vacillates between the two claims, that you *do* not, and that you *could* not, have any impression of the self. First, it is necessary to appreciate that, if you did have such an impression, it would be an internal impression of something mental.

---

[9] *Treatise*, pp. 251–2. The last sentence means only that we have no idea of the self as anything *extra* to our ordinary impressions and ideas, suitably related; just as, when he denies that we have any idea of necessity in objects, he only means that we have nothing more than our own natural tendency to make audacious causal inferences and the inner feeling of their inevitability. See above, ch. 1 n. 12, pp. 78–9, and pp. 112–13.

[10] *Treatise*, p. 253.

So when he denies its occurrence, he is opposing an internal version of Naïve Empiricism. If such an impression did occur, it would be an ever-present indicator to the mind of the ultimate subject within it. We may compare the field of consciousness to the visual field and say that an internal impression of the self would be like an impression of the blind spot which indicates where the optic nerve is attached to the retina. The point is that, though neither of these kinds of impression ever occurs, they would be like one another, if they did occur.

Why is Hume not content to establish that there is no such internal impression, just as there is no visual impression of the point where what is seen is collected and transmitted to the visual centre of the brain? He seems to realize that his usual criticism of Naïve Empiricism is not enough in this case, and that he is really in a position to demonstrate that there is something unintelligible in his opponents' thesis. For he goes on to argue that each of your ordinary impressions and ideas is an independent entity capable of existing on its own without the support of a substantial self, and he challenges his opponents to give an intelligible account of the way in which a substantial self could succeed in owning all these independent entities and support them.[11]

There are, of course, no resources in his system for explaining this ownership. But that is not enough to justify him in accusing his adversaries of 'a manifest contradiction and absurdity'. They may be contradicting him,[12] but they are not contradicting themselves. It is hard to avoid the suspicion that there is some undercurrent here, some disturbing thought which does not quite reach the surface of his text, and the most plausible suggestion is that in this case ownership involves awareness. If this is right, the self would be the subject of awareness, and there might well be reasons for denying that any internal impression could possibly be an impression which indicated the continuing identity of such a self.

Consider, for example, your own identity over a period of twenty-four hours. Suppose that you really did have an internal impression of your self as subject and that you fell asleep contemplating it. Next

[11] Ibid. 252: 'After what manner do they belong to self, and how are they connected with it?'

[12] His view is given on p. 233: 'since all our perceptions are different from each other, and from every thing else in the universe, they are also distinct and separable, and may be consider'd as separately existent, and may exist separately, and have no need of anything else to support their existence. They are, therefore, substances, as far as this definition explains a substance.' See below, p. 141.

morning, how could you possibly tell that the apparently similar internal impression with which you awoke was an impression of the *same*
subject-self? Whatever you *seemed* to remember about it from the night
before would be reliable only if you, as recollector this morning, carried on the identity of the subject of last night's experience in some
other way. But, given that condition, it would not matter what you
remembered from the previous night—it would have been just as good
if you had remembered taking a sleeping-tablet—and, in default of
that condition, there would be no reason to rely on any memory. For a
recording system always needs something independent to support its
own identity. If that support, whatever it may be, is projected outwards
and treated as an object, the identity of that object cannot possibly be
validated by the system itself. It is easy to see that a physical version of
this procedure would be circular—for example, if someone said 'The
identity of my mind is guaranteed by the fact that I remember that my
fingerprints always looked like this.' When Hume's adversary postulates an impression of the self, he is making a mistake of the same kind,
and the only reason why it is not so easy to diagnose is that the
mentalistic version, which appeals to an internal impression of the self
instead of an external impression of the body, is very unrealistic and
the lack of realism masks the absurdity.

There is another way of appreciating the absurdity of the theory that
Hume is attacking. Suppose that, instead of considering the identity of
your mind over time, you concentrate on its present contents, as he
recommends. Let us say that you find among them an impression
which, you suspect, might be the internal impression of your self. But
how could you possibly tell that that was what it was. In the physical
world your body channels your external impressions into your mind,
and you can discover by experiment that it does so, and also, more
specifically, that you see with your eyes, hear with your ears, and so on.
But what experiment could possibly assure you that a mental entity, of
which you had an internal impression, really was the subject contemplating everything else in your mind? The uncritical assimilation of the
mental role of the ego to the physical role of the eye immediately fails
for lack of resources. In the mind there is no medium, no mobility, and
no controllable interruption of receptivity.

Hume does not push the investigation as far as this. He does charge
his opponents with 'manifest contradiction and absurdity', but he does
not explain how he would support the charge. He evidently suspects
that the problem goes much deeper than his opponents suppose.

However, he too fails to plumb its depth, and so he criticizes their theory on a superficial level, as if its faults were no deeper than the faults of the theory that material objects are individual substances. To put this interpretation in the form in which it was presented earlier, he assumes that his treatment of physical objects can be transferred, more or less unaltered, to minds. However, this assumption is profoundly mistaken, and, as will soon become apparent, the mistake generates the faults in his own theory, which eventually led him to recant it.

The mistake is a simple one, neglecting the body. It is obvious that the identities of physical objects are not generally founded on the identities of anything else supporting them. This makes it easy for a philosopher in the Cartesian tradition to assume that the same is true of the identities of minds. Hume, of course, rejects the suggestion that minds are individual substances, but he fails to reject the more general underlying idea that their identities are independent of any support that might be provided by the identities of any other kind of thing associated with them. He thus puts himself in the same impossible position as his opponents, and that is why he can only criticize them in a comparatively superficial way. However, in his chapter 'Of Personal Identity' he does give signs of his uneasy suspicion that the problem is deeper than either he or they realize, and later, in the Appendix, he retracts his own solution to it. So one way to read his account of personal identity is to take his theory and his retraction together, and to construe them as a *reductio ad absurdum* of the assumption that the identities of minds are not founded on the identities of anything else supporting them.

If persons are not merely minds but mind–body couples, neglect of the body will result in a lame account of the criteria of personal identity over time. That is obvious and it need not be elaborated here. What is not so obvious is the effect of Hume's neglect of the body on his account of the identities of minds.

The effect, to describe it briefly first, is a crippling reduction of resources. The mentalistic theories of both Hume's opponents and Hume himself are desperate reactions to this conceptual impoverishment. Both sides strive to give the mental structure of a person a strength which it could never achieve without the body, and, from this point of view, the main difference between them lies in their attitudes to their efforts. Hume's opponents are satisfied with the unifying power of the self as a substance. Hume is at first happy to mock this power as something purely mythological and to substitute a much weaker empiricist version of the structure of a mind; but later he sees that this will not do, although he can find no way of improving on it.

The magnitude of the predicament in which both sides find themselves can be gauged by the difficulties encountered by Hume when he tries to make use of memory in his analysis of the problem of personal identity. Unlike Locke, he does not treat memory as any kind of criterion of personal identity. He allows that it provides us with the data, our past impressions and ideas, and the relations that bind them together into a single person, but he denies that it settles questions of personal identity. The reason that he gives for this denial is, as far as it goes, convincing; our lives extend beyond our capacity to remember them and so 'memory does not so much *produce* as *discover* personal identity'.[13] This is just what we would expect from a philosopher dedicated to the science of human nature: *A* can be the same person as *B*, even if he is unable to remember perceiving, thinking, and doing everything that *B* perceived, thought, and did. There are other, objective relations between the stages in the life of a mind and they do not need to be reinforced every time by the subjective link that is provided by experience-memory.

So far, so good. But even if experience-memory is not criterial, it is certainly needed by anyone with a sense of his own identity. It is also needed by anyone who merely makes a collection of data and asks himself whether they are related to his present data in the ways that Hume counts as establishing his identity-line back into the past. For example, he might say 'Someone left those footprints on the wet pavement. Am I that person?' Here, then, are two ways in which memory functions in Hume's system, and the question is whether he has given it enough resources to support these two functions.

It was pointed out above that any recording system must rest its identity on something independent of its own deliverances. In the case of a mind, the obvious candidate for this supporting role is the body, or the brain. However, Hume makes no use of the body at this crucial point. This is not because he was a sceptic about the physical world and, therefore, felt himself unable to use the human body at this point. It is merely that he preferred not to make use of it, because the aim of his science of human nature was to describe and explain the inner working of the mind, and he believed that he could achieve this aim most clearly and convincingly if he detached the mind from its

---

[13] *Treatise*, p. 262.

entanglements with the physical world. In the Appendix, when he admits the failure of his enterprise, he says:

I had entertained some hopes, that however deficient our theory of the intellectual world might be, it wou'd be free from those contradictions, and absurdities, which seem to attend every explication, that human reason can give of the material world.[14]

This explains why he tried to set up the mind on a completely independent basis. But we still need to know why that was an impossible enterprise.

His own view of the reasons for his failure will be examined in the next chapter, after his theory of personal identity has been explained. Here we are only concerned with one aspect of his failure, his inability to base the identity of a mind on its own unchecked deliverances. His predicament was the direct result of his self-frustrating refusal to use the body. For without the body, how could a mind ever set up the distinction between memory and fantasy? Fantasy is free, but memory is tied to the success of certain patterns of behaviour, like returning to the place where you think you remember putting something that you now need. Even when what you remember doing is something purely mental, like thinking a certain thought, the correctness of the memory requires that the remembering mind be a genuine continuation of the mind that had the thought, and how could that be established without reference to the brain? If there were no causal link between the original thought and the later 'memory' of it, the so-called 'memory' would merely be a coincidental match, and only the brain is capable of carrying the required causal link.

This does not mean that you have to check the history of your brain before making any particular memory-claim, like the claim that you had a certain thought or a certain experience yesterday. You know such things immediately from inside the system of your mind. However, that system does need general support from the body, since, without it, the reliability of the immediate deliverances of memory would vanish. Indeed, if the required physical support had never been available, the concept of memory, as distinct from fantasy, would never have been set up.

When a philosopher working in the Cartesian tradition contemplates this scene, he will always underestimate the role of the human body. The fact is that if the mind lacked the general support provided by

[14] Ibid. 633.

the body, our concept of mind would disintegrate. However, the dependence of mind on body is not obvious, because the ordinary transactions of the mind do not include any check on their own physical basis. Indeed, if they did include such a check, and if you had to carry it out alone, you would be reduced to the circularity of the argument 'My memory of yesterday's thought is reliable, because I can see from my fingerprints that it has been carried by the same body.'

This collapse can never be avoided with purely mental resources. When Hume's adversaries tried to tighten up the unity of the mind by postulating an impression of the self, they could not possibly succeed. However, his diagnosis of their failure was only a superficial one. He was quite right to give a more limited, empiricist account of the contents of the mind, but he underestimated the difficulty of the problem which their more extravagant account was designed to solve. Later, when he got the measure of the problem, he realized that he too had failed to solve it, and the reason why he failed was that he shared his adversaries' crippling assumption that the solution was to be sought entirely within the mind.

The deficiency in his account of personal identity becomes especially clear when we examine the other function of memory, extending one's identity-line back into the past. In this case it almost looks as if he was not really concerned with the criteria for answering questions of personal identity spanning periods of time. Certainly, his main interest was in the question how much unity or integration is achieved by a sequence of impressions and ideas, which are already known to belong to a single person.

This is exactly what we would expect, given his treatment of the contemporary impressions and ideas which, he already knows, belong to a single person, namely himself. In both cases the lines of demarcation between one person and another are neglected. What are the grounds for attributing a set of impressions and ideas, either at the present moment or over a period of time, to a single person? We are not told. Instead, we get an account of the internal unity of the set, which cannot possibly serve to mark it off from other sets. It is as if he believed that the attribution of a particular item to a particular collection could be decided by its effect on the structure of the collection — or perhaps it would be fairer to say that he was so concerned to give an empiricist account of the structure of a collection that he lost sight of the prior question of attribution or ownership.

Consider the way in which I would try to extend my identity-line back into the past. There are two kinds of question that I might ask myself. An example of the first kind would be 'What did I do last night?' This question merely seeks to add to my autobiography, and so it rests on the general assumption that my identity-line is there to be traced back for at least twenty-four hours. It is, of course, true that some additions to my autobiography will settle particular questions of identity, like the question 'Am I the person who left those footprints on the wet pavement last night?' However, if I am going to ask myself that question, I will need independent evidence that someone did walk last night on that pavement. The reason why my evidence for that fact must be independent is this: it must leave the question of identity open. For an identity-question of this kind makes two references and then goes on to ask whether the persons picked out by them are identical or not.[15] But if I relied on my memory for the past reference, I would be presupposing an affirmative answer to the question of identity.

The only way for me to get an independent reference to the person last night is to make some use of his body. But Hume refuses to let me do that and instructs me to rely entirely on my memory. However, if I do trust my own memory for the existence of that person, I can no longer treat the question of my identity with him as an open one. So when I accept the constraints of Hume's system, I cannot even ask a typical identity-question about myself, because the evidence which supports its earlier reference will immediately settle the question of identity.

This shows very clearly that Hume neglects the lines of demarcation between one person and another. He assumes that he already knows which set of impressions and ideas constitute himself, and he goes on to ask about their internal relationships. But how could the answer to this further question possibly affect the answer to the original question of identity? To revert to the example used above, if I really do remember the experience of walking on the wet pavement, then it will not matter if the complete sequence of my impressions and ideas does not have a well-integrated structure. I could be distraught.

So Hume's account of personal identity is in trouble. His refusal to make any use of the body frustrates his attempt to use memory even in the posing of typical questions about one's own identity. It also undermines the very distinction between memory and fantasy. He faces up

[15] See above, p. 121. Cf. Frege, 'Sense and Reference', trans. M. Black, in *Philosophical Writings of Gottlob Frege*, ed. P. Geach and M. Black, 2nd edn. (Oxford: Blackwell, 1960).

neither to these difficulties nor to the related difficulties of demarcation which arise when a person is attributing contemporary impressions and ideas to himself and others. Instead, he devotes himself to developing an account of the internal structure of a collection which is *already* taken to be a single person. The trouble is that no structural theory of identity of mind can possibly serve as a substitute for a theory of mind based on body. Whatever relations between impressions and ideas are chosen to constitute the unity of a mind, they will never succeed in explaining the original individuation of different minds.

In the next chapter, Hume's choice of unifying relations will be examined from this point of view, and an interpretation of his own confession of its failure will be attempted.

9

Personal Identity: Hume's Solution and his Later Recantation

HUME'S views about the unity and structure of an individual mind are set forth in two chapters near the end of Book I, 'Of the Immateriality of the Soul' and 'Of Personal Identity'. He starts with this bold claim:

> The intellectual world, tho' involv'd in infinite obscurities, is not perplex'd with any such contradictions, as those we have discover'd in the natural. What is known concerning it, agrees with itself; and what is unknown, we must be contented to leave so.[1]

He then proceeds to give an account of personal identity which is another example of 'Sophisticated Empiricism'.[2] However, in the Appendix to the *Treatise* he retracts it:

> I had entertained some hopes, that however deficient our theory of the intellectual world might be, it wou'd be free from those contradictions, and absurdities, which seem to attend every explication, that human reason can give of the material world. But upon a more strict review of the section concerning *personal identity*, I find myself involv'd in such a labyrinth, that, I must confess, I neither know how to correct my former opinions, nor how to render them consistent.[3]

So there are two things to be explained in this chapter, his theory of personal identity and his reasons for retracting it.

The theory relies entirely on the available mental resources. A person—or, to be more precise, a mind—is merely a sequence of impressions and ideas held together by certain relations. These relations give the sequence the internal structure which deceives us when we contemplate it. What we really see is only the endless replacement

---

[1] *A Treatise of Human Understanding*, ed. P. H. Nidditch (Oxford: Clarendon Press, 1989), 232.

[2] See above, pp. 65–6.

[3] *Treatise*, p. 633.

of each set of impressions and ideas by the set that immediately follows it, but the relations between one set and the next make the transition so smooth that it is almost imperceptible. This makes us feel that something must remain unchanged as we voyage through time. What else could possibly justify the strong sense of identity that each of us has? So the conviction that we must somehow be achieving genuine identity through time becomes unavoidable. Nevertheless, it is, according to Hume, an illusion. We are like travellers on a road so perfectly constructed that we do not feel that we are moving, or, rather, to bring this illusion closer to the case of personal identity, we feel that we must be taking our part of the road-surface with us, like toy soldiers, each on his own toy patch of ground.

But what are the relations between the successive stages of our mental development which produce this powerful effect on us? Hume's answer to this question makes it seem easier than it really is:

> The only question, therefore, which remains, is, by what relations this uninterrupted progress of our thought is produc'd, when we consider the successive existence of a mind or thinking person. And here 'tis evident we must confine ourselves to resemblance and causation, and must drop contiguity, which has little or no influence in the present case.[4]

This selection of only two out of the three natural relations[5] is puzzling. He is evidently contemplating the development of his own mind in much the same way that he would observe the development of a well-structured physical object. Each stage in the growth of a plant resembles, and is caused by, the preceding stage and similarly, within his mind, ideas are caused by impressions that resemble them. This is at least an over-simplification. For if he is going to record the world around him and think about it, the patterns of resemblance and causal linkage will have to be enormously more complex than this account of the structure of his mind suggests, and some of the complications have already been described in previous chapters. But there is another, more radical problem confronting him at this point. Causation, according to him, involves contiguity.[6] So if he appeals to causation to explain the development of his mind, how can he 'drop contiguity'?

Perhaps he would have answered this question by pointing out that

---

the mind is not a place, and that things within the mind cannot stand in spatial relations to one another. So if 'contiguity' is understood in the way in which he originally introduced it, as 'contiguity in time and place',[7] it cannot possibly be included among the relations that give a mind its internal structure.

However, that is not a sufficient answer. For we have already found that the role played by contiguity in time and place in his account of causation is an essential one: it tells us when and where to look for the effect of a given cause, or the cause of a given effect.[8] Consequently, if the mind owes its internal structure partly to causation, and if this essential role cannot be played by contiguity in time and place, some substitute must be found. What, then, is the substitute?

Hume himself tries to supply the necessary substitute in his chapter 'Of the Immateriality of the Soul'. He proposes contiguity in time alone.[9] In fact, his main argument in that chapter is that 'our endeavouring to bestow a place on what is utterly incapable of it . . . . arises from our inclination to compleat a union, which is founded on causation, and a contiguity of time, by attributing to the objects a conjunction in place'.[10] It is surprising that, having offered this substitute in the first of his two chapters on this topic, he should forget it in the second one, 'Of Personal Identity', and propose that we simply 'drop contiguity'.

It is hard to follow his line of thought at this crucial point, because so much is left to work itself out below the surface of his text. The problems which first make themselves felt when we ask how mental causation is supposed to function in his theory of personal identity really go much deeper than that. We certainly need a way of telling when and where to look for the effect of a given cause, or the cause of a given effect. However, our troubles would not necessarily be at an end when this deficiency in the theory had been made good. For causation does not keep within the confines of a single mind, and so, though the internal structure of each mind owes much to the causal processes that go on within it, the lines of demarcation between one mind and another cannot possibly be determined by causation alone. Nor can this deficiency be made good by an appeal to resemblance. For that too is a relation which holds not only between things in the same mind, but

---

[7] Ibid.
[9] *Treatise*, p. 237.

[8] See above, pp. 71–2.
[10] Ibid. 238–9.

also between things in different minds. So there seems to be a more radical weakness in Hume's theory of personal identity.

At this point we should remind ourselves of the several different problems that the theory ought to have been able to solve. First, there is the question how we identify the owner of an experience at the time when it is had. An answer to this question would obviously tell us a lot about the boundaries between minds, but Hume never tries to answer it. Secondly, there is the question how unified or integrated the mental life of a single person is. He does deal with this question, but he takes it as a question about a particular mind, already identified in some way, and so already distinguished from other minds. Thirdly, there is the question by what criteria we establish the identity of a person over time. This is a much-discussed problem today, but he does not put it in the forefront of his treatment of personal identity. In fact, as we have seen, a typical inquiry about the identity of a person over time would start with two independent personal references, and then go on to settle whether their targets were, or were not, the same person, but this schema cannot even be set up with the resources available in Hume's system.[11]

Much has been written about the defects of his theory of personal identity and about his own view of what they were. He evidently wanted to extend to the mind the Sophisticated Empiricism which, he thought, had proved successful with physical objects. This suggests two lines of inquiry. Had that treatment really succeeded with physical objects? And if it failed, or failed more radically when it was extended to minds, what differences between minds and physical objects would explain its failure? These two lines of inquiry will be followed in the remainder of this chapter. It is important not to omit the first one. For though Hume was obviously right in thinking that his Sophisticated Empiricism encountered special difficulties when it was applied to the mind, his assumption that it gave a satisfactory account of the identities of physical objects is questionable.

So that is the point where we must start. Now the most striking feature of his treatment of the identity of a physical object is the strictness of the standard that he requires it to meet. Either there must be no change in its composition, or else there must be a permanent substance to which its changing parts successively belong. The first requirement, according to him, is met only by a rather special case:

---

[11] See above, pp. 132–3.

... suppose any mass of matter, of which the parts are contiguous and connected, to be plac'd before us; 'tis plain we must attribute a perfect identity to this mass, provided all the parts continue uninterruptedly and invariably the same, whatever motion or change we may observe either in the whole or in any of the parts. But supposing some very *small* or *inconsiderable* part to be added to the mass, or subtracted from it; tho' this absolutely destroys the identity of the whole, strictly speaking; yet as we seldom think so accurately, we scruple not to pronounce a mass of matter the same, where we find so trivial an alteration.[12]

The alternative requirement—according to him, the only alternative—that there be a permanent substance, is never met, because, he thinks, the whole notion of such a substance is an illusion. So physical objects very seldom achieve genuine identity through time, and when they do achieve it, it is always by meeting the first requirement, of unchanging composition, which, as we saw in the previous chapter, can never be met by a mind.[13]

This phase in his discussion of identity has caught the attention of commentators, who protest that his strict way of speaking is too intolerant. They do not want to revive the Naïve Empiricist's notion of substance, but, rather, to relax the conditions specified in Hume's alternative recipe for genuine identity. Why insist on sameness of composition? Why treat a river like a sealed reservoir? Surely, with most types of thing, the internal structure and organization of the parts are more important than their preservation without any augmentation or diminution? These protests are justified, and their effect is to discredit the exorbitant demands that he makes for strict identity. When he accuses his adversaries of fantasizing some way of meeting these demands, they retort that the demands themselves are a product of fantasy.

This controversy about 'genuine and ersatz identity has taken people's minds off the question that needed to be asked first, which is the question how we count things. To use some of Hume's examples, what are the differences between being confronted by one building and by two, or by one tree and by two, or by one mind and by two? These basic questions about the lines of demarcation between two juxtaposed individuals of the same type need to be answered before any questions are posed about their identities through time. They are, of course, often easy to answer, but we still need to know how to answer them, and, because they are basic, we need to know that first.

---

[12] *Treatise*, pp. 255-6.   [13] See above, pp. 124-5.

Unfortunately, it is not only Hume's commentators who have been diverted from these basic questions by the controversy about genuine and ersatz identity. For he himself fails to give them the attention that they deserve. He tells us a lot about objects which are supposed to maintain their identities through time—'they are such only as consist of a succession of parts, connected together by resemblance, contiguity and causation'[14]—but he says nothing about the separateness of different objects which are observed simultaneously. True, there is often not much to be said: they are usually disconnected and contiguous in time, but not in space. Sometimes, of course, it will not be easy to count simultaneously observed individuals—for example, there can be difficulties about streets and houses. But, easy or difficult, we still need to know how it is done. The theory of identity over a period of time cannot be detached from the theory of differentiation at a moment of time, and, when Hume sets out to develop the first of these two theories without the second one, he is bound to run into difficulties later.

At first, when he is discussing physical objects, we let him off giving an account of their differentiation at a given moment. We grant him his single acorn and allow him to describe the spatio-temporally successive stages of the sapling and the oak-tree. He is concentrating on this tree and it would not occur to us to question whether a particular stage might not perhaps belong to the development of a different tree. Once he has his starting-point, the acorn, contiguity in time and space will keep him on the track of its development. So it does not worry us that he concentrates entirely on the internal structure of the life of the tree. For, given that he starts with a separate individual, its internal development will maintain its difference from other individuals of the same type.

Of course, he ought to have completed this part of his theory and told us exactly how we pick out one individual of a given type from others. But the analysis of this stage in our thought about the world is easy when the individuals are all presented on the same level, as physical objects are. We simply pick one off the plate and follow its development from that point onwards. So we read this part of Hume's theory of identity charitably, and do not demand a thorough analysis of anything so straightforward and obvious as the original discrimination of physical objects. However, this laxity is going to produce trouble later. For he postpones the problem when it first arises about physical

[14] *Treatise*, p. 255.

objects and would be easy to solve, and later when it arises for minds and is much more difficult, faces it without having done the necessary groundwork.

If individual physical objects can simply be picked out of the field of present perception, how is it with individual minds?

> Whatever is clearly conceiv'd may exist; and whatever is clearly conceiv'd, after any manner, may exist after the same manner. This is one principle, which has already been acknowledg'd. Again, every thing, which is different, is distinguishable, and every thing which is distinguishable, is separable by the imagination. This is another principle. My conclusion from both is, that since all our perceptions are different from one another, and from every thing else in the universe, they are also distinct and separable, and may be consider'd as separately existent, and may exist separately, and have no need of any thing else to support their existence. They are, therefore, substances, as far as this definition explains a substance.[15]

When we read this, we will probably picture our perceptions floating freely in space and time, like stars which do not depend on grouping in constellations for their existence. But that is not what Hume means. For two pages later in this chapter, 'Of the Immateriality of the Soul', he 'delivers a maxim':

> This maxim is *that an object may exist, and yet be no where*; and I assert, that this is not only possible, but that the greatest part of beings do and must exist after this manner. An object may be said to be no where, when its parts are not so situated with respect to each other, as to form any figure or quantity; nor the whole with respect to other bodies so as to answer to our notions of contiguity or distance. Now this is evidently the case with all our perceptions and objects, except those of the sight and feeling.[16]

So our perceptions (impressions and ideas) are individual mental things, existing in time but not in space, and standing in no need of each other's support for their existence. This is an uncompromising thesis, but, given his treatment of contiguity, no other conclusion was possible. For if the contiguity of mental things is only temporal and never also spatial, then the original identification of a mind, which is merely a group of such things, can only be temporal, and the subsequent unity of the group can only be maintained temporally. So it

---

[15] Ibid. 233.

[16] Ibid. 235–6. The exception mentioned in the last sentence seems to betray a confusion in Hume's mind. It is true that impressions of sight and touch give us our concept of the space around us, but it by no means follows that they exist in that space.

will have to be maintained by temporal contiguity functioning in the two ways that have already been described,[17] as simple juxtaposition in time, and as the relation which underpins causation.

When we focus our attention on the resources offered by this theory of mind, we can immediately see that they are hopelessly inadequate. If the relation underpinning mental causation is only *temporal* contiguity, what is there to prevent one of my ideas from being the *direct* cause of one of yours? Of course, it would not be an objection to Hume's theory that one of mine might be an *indirect* cause of one of yours. For that is precisely what happens when people communicate with one another. But *direct* mental causation is one of the two main connections which, according to him, give a mind its unity, and so it is a fatal objection to his theory that it is a connection which can cross the boundary between one mind and another, if it only needs to be supported by temporal contiguity. Even if telepathy never in fact occurs, that can hardly be what enables us to draw a line between one mind and another.

The other main connection which, in his theory, gives a mind its unity, is temporal contiguity functioning as simple juxtaposition in time. This is obviously vulnerable to the same objection. Nor will his theory get any help from resemblance at this point. For resemblance is evidently another relation which crosses the boundary between one mind and another. In fact, its importance as a unifying relation is much exaggerated by Hume, perhaps because of its role in creating the 'illusion of genuine personal identity'.

It is worth pausing to dramatize the inadequacy of this part of Hume's theory of personal identity. His account of the relations that give a mind its unity allows him no way of distinguishing a stage in the development of his own mind from a stage in the development of some other mind. Imagine a theory about the identity of physical objects which puts us in the same predicament. You plant three acorns in a row and the theory only allows you to use temporal contiguity and never also spatial contiguity when you are assigning later stages to the development of each of the three saplings. In that case your conception of the unity of each plant would be hopelessly inadequate because it would be based on relations which crossed the lines of demarcation between them.

Once this is pointed out, it is so obvious that we may wonder why we ever begin to go along with Hume's theory, and do not immediately

---

[17] See above, pp. 136–7.

protest that it cannot possibly work. Equally, we may wonder why he does not pull himself up short, and never even expresses the slightest doubt about it in the main text of his book. The reason, to put it briefly at first, is that he does not draw a sufficiently firm line between our pre-theoretical conceptual scheme and his own theory about it. His theory ought to explain the way in which we conceptualize the world, but he underestimates the stringency of this requirement, because, at the point where his theory falls short, he simply helps himself to some of the raw material, merely appealing to certain familiar features of our pre-theoretical scheme and forgetting that he is supposed to be offering a theory that explains them.

But how does he fall into such an obvious trap? It seems that he is misled by what might be called the 'any-personal' character of his presentation of the data. He writes in the first person about what he finds when he 'looks into his own breast', but he freely conjectures that his findings would be the same if he were able to 'look into the breast of another'. So he discards the body and writes in the first person plural about the structure of any mind, without pausing to ask himself how he ever got into a position to generalize his findings in this way.

The answer to this question, if he had given it, would certainly not have been that he started with an impersonal view of everybody's impressions and ideas and then split them up into groups, like an astronomer distinguishing one constellation from another. That is easily understood. What is not so easy is to understand exactly why such an answer would be absurd.

The reason goes much deeper than the evident fact that, unlike stars, impressions and ideas are not spatially related to one another. He himself makes that point,[18] but it does not yield a complete explanation of the absurdity of the simple analogy between his scientific investigation of human minds and astronomy. For when he excludes spatial contiguity from the mind and tries to base mental unity on temporal contiguity alone, he ends with a theory which is hopelessly inadequate. The remedy, of course, is not to bring back spatial contiguity, but to find something else to take its place. The discovery of the right substitute is needed in order to complete the explanation of the absurdity of the simple analogy.

The right substitute was not to take impressions and ideas which had already been identified and find a new relation between them. The

---

[18] See above, pp. 136–7.

only way to correct his theory was to go back to the beginning and to describe how a person originally identifies impressions and ideas. It was no good looking for a stronger relation, overlooked by him when he formulated his theory, a relation which would bind together the impressions and ideas of a single person more tightly and exclude those of other persons. That was not the way to correct the inadequacy of his theory. What was needed was a different kind of correction, the development of the first and most basic part of any theory of identity, which he had omitted both when he was dealing with physical objects and when he was dealing with minds. How did we originally distinguish them from one another?

The full development of this part of his theory would make a lengthy appendix to the *Treatise*, but the two main points are clear and simple. If anyone finds that he is directly aware of an impression or idea, then there is no further question about its ownership—it is his. If, on the other hand, his awareness of an impression or idea is indirect, then it can only have come through the body of whichever other person owns it. In the example used earlier, if you yourself witness the assault, the visual impressions are, undoubtedly and without any further investigation, yours. But when you find the footprints of another person, who, you infer, must have witnessed it, the visual impressions of the assault are his. These two points are enough to show that nobody starts by identifying an array of impressions and ideas and then has to face the task of sorting them into bundles, one of which will be himself, while the rest will be other people. The analogy with stars and constellations is fundamentally and completely wrong.

The next point in this rewritten appendix to the *Treatise* would be more complicated. It is a natural reaction to the first two points to suppose that a person's body is not needed for the possession and direct awareness of his own impressions and ideas, but only needed to signal them to others and give others indirect awareness of them. However, that would be a mistake. Memory is needed in order to give a person any sense of the identity of anything through time, and if we really were confined to the resources of our own minds, without any help from our bodies, we would not even have the concept of memory. For memory is a faculty with a function—to get past facts right—and, if we never had any independent test of right and wrong, the very idea of such a faculty would be beyond our comprehension. But the only way to get the necessary independent test is through our bodies. To adopt the earlier example, if I think I remember walking past the scene of the crime, my footprints may confirm the correctness of my memory.[19] Naturally, such tests are not always needed, but they must sometimes be available, and a theory of personal identity which altogether dispenses with them is bound to fail.

If we now look back from this vantage-point at the theory of personal identity offered by Hume in the two chapters which he devotes to the topic in the *Treatise*, we can give a firm diagnosis of its failure. It fails because it rejects all help from the body. That is a double handicap. First, since a person is a mind–body couple, it produces a necessarily incomplete theory of personal identity. Secondly, the theory cannot succeed even when it only purports to explain the continuing identity of a mind.

It is true that, when it is judged as a theory of the identity of a mind, it starts well, with the exclusion of spatial contiguity from the world of impressions and ideas. However, instead of looking for an effective substitute for spatial contiguity, Hume offers an account which completely fails to explain the boundaries between one mind and another. The fact is that we do succeed in individuating minds with the help of bodies, and he exploits this fact without acknowledging it. He writes from his own point of view, secure in his single mind, and he says nothing about the physical scaffolding which made it possible for him to take up this mental position. The result is a theory like a trick performed by an illusionist. We watch him adopting his own point of view in a world of impressions and ideas waiting to be appropriated by him or by others, and we see him doing this without making any visible use of his body or of theirs. We know that this is impossible, but the performance is so good that we cannot immediately see where it relies on physical props, and we have to work out afterwards how it was done.

At this point the analogy with a conjuring trick breaks down, because he too is fooled. In his Appendix, when he explains his reasons for retracting his earlier theory, he shows absolutely no awareness that in the mental world the right substitute for spatial contiguity is not some purely mental relation that he had overlooked, but an intricate pattern of dependence on the physical world. After reviewing his theory, he admits that

---

[19] So Hume's refusal to appeal to the body in this kind of case produces two different effects. It deprives him of an independent reference to the person with whom he is questioning his own identity (see above, pp. 132–3); and it deprives him of the so-called 'memory criterion' of personal identity, which he might otherwise have used to settle the question, or, at least, to help him to settle it.

... having thus loosen'd all our particular perceptions, when I proceed to explain the principle of connexion, which binds them together, and makes us attribute to them a real simplicity and identity; I am sensible, that my account is very defective, and that nothing but the seeming evidence of the precedent reasonings cou'd have induc'd me to receive it. If perceptions are distinct existences, they form a whole only by being connected together. But no connexions among distinct existences are ever discoverable by human understanding. We only *feel* a connexion or determination of the thought, to pass from one object to another. It follows, therefore, that the thought alone finds personal identity, when reflecting on the train of past perceptions, that compose a mind, the ideas of them are felt to be connected together, and naturally introduce each other. However extraordinary this conclusion may seem, it need not surprize us. Most philosophers seem inclin'd to think that personal identity *arises* from consciousness; and consciousness is nothing but a reflected thought or perception. The present philosophy, therefore, has so far a promising aspect. But all my hopes vanish, when I come to explain the principles, that unite our successive perceptions in our thought and consciousness. I cannot discover any theory, which gives me satisfaction on this head.

In short there are two principles, which I cannot render consistent; nor is it in my power to renounce either of them, viz. *that all our distinct perceptions are distinct existences*, and *that the mind never perceives any real connexion among distinct existences*. Did our perceptions either inhere in something simple and individual, or did the mind perceive some real connexion among them, there wou'd be no difficulty in the case. For my part, I must plead the privilege of a sceptic, and confess, that this difficulty is too hard for my understanding. I pretend not, however, to pronounce it absolutely insuperable. Others, perhaps, or myself, upon more mature reflection, may discover some hypothesis, that will reconcile those contradictions.[20]

The main lines of this criticism of his earlier theory are clear. It gave an inadequate account of the unity of a person's mind, and there was no hope of correcting the deficiency either by bringing back the self as an individual mental substance, or by finding some stronger connection between the impressions and ideas of a single person. His complaint is not that the principles, which rule out the two remedies, are inconsistent with one another, but, rather, that together they cannot be reconciled with an adequate account of the phenomena.

The first of those two remedies was obviously hopeless. It is, of course, easy to say 'If my mind holds together the world as I find it, surely there must be something holding my mind together.' But the

[20] *Treatise*, pp. 635–6. He is taking back his earlier claim that 'The intellectual world, tho' involv'd in infinite obscurities, is not perplex'd with any such contradictions, as those we have discover'd in the natural' (*Treatise*, p. 232; quoted above, p. 135).

emptiness of this thought becomes apparent when we reflect that the ultimate unifier would need the same internal complexity as the mass of impressions and ideas that it unified. Or there are Hume's own arguments against the postulation of any subject to view the contents of a mind from within.

At first sight, the second remedy seems equally hopeless. How could there be any stronger connection between distinct impressions and ideas than resemblance, contiguity in time, and causation? It seems quite impossible that a solution should be found in that direction. Here it must be remembered that the impressions and ideas of a single mind are being considered as particulars, each occurring at a definite time, and we do not need to ask *of what* they are impressions or ideas — their contents are irrelevant. As such, it seems obvious that their connections with one another can only be contingent. No doubt, Hume can see that the unity of a single mind is greater than his theory allows. But how can he possibly augment it either by making it more closely knit or by making it more exclusive?

He was evidently thinking too much about the first of these two ways of dealing with the problem when he ought to have been thinking of the second way. But that is only the first step in the diagnosis of his mistake. The next step is to see something which he altogether failed to see — that the original identification of any impression or idea places it necessarily in the mind in which it occurs, and does that not in virtue of its content but simply by taking it as a particular. The trouble was that he started his inquiry at a later stage, when his own impressions and ideas had already been grouped together, and he then reviewed the group, searching for the kind of relation between its members which would establish a strong line of demarcation between it and other groups.[21] At this stage of the inquiry, it seemed to him that the requisite relation could only bind impressions and ideas together through their contents. But then it struck him as obvious that no such bond could possibly be available. So he was at an impasse.

This line of diagnosis is worth pursuing, but, before it is taken any further, there is an alternative interpretation which ought to be examined. Paul Grice and John Haugeland suggest that Hume retracted his theory because he saw that it moves in a circle.[22] He rests the identities of minds on causation, but explains causation in a way that

---

[21] See above, pp. 129–34 and 143–4.
[22] In an unpublished article on Hume's retraction of his theory in the Appendix to the *Treatise*.

requires impressions and ideas to be *already* sorted into the different groups that count as different minds in his theory. But how is that prior grouping supposed to have been done? How are the lines of demarcation between one mind and another supposed to have been drawn? If he uses causation when he draws them, he is moving in a circle, and yet he is unable to find any other explanation of the way in which it is done. This interpretation of his quandary is taken up and modified by Barry Stroud in his book.[23] Stroud tries to defend Hume against the charge of circularity by arguing that he can rely on the pre-theoretical concept of an individual person, but he does agree that he offers no convincing theoretical explanation of the grouping of impressions and ideas to form different persons. For since each person observes a different part of the physical world, Hume is unable to explain how causal sequences can be discovered in the original position before impressions and ideas have been sorted into different personal groups.

The general line taken by these two interpretations of Hume's difficulty is the same as that taken by the interpretation put forward in this chapter: he fails to explain the way in which impressions and ideas are grouped together to form individual minds. But there are many important points of difference, and they will begin to emerge when we ask exactly why the advocates of these rival interpretations suppose Hume's theory of causation to require that impressions and ideas be already sorted into such groups.

The reason given by Grice and Haugeland starts from the observation that people vary in their experience and in their sensitivity to constant conjunctions. Consequently, a true causal statement about the physical world will not be supported by an association of ideas at every point in the total set of everyone's impressions and ideas. There will be bad patches, where the association fails, and these bad patches cannot be identified and discounted until the total set has been split up into individual minds. Stroud offers a different criticism in the same area. According to him, the difficulty is not presented by the trustworthiness of different observations, but by their interpretation. For in the original position there would be no way of locating physical events at particular points in physical space. But physical causal sequences require spatial contiguity, and an impression of A received at one point in space and immediately followed by an impression of B received at another point would not count as evidence for an AB causal sequence.

<hr/>

[23] *Hume* (London: Routledge and Kegan Paul, 1977), 130–40.

So Stroud's criticism is that in Hume's original position there would be no way of assigning physical events to the sequences to which they belong, and so no concept of causation.

These epistemic arguments are not easy to assess. They are concerned with the apprehension of external causal sequences, which have to be reflected in minds by conjunctions of sense-impressions producing associations of ideas. Both arguments start from Hume's original position, as it is before the groups that form different minds have been separated from one another. Grice and Haugeland argue that, in that situation, the evidence for external causal sequences would be too unreliable to give the total mind the concept of causation. Stroud argues that, when anyone makes causal statements of this kind from his own point of view, he needs to restrict himself to constant conjunctions based on sense-impressions which have been received by his own mind. For sense-impressions received by other people's minds will have come from different parts of the physical world and so they will be irrelevant. However, though in real life he is able to restrict himself in this way, he cannot give a theoretical explanation of his ability to do so before he has established the boundary between his mind and other minds.[24]

The reason why these epistemic arguments are hard to assess is that we cannot be sure of the rules governing the collection of evidence for causal statements about the physical world in Hume's original position. It is so different from our position that it is unclear what the constraints on the collection of evidence would be. Grice and Haugeland suppose that in Hume's original position the unreliable patches, which would correspond *later* to the evidence collected by untrustworthy observers, could not be identified and discounted, because the total mind had not yet been split up into individual minds. But that, according to Hume, would require well-founded causal statements, which, they argue, would not yet be available in Hume's original position.

But the fault in Hume's system seems to run much deeper than this. The causal statements which, in their view, and in Stroud's, put him in a quandary, are about the physical world. But if the interpretation proposed in this chapter is right, his quandary is produced by causal statements about impressions and ideas *considered as mental particulars*. These statements cannot involve *spatial* contiguity, and the only available substitute is attachment to different bodies. So Hume's more

---

[24] It is not clear why Stroud thinks that Hume can rely on the pre-theoretical concept of an individual mind, even if he cannot explain it. See above, pp. 72–4 and 142.

profound error at this point is his refusal to individuate minds by their locations in bodies.

It is true that this refusal jeopardizes the evidence for causal statements about the physical world. But it produces this effect not only by preventing the division of the total mind into individual minds, but also by making it impossible to connect the evidence collected by any mind, individual or total, with any particular part of the physical world. For what puts causal statements about the physical world in jeopardy is the *general* fact that, if no use is made of the location of minds in bodies, there is no way of connecting the evidence collected by any mind with the physical world. However, since this effect and the refusal to locate minds in bodies affects individual minds as well as the total mind, it does not pick out what is peculiarly wrong with causation in Hume's original position. What is needed is a more discriminating diagnosis, and, if the line taken in this chapter is right, it will draw on the special difficulty in the original position of accounting for causal statements about impressions and ideas considered not as the bearers of their contents, but as mental particulars.

In any case, Hume does not seem to be charging his earlier theory with circularity. If that had been his criticism, he would have admitted that his account of causation was in just as much jeopardy as his account of personal identity, because the burden of the fault would be equally divided. But that is not an admission that he ever makes. This suggests that he saw the need to mark off his own mind from others but simply did not see how to do it. Now if the trouble is not circularity, we do not have to assume that the need had any *special* connection with the apprehension of external causal sequences. Stroud seems to be right when he claims that such sequences could not be apprehended by the total mind. But that is at least partly because Hume does not give it any connection with the physical world, and this deficiency in his theory would still have spoiled it, even if he had succeeded in splitting up the total mind into individual minds.[25] It is, in any case, a deficiency which jeopardizes all kinds of statement about the physical world, and not only causal statements.

So we are free to revert to the interpretation offered in this chapter: Hume set himself the task of individuating minds by the causal connections between impressions and ideas *considered as mental particulars.* On the face of it, this method of individuation would require them to

---

[25] Unless, of course, he used location in different bodies to split it up.

be related by spatial contiguity. However, that requirement obviously cannot be met, and he failed to find the one and only viable substitute for spatial contiguity, dependence on a body. If he had found it, he might have realized that its function as an individuator is performed right at the start, when impressions and ideas are first identified as particulars, and that there is no need to rely on it for the individuation of minds at a later stage, when it comes in again to support direct mental causation.

It is no part of this interpretation that he realized what had gone wrong. His theory and his recantation of it may be read as a *reductio ad absurdum* of the theory that minds have independent identities. As such, they are a brilliant achievement, but he never located the false premiss and so was never able to follow it up with an alternative theory.

However, as sometimes happens in such cases, he was quite near to finding out what had gone wrong. When he rejected the second remedy—the discovery of a stronger connection between the impressions and ideas of a single person[26]—he could have focused more closely on to the nature of his inquiry. It was concerned with impressions and ideas considered as particulars, and that ought to have put him on to the ways in which they are first identified as particulars. Regardless of their content, one of yours could not have belonged to anyone else, and that really does make a stronger bond than any that he discovers between the impressions and ideas in a single mind. For it is a conceptual bond and not one discovered by scientific investigation.[27]

[26] This would be the Rationalist's solution to the problem. See above, ch. 8 n. 5.

[27] See the chapter 'Hume on Personal Identity' in my *Questions in the Philosophy of Mind* (London: Duckworth, 1975).

10

Sense-Perception: Hume's Assessment of the Problem and his Strategy for Eliminating Current Solutions

THE passage in which Hume poses the problem of perception, as he sees it, is worth quoting again:[1]

Thus the sceptic still continues to reason and believe, even tho' he asserts, that he cannot defend his reason by reason; and by the same rule he must assent to the principle concerning the existence of body, tho' he cannot pretend by any arguments of philosophy to maintain its veracity. Nature has not left this to his choice, and has doubtless esteem'd it an affair of too great importance to be trusted to our uncertain reasonings and speculations. We may well ask, *What causes induce us to believe in the existence of body?* But 'tis in vain to ask, *Whether there be body or not?* That is a point, which we must take for granted in all our reasonings.[2]

It may seem that he is asking us to take too much for granted at the beginning of a philosophical discussion of perception. However, when he speaks of 'body' in this passage, he is not thinking of physical objects as things lying beyond our sense-impressions and causing them. Nor, of course, is he thinking of them as sense-impressions contrasted with external physical objects. He is trying to express the pre-theoretical belief in body as it would be held by non-philosophers, who, he thinks, never ask themselves in which of the two ways they think of body. His idea is that the difference between treating bodies as irreducibly physical and reducing them to a mental basis is one that never even occurs to 'the vulgar'. They simply take what is given as it comes without making any attempt to categorize it.

---

[1] See above, p. 99.
[2] *A Treatise of Human Nature*, ed. P. H. Nidditch (Oxford: Clarendon Press, 1989), 187.

This view of what Sartre would call 'pre-reflective consciousness' is questionable, and some may find its ascription to Hume incredible. However, the following passages make it clear that it really was his view:

... the vulgar confound perceptions and objects, and attribute a distinct continu'd existence to the very things they feel or see.[3]

This view of 'the vulgar' is explained a few pages later in a way that puts its interpretation beyond doubt:

Now we have already observ'd, that however philosophers may distinguish betwixt the objects and perceptions of the senses; which they suppose co-existent and resembling; yet this is a distinction, which is not comprehended by the generality of mankind, who as they perceive only one being, can never assent to the opinion of a double existence and representation. Those very sensations, which enter by the eye or ear, are with them the true objects, nor can they readily conceive that this pen or paper, which is immediately perceiv'd, represents another, which is different from, but resembling it. In order, therefore, to accommodate myself to their notions, I shall at first suppose; that there is only a single existence, which I shall call indifferently *object* or *perception*, according as it shall seem best to suit my purpose, understanding by both of them what any common man means by a hat, or shoe, or stone, or any other impression, convey'd to him by his senses. I shall be sure to give warning, when I return to a more philosophical[4] way of speaking and thinking.[5]

The ascription of this view to non-philosophers is so paradoxical that Hume inadvertently represents them as *confusing* two kinds of thing, when what he really means is that it *never occurs to them to distinguish* them or to name them in a way that would indicate their different categories. It is very important to bear in mind throughout his discussion of perception that he regards the pre-theoretical belief in body as an ontologically neutral belief, which, according to him, antedates the categorial question and does not presuppose an answer to it.

So he starts with an ontologically neutral account of our belief in body and with the avowed intention of explaining what causes us to hold this belief, rather than assessing its acceptability. He then proceeds to offer an explanation of the route by which we arrive at the belief which makes it almost impossible to understand why we rest content with it. Nature presumably will not allow us to abandon it, but

---

[3] Ibid. 193.
[4] As usual, 'philosophy' includes science.
[5] Ibid. 202.

if Hume's account of the manœuvres that we need to make in order to retain it is accurate, nature makes fools of us. There is worse to come when he finally splits up the ontologically neutral belief which he ascribes to us and submits the two alternatives, that it is impressions that fill the gaps in observations and that it is physical objects, to a philosophical examination. For it emerges that in each of these two forms the belief is intellectually unacceptable.

If we are going to understand Hume's system, we must appreciate that he puts belief in body in a far weaker position than belief in causation or belief in personal identity.[6] It is easy to miss this difference, because he treats all three problematical beliefs in broadly the same way: all three are, in the sense explained earlier, audacious,[7] and so all three must be products of the imagination. The differences become apparent when we ask for an accurate account of the content of our belief in body, or for a full description of the way in which imagination produces it. It then emerges that his answers to these two questions are far more discrediting than his answers to the same two questions when they were asked about causation and personal identity.

His answers to the two questions about our belief in body will be analysed in the next chapter, and the way in which that belief gets into such an exceptionally weak position in his system will be explained. Naturally, he was not worried by this feature of his system while he was actually developing it. For his aim was to demonstrate that, however much disorder there might be in the 'natural world', there is none in the 'intellectual world'.[8] However, in his Appendix he admits that he did not succeed in this demonstration, and the diagnosis proposed in the previous chapter of his failure to solve the problem of personal identity was that it is not possible to explain the unity of a mind in complete detachment from the physical world.

If that was a correct diagnosis, he needed to rewrite his account of belief in body in order to make it at least as supportive as his account of causation. In fact, he needed to do rather more in this case than gesture in the direction of his adversaries' theory, as he did in the case of causation. He had to produce an account of belief in body which would support a rewritten solution to the problem of personal identity. However, he let his account of belief in body stand, in the ontologically

---

[6] Not, of course, in his Appendix, but in the main text, where his theory of personal identity is developed.

[7] See above, p. 78.

[8] Cf. the passages quoted above, p. 135.

neutral and, therefore, completely unsupportive form in which he developed it in the main text of the *Treatise*. His difficulty was an obvious one: any strengthening of his account of belief in body would not have met the requirements of his theory of meaning. But it is also worth observing that what he leaves standing in the text of the *Treatise* is an account of belief in body which fails to conform to his theory of truth and evidence even on the pre-theoretical level.

He opens his investigation with a distinction:

> We ought to examine apart those two questions, which are commonly con-founded together, *viz.* Why we attribute a CONTINU'D existence to objects, even when they are not present to the senses; and why we consider them to have an existence DISTINCT from the mind and perception. Under this last head I comprehend their situation as well as relations, their *external* position as well as the *independence* of their existence and operation.[9]

He applies this distinction to cases in which there is a gap in percep-tion. For example, he is alone in his room watching the fire in his hearth, goes out, and returns to find it still burning. The first of the two questions asks why he believes that the 'object' (whatever its category) continues to exist throughout the gap in his observation of it. The second question asks why he believes its existence to be independent of his mind.

Having distinguished the two questions, he goes on to remark that they are

> ... intimately connected together. For if the objects of our senses continue to exist, even when they are not perceiv'd, their existence is of course independent of and distinct from the perception; and *vice versa*, if their existence be independent of the perception and distinct from it, they must continue to exist, even tho' they be not perceiv'd.[10]

So the second question — the one about independent existence — is not asking whether there are *two kinds of object* involved when the person watches his fire, namely his visual impressions and the thing outside him in physical space which causes them. If that had been what the second question was asking, the answer to it would not have followed automatically from the answer to the first one. For he could have answered the first question by saying that he believes in the continued existence of his unperceived fire, because 'nature has not left this to his

---

choice', but that he does *not* believe that, when he does perceive it, it is an object in physical space, distinct from his visual impression and causing it: it *is* his visual impression, no more and no less.

He goes on to explain very clearly that his second question is not about what he calls 'the opinion of a double existence and representation'.[11] For he ends his presentation of the distinction between the two questions with these words:

> But tho' the decision of the one question decides the other; yet that we may the more easily discover the principles of human nature, from whence the decision arises, we shall carry along with us this distinction, and shall consider, whether it be the *senses, reason*, or the *imagination*, that produces the opinion of a *continu'd* or of a *distinct* existence. These are the only questions that are intelligible on the present subject. For as to the notion of external existence, when taken for something specifically different from our perceptions, we have already shewn its absurdity.[12]

So his second question—the one about independent existence—is not asking what leads the person watching his fire to believe that there is an independent object located in space *beyond* his visual impressions. It is only asking what leads him to believe that the object of his perception does not depend on his perception for its existence.

This is, at first sight, surprising. For what sort of person could believe that the object of his perception was not located in space beyond his visual impressions, and yet did not depend on his perception for its existence? But we already know Hume's answer to this question—one of 'the vulgar'. For, according to him, it does not occur to 'the vulgar' to ask themselves to which of the two categories their 'objects' belong, the mental or the physical. So he will argue later that it is only the carelessness produced by their lack of sophistication which allows them to believe that their 'objects' do not depend on being perceived for their existence, without believing that they are located in space beyond their sense-impressions.

It is not easy to keep a grip on the development of Hume's ideas about perception. On first reading, he seems to be heading for phenomenalism. That is certainly the impression given by the famous passage in which he demonstrates the absurdity of 'the notion of

---

[11] See *Treatise*, p. 202, quoted above, p. 153.

[12] *Treatise*, p. 188. This is an application of his theory of meaning. His theory of truth and evidence is not the only resource that he uses in his treatment of perception. The passage to which he refers in the last sentence is *Treatise*, pp. 67–8, quoted below, p. 157.

external existence, when taken for something specifically different from our perceptions':

> Now since nothing is ever present to the mind but perceptions, and since all ideas are deriv'd from something antecedently present to the mind; it follows that 'tis impossible for us so much as to conceive or form an idea of any thing specifically different from ideas and impressions. Let us fix our attention out of ourselves as much as possible; let us chace our imagination to the heavens, or to the utmost limits of the universe; we never really advance a step beyond ourselves, nor can conceive any kind of existence, but those perceptions, which have appear'd in that narrow compass. This is the universe of the imagination, nor have we any idea but what is there produc'd.[13]

However, he certainly does not ascribe phenomenalism to 'the vulgar'. For he represents them as believing that something continues to exist in the gap between the two observations of the fire, whereas a phenomenalist would claim that all that can be said about this gap is that, if the observer had eliminated it by observing the fire continuously, he would have received the appropriate visual impressions, and that is only a conditional proposition.

It is this difference that is going to prove important later when Hume analyses the content of the plain man's belief in the continued and distinct existence of 'objects'. The content of the phenomenalist's version of this belief is clear enough—it is about sense-impressions—but it is only a belief in a *conditional* proposition. What 'the vulgar' believe is, he thinks, a *categorical* proposition—something actually exists in the gap. But *what* is it that exists in the gap? He tells us that 'the vulgar' do not even ask themselves that question, and, as we shall see later, when he himself asks it, he finds that there is no acceptable answer to it, and he concludes that the plain man's belief has no reliable basis and no coherent content.

One reason why Hume's introductory remarks, which set the scene for his discussion of perception, are not easy to follow, has now been explained. The belief which he ascribes to 'the vulgar' is extremely unsophisticated. How can they possibly fail to ask themselves to what category, the mental or the physical, their 'objects' belong. Still, there is no doubt that he does ascribe such a vaguely formulated belief to them, and so, according to him, they neither take the 'distinct existence' which he represents them as ascribing to their 'objects' to be

---

[13] *Treatise*, pp. 67–8.

physical existence in space, nor do they take it to be mental existence within a mind.

There is also something else which makes it hard for us to understand this *mise-en-scène*. When Hume is setting it up, he says that under the heading *The distinct existence of objects* he includes 'their situation as well as relations, their *external* position as well as the *independence* of their existence and operation'.[14] But that cannot be the right way to set the stage for the subsequent discussion. For if 'distinct existence' involves external position, anyone who believes in it is committed to the 'opinion of double existence and representation'. But, as we have seen, Hume makes it quite clear that belief in the continued and distinct existence of objects does not commit the plain man to that opinion.

This error is not a slip of Hume's pen. For, as we shall soon see, when we examine his argument for denying that it is *sensation* that gives us the idea of distinct existence, he makes the same mistake again, treating that suggestion as if it really were the 'opinion of double existence and representation'.[15] Nor is this a trivial mistake. It is extremely difficult, if not impossible, to see how the plain man's belief in the distinct existence of objects could accommodate their spatial relations without making them physical.[16] So it is hardly surprising that Hume fails to maintain the requisite naïve impartiality between the two categories, physical and mental, in his characterization of the plain man's belief.

There is one more point that needs to be made, by way of introduction, before we examine his arguments in detail. It was remarked above that our belief in the continued and distinct existence of unperceived objects occupies a much weaker position in his system than the other two problematical beliefs, in causation and in personal identity. It may seem surprising that there should be so much difference between his treatment of unobserved objects and his treatment of causation. For in both cases the problem is created by an audacious inference. Or, to put it in another way, in both cases the belief is at no time completely supported by the available evidence. So how can unperceived objects end up in a weaker position than causation? The answer to this question may throw light on the way he sets the scene for the discussion of perception.

[14] *Treatise*, p. 188, quoted above, p. 155.
[15] See below, pp. 161–5.
[16] This is a problem that Neutral Monism must somehow solve.

Suppose that he had been a phenomenalist. Then he would have said that belief in the continued existence of the unobserved fire was merely belief in a set of conditional propositions about sense-impressions. The assumption that the fire continued to exist in the gap between the two observations would then not imply that anything actual occupied the gap. If that had been his view, the problem of unobserved objects would merely have been a special case of the problem of causation. For, according to him, all inferences from the observed to the unobserved are causal inferences,[17] and the only peculiarity of the inference about the fire would have been that it was expressed by a counterfactual conditional, and, therefore, unverifiable; but so too is any ordinary causal inference about what would have happened on the billiards table if a player had hit the ball at a different angle.[18]

However, he was not a phenomenalist, and so the belief that he ascribed to the plain man was not about what would have filled the gap, if observation had covered it, but about what actually filled it, in the absence of observation. He realized, of course, that the plain man did believe the counterfactual conditional, but that was not the problem for him. The problem was the plain man's further belief in the underlying categorical proposition specifying the actual situation because of which the counterfactual conditional was true. What exactly was the content of that categorical proposition, and what were the grounds for believing it?

So, though causation and perception both involve audacious inferences, there are differences between the structures of the problems that they present to Hume. In the case of causation, a particular effect is inferred from a particular cause and he does not regard the necessity underlying what can be observed as a further fact of the same kind which, unfortunately, cannot be observed. But, in the case of perception, it *is* the underlying fact that is inferred and not the sense-impressions which would have been yielded by observation, if there had not been a gap in observation. That is one difference between the structures of the two problems.

Another difference is that, in the case of causation, he is not especially concerned with unobserved sequences or counterfactual inferences, but his examination of perception is focused exclusively on to the problem of unobserved objects. To put this difference in

---

[17] See above, pp. 46–7 and 70–3.   [18] See above, pp. 82–3.

another way, he might have taken unobserved objects together with objects that may or may not be observed in the future, and, if he had done that, his treatment of perception would have been more like his treatment of causation, which concentrates on inferences to future effects. However, he does not do that, and the reason why he does not do it is evident: in the case of perception, his question is 'What do we believe about actually existing unobserved objects, and on what grounds?', and a discussion of inferences to objects that may or may not be observed in the future would leave that question untouched.

Enough has been said to indicate the originality of Hume's treatment of perception. He starts not with the theories of philosophers, but with the plain man's beliefs. These beliefs are examined in a scientific spirit and the purpose of the examination is to discover their content and the grounds on which they are adopted. The programme is the same as it was with the other two difficult cases, causation and personal identity. However, it will soon appear that his conclusions are far less favourable to belief in unobserved objects than they were to belief in causation and even to belief in personal identity.[19]

His arguments must now be examined in detail. As usual, he starts by assuming that there are three possible answers to his question about the continued and distinct existence of unperceived objects, the Naïve Empiricist's answer, the Rationalist's answer, and the answer which he himself is going to give as a Sophisticated Empiricist. We have to 'consider, whether it be the *senses*, *reason*, or the *imagination*, that produces the opinion of a *continu'd* or of a *distinct* existence'.[20] He then proceeds to argue against the first two explanations of the opinion, and, having dismissed them, he develops the third explanation, only to find that in the end it leaves the opinion in a very weak position.

The remainder of this chapter will deal with his objections to the first two theories—that our belief in the continued and distinct existence of objects is produced by the senses, and that it is produced by reason. Some of the details of his arguments will be difficult and a short preview is needed.

If we may leave out the details for a moment, his criticisms of the first two theories are essentially very simple. The plain man lives in the world that he perceives and sensation gives him the objects which constitute that world. He does not ask himself to what general category

---

[19] In the main text. His recantation of his theory of personal identity came later, in the Appendix.

[20] *Treatise*, p. 188. The passage was quoted at greater length above, p. 156.

they belong, and it never occurs to him that there might be another world behind the one in which he lives. His world is, for him, the one and only world, and, if he thinks of it as phenomenal, he will not be using that word mentalistically or pejoratively.

However, he does believe that something occupies the gaps in his observation of his world, and the question is 'Why does he believe this?' Hume argues that it cannot be sensation which gives him the belief, because his senses are not operating in the problematical gaps. Nor can it be reason that gives it to him. For a priori reasoning merely traces the necessary connections between our ideas and so is incapable of supporting an audacious inference. The only kind of reasoning that would support the audacious inference, if it could be used in this case, is causal reasoning. However, unperceived objects cannot figure in the experienced constant conjunctions that would be required for causal reasoning. Therefore, it cannot be causal reasoning that produces the plain man's belief that the gaps in his observation of his world are filled by objects.

When we examine the details of these arguments, their clear structure is clouded by uncertainties. The first doubt is one that has already been mentioned. Hume ought to be preserving the categorial neutrality of the objects to which the plain man ascribes continued and distinct existence when he is not perceiving them. But does he really do so?

His first claim, that sensation alone cannot give us our belief in the continued existence of objects, is all right. Sensation alone really cannot give us a belief about something which is outside the scope of its operations.[21] This argument does not depend on any categorization of the objects that we believe to continue to exist.

It is his second claim, that sensation cannot give us our belief in the distinct existence of objects, which runs into trouble. What he ought to mean by 'distinct existence' is existence outside any mind, and this should cover impartially the two possible ways in which an object might exist independently of any mind: it might be an impression existing in complete isolation from the impressions and ideas which constitute any mind, or it might be a physical object in physical space. However, the moment he embarks on this argument, he forgets the need for ontological impartiality and concentrates exclusively on the second of these two alternatives:

That our senses offer not their impressions as the images of something *distinct*,

[21] *Treatise*, p. 188.

or *independent*, and *external*, is evident; because they convey to us nothing but a single perception, and never give us the least intimation of any thing beyond. A single perception can never produce the idea of a double existence, but by some inference either of the reason or imagination.[22] When the mind looks farther than what immediately appears to it, its conclusions can never be put to the account of the senses; and it certainly looks farther, when from a single perception it infers a double existence, and supposes the relations of resemblance and causation betwixt them.[23]

One sentence in this passage is compatible with ontological neutrality: 'When the mind looks farther than what immediately appears to it, its conclusions can never be put to the account of the senses'. But the remainder makes it perfectly clear that he is only thinking of belief in physical objects lying beyond our impressions and causing them.[24] To put the point in another way, he is not thinking of the Neutral Monism to which H. H. Price took him to be committed by his treatment of the plain man's belief.[25]

If this passage left any doubt about what he means by 'distinct existence', it would be removed by the sequel. His next move is to argue that our impressions do not 'present themselves as distinct objects', and that our senses do not 'present our impressions as external to, and independent of ourselves'.[26] This is all right, because it is compatible with categorial neutrality. But he immediately goes on to argue that our senses do not present our impressions as exterior to *our bodies*, and this argument is hardly compatible with categorial neutrality.[27]

It is worth pausing to look at the very different tendencies of these two similar-looking arguments. The self, according to Hume, is a sequence of impressions and ideas, and so the first argument only claims that the senses do not present our impressions as objects distinct from, and external to, these sequences. This is an objection both to the physical and to the mental versions of our belief in distinct existence. But the second argument claims that the senses do not present our impressions as objects distinct from, and external to, our bodies, and this is an objection to the physical version of our belief in

---

[22] These are the two kinds of reasoning which might have given us our belief in the distinct existence of objects, but, according to Hume, do not do so. See above, pp. 64–5.

[23] *Treatise*, p. 189.

[24] i.e. the theory adopted by Locke.

[25] H. H. Price, *Hume's Theory of the External World* (Oxford: Clarendon Press, 1940).

[26] *Treatise*, p. 189.

[27] Ibid., continuation.

distinct existence. For it seems that our objects could be external to our bodies only if they existed in physical space.

To be fair to Hume, it must be admitted that it is very hard to be sure when he is abandoning categorial neutrality. For he might defend himself against the last criticism by pointing out that 'properly speaking, 'tis *not* our body we perceive ... but certain impressions, which enter by the senses'.[28] He could then use this point to rebut the charge that he is focusing exclusively on the physical version of our belief in the distinct existence of objects. That may be a valid defence of his categorial neutrality in this part of his argument. It is hard to be sure, because the Neutral Monist's views about space are very difficult, if not impossible, to develop coherently. However, there is no doubt that he abandons categorial neutrality in the passage quoted above.[29]

Is this inconsistency important? Earlier, the point was made that Hume's interpretation of the plain man's belief is almost incredible. How can he suppose that the objects that continue to exist independently of his observation might be mental? The point can now be developed further. Having ascribed this extraordinary belief to the plain man, Hume cannot help removing the feature that makes it extraordinary, when he goes on to examine it. He inadvertently, but quite naturally, tacitly restricts the plain man's belief to its physical version: his objects, unlike his impressions, are physical. It is then easy for him to show that the senses alone cannot give him this belief in a 'double existence', when what he ought to have shown is that they can neither give him that belief nor a belief in a single, mental existence extending into the gaps in his observation.

We might think that this does not matter, because, either way, reason or imagination are going to be needed. But, quite apart from the merits of consistency, Hume's mistake produces an effect which we shall later find to be damaging. Having given his extraordinary, categorially neutral interpretation of the plain man's belief, he is able to present the theory of 'double existence' as one which would only occur to a philosopher, and which has nothing to recommend it but sophisticated and untrustworthy abstract reasoning. That is a much more serious error on his part.

The second theory, that it is reason that produces our belief in the continued and distinct existence of objects, fares no better than the theory that it is sensation. There are two versions of the second theory;

[28] Ibid. 191. [29] See pp. 161–2.

because the reasoning may be a priori or a posteriori. The Rationalist would claim that it is a priori. But this succumbs immediately to Hume's objection that the only kind of inference that could possibly take us from the observed to the unobserved is causal inference:

> The only existences, of which we are certain, are perceptions, which being immediately present to us by consciousness, command our strongest assent, and are the first foundation of all our conclusions. The only conclusion we can draw from the existence of one thing to that of another, is by means of the relation of cause and effect, which shews, that there is a connexion betwixt them, and that the existence of one is dependent on that of the other.[30]

That gets rid of the suggestion that the inference to objects existing in the gaps in our observation might be a priori. A priori reasoning merely takes an idea derived from an impression and analyses its structure; it cannot move from one idea to another derived from a separate impression.[31]

However, though causal inference is the right device for moving from the existence of one thing to the existence of another, Hume argues that it will not be able to take us from observed objects to unobserved objects. For, he continues,

> The idea of this relation is deriv'd from past experience, by which we find, that two beings are constantly conjoin'd together, and are always present at once to the mind. But as no beings are ever present to the mind but perceptions; it follows that we may observe a conjunction or a relation of cause and effect between different perceptions, but can never observe it between perceptions and objects. 'Tis impossible, therefore, that from the existence or any of the qualities of the former, we can ever form any conclusion concerning the existence of the latter, or ever satisfy our reason in this particular.[32]

Perceptions are perceived and unobserved objects are not perceived. Therefore, causal inference, which is always based on perceived conjunctions, cannot bridge this gap.

The argument used by Hume here is a familiar one, but it does need to be scrutinized closely. The first question to ask is one which he never faces squarely: 'What exactly is the difficulty presented by unobserved objects?' There are, as we have seen, two ways of developing

---

[30] *Treatise*, p. 212.
[31] The point was made above, in the discussion of causation, p. 65. Cf. *Treatise*, p. 69.
[32] *Ibid.* 212.

the plain man's belief in them. One version takes them to be just like the objects that he perceives, except, of course, that they are not perceived. The other version treats them as a class of objects which may differ in kind from any that are perceived: the objects that we perceive are always sense-impressions, but the objects that continue to exist in the gaps in our observation are of a problematical kind, and they may be physical objects, lying beyond our sense-impressions and causing them. But which version does Hume have in mind when he argues that causal inference can never produce the plain man's belief in unobserved objects?

The question is not easy to answer. We may begin by reminding ourselves that he is not a phenomenalist. He believes, and assumes that the plain man believes, that *something actually exists* in the gaps in observation. If he had been a phenomenalist, he would have been content with the theory that if observation had extended into the gaps, more sense-impressions would have occurred. In that case, the problem of perception would merely have been a special aspect of the problem of causation: the inferences covering the gaps in observation would simply have been counterfactual causal conditionals.[33]

But, given his assumption that we believe that something actually exists in the gaps, the problem becomes more difficult. However, we cannot tell exactly how difficult it becomes, until we know *what kind of thing* is supposed to continue to exist unobserved.

Consider the alternative which he tends to neglect in this part of his investigation:[34] unobserved objects are exactly like observed objects, because they are sense-impressions existing independently of any mind. This may be an incoherent suggestion, but, if we assume, for the moment, that it is not incoherent, would it be impossible for us to base our belief in such objects on causal inferences?

In this part of his inquiry Hume does not pose this as a distinct question to be answered separately, because he does not develop his criticism of the inferential theory in full detail. For example, we find him saying,

To which we may add, that as long as we take our perceptions and objects to be the same, we can never infer the existence of one from that of the other, nor

---

[33] See above, pp. 79–83.

[34] He does focus on to this alternative later, when he is explaining why our belief in the continued and distinct existence of objects is in an especially weak position. See below, pp. 189–91.

form any argument from the relation of cause and effect; which is the only one that can assure us of matter of fact.[35]

If this means that we must distinguish perceptions and objects, as Locke does, before we can claim that the latter cause the former, it is true. But what about causal inferences from sense-impressions which are, to those which are not, part of any mind? As usual in this part of his investigation, Hume ignores this development of the plain man's belief. No doubt, he would defend his neglect of it by pointing out that he was maintaining categorial neutrality. But that would not be a true defence, because in fact he gives preferential consideration to the other theory, that unobserved objects are physical objects in space.

Behind the screen of all these manœuvres he makes a really fundamental mistake: he treats unobserved objects as objects of a determinate problematical kind. But whatever category the objects of perception are taken to exemplify, unobserved objects will not be a determinate species of objects in that category. To put it in another way, there will not be a well-formed class of inferences to unobserved objects. This applies to what is in fact (although Hume denies the fact) the plain man's view, that observed and unobserved objects are physical objects in space. But it is equally applicable to the strange theory that they are sense-impressions which belong to a mind when they are observed, but when they are unobserved do not belong to any mind. Either way, there does not seem to be any special difficulty about causal inferences to unobserved objects. If I observe a plume of smoke and infer a ship which, it turns out, I can also see, am I going to refuse to infer another ship, below the horizon, from another plume of smoke above the horizon? Or am I going to refuse to make the idealist's version of this inference for Hume's reason—i.e. because unperceived impressions are a determinate species of impression?

This fundamental mistake will be analysed in the next chapter. Hume's concentration on the notion of 'a double existence'[36] and his neglect of the other development of the plain man's belief make it difficult to detect the mistake and diagnose it. For physical objects really do differ in kind from impressions. But that is beside the point. The point is that *unobserved* physical objects are not objects of a determinate, problematical kind.

Let me end with a warning. It is important not to exaggerate Hume's departure from categorial neutrality in his interpretation of the plain man's belief. At the start of his inquiry he explicitly refuses to categorize its objects, and again, at the end of his inquiry, when he complains that the belief is ill-founded and incoherent, he examines both the physicalistic and the mentalistic developments of it.[37] The criticism is only that, when he is assessing the claim of reason employed in causal inference, he neglects the mentalistic development, as he neglected it earlier, when he was assessing the claim of sensation, and so comes to focus exclusively on the physicalistic development.

That makes this part of his discussion very baffling. We think that it is about the problem of gaps in our observation and the difficulty of horizontal inferences covering those gaps. However, when we look more closely, we find that a large part of the problem concerns our knowledge of the objects, if there are any, which lie beyond our sense-impressions when we are actually having them. Are Locke's vertical inferences really legitimate?[38] But what if they are not? Would that also disqualify horizontal inferences? It seems that it would not.

---

[37] See below, pp. 189–94.

[38] The furthest that Hume ever goes in Locke's direction is to concede that we may have a 'relative idea' of objects '*specifically* different from our perceptions' (*Treatise*, p. 68). But that is not a concession sufficient to reinstate causal inference from sense-impressions to objects lying beyond them.

I I

Sense-Perception: Hume's Heroic Solution

IF neither sensation nor reason are capable of producing our belief in the continued and distinct existence of objects, then 'that opinion must be entirely owing to the *imagination*: which must now be the subject of our inquiry'.[1] So there has to be something which puts into our minds the ideas of objects existing in the gaps in our observation, and there also has to be something which gives them the vivacity which, according to Hume, constitutes belief. But what are the causes which produce these two effects? As usual, the inquiry belongs to the scientific investigation of the human mind.

It is divided into two parts. First there is a lengthy search for the causes of our belief in body, and when he is carrying out this part of his task, the category of the objects in whose continued and distinct existence we believe is left unspecified. This is because the formulation of the belief is pre-theoretical, and the question whether we take our objects to be physical or mental has not yet been asked.[2] Then in the second part of his inquiry he does ask the question, and he argues that, whichever of the two answers is given to it, our belief is deficient both in its justification and in its content. As usual, the question is not only *why* we believe, but *what* we believe—not only about truth and evidence, but also about meaning.[3]

Before Hume's arguments are analysed, there is a point that needs to be made and borne in mind throughout the exposition and criticism of his answers to the two questions. If we really did not distinguish between our sense-impressions and objects lying beyond and causing

---

[1] *A Treatise of Human Understanding*, ed. P. H. Nidditch (Oxford: Clarendon Press, 1989), 193.

[2] See above, pp. 152–4.

[3] However, Hume makes almost no use of his theory of meaning in his discussion of perception. This might seem to lend support to the interpretation which downgrades the importance of his theory of meaning in the *Treatise* (see pp. 9–10). But an alternative explanation will be given below. See pp. 191–4.

them, it would not even occur to us that gaps in our observation might be explained in the two different ways in which we are accustomed to explaining them in our daily lives. One of our explanations is that the existence of the object under observation has been interrupted—for example, the song of a bird has stopped—and the other one is that the operation of our senses—in this case, hearing—has been interrupted in some way. This is a difference between two kinds of explanation which simply would not occur to us, unless we distinguished between sense-impressions and physical objects.

When Kant criticized Hume's account of causation, he exploited this difference between changes attributable to the observer and changes attributable to the phenomena themselves. Whether his criticism was effective or not, it certainly drew attention to the need to distinguish causal connections between two occurrences at least one of which is mental from causal connections between two non-mental occurrences. The distinction that has just been adduced as a difficult one for Hume's theory of perceptual belief is similar, but more radical. For the difference, which is hard for him to accommodate so long as he gives a categorially neutral account of what we think about the gaps in our observation, is the difference between an interruption in the perception of an object and an interruption in the existence of the object itself. This is a distinction which needs to be drawn at the beginning of any account of perception, and when Hume postpones it to the end, he leaves it too late to do justice to it. So here we find another fault of the same kind as the fault in his theory of personal identity.

His difficulty can be presented in a very simple way. If, as he asserts, we did not distinguish between our sense-impressions and the objects that we observed with their aid, what valid reason could we possibly have for believing that *anything* existed in the gaps in our observation?[4] We would be like people who lived in a physical world which underwent completely inexplicable intermissions, so that they were reduced to saying that things simply took time out. Their 'space' and the

---

[4] He realized that we could not have a valid reason for this belief *in those circumstances* (see *Treatise*, pp. 197–8), but, instead of drawing the conclusion that his description of *our actual circumstances* must be mistaken, he inferred that the belief was in an exceptionally weak position. Really, he ought to have treated his demonstration of the weakness as a *reductio* of his theory of perception, thus bringing it into line with his rejection of his theory of personal identity (in the Appendix). But he did not do this. However, he did see that his theory of causation was far the most successful of the three applications of his theory of mind to difficult problems.

'objects' in it would suddenly be replaced by a void and then, after an interval, the status quo ante would be restored. How could those people possibly believe, or even, perhaps, understand, that their 'objects' did, or did not, continue to exist in these gaps? When Hume refuses to allow that we distinguish between the continued and distinct existence of mental objects and that of physical objects in the gaps in our observation, he puts us in an analogously hopeless predicament.

The validity of this analogy might be questioned for several reasons. First, in the analogy itself, it is not clear what is supposed to happen to the observers in the intermissions or how they manage to preserve any sense of time while the world takes its holidays. We seem forced to suppose that they enjoy a godlike existence, without bodies and so without any position in space, but that they do remain in time and somehow preserve their sense of time. However, the fact that we are forced to say these unconvincing things is no objection to the analogy, because it is a direct consequence of the extraordinary character of the predicament that it has to illustrate—our predicament, as Hume describes it.

There are two more features of the analogy that need to be noticed and understood. One of them is a feature which it shares with the predicament in which Hume places us. There is no intermission of consciousness produced by sleep, fainting, or, of course, death.[5] Similarly, when Hume finds a gap in his observation of the fire in his study, he remains in full possession of his faculties.

The other feature of the analogy is *not* shared with the predicament in which Hume places us: the reason why he no longer observes his fire is that he has walked out of his study, but in the analogy what immediately precedes the interruption in observation is nothing definite, and certainly not any movement of the observers in space. However, that is not a fault in the analogy. For if, in Hume's version of your life, you really did not draw any distinction between physical and mental objects, you would not be able to say that you walked out of the room. All that you could say would be that the impressions in your visual field were replaced by other, very different impressions. You would have no way of separating changes attributable to yourself, as observer, from changes attributable to the objects of your observation.

No doubt, Hume would object that your movements in space can be

---

[5] The connection between mentalistic theories, like idealism or phenomenalism, and death is exploited by Schopenhauer, when he argues that a person's death is not an event in his world.

described by you in a way that is neutral between the two categories, mental and physical. But though it may be true that the sensory effects of your movements are describable in neutral terms, the separation of changes attributable to you as observer from changes in the objects of your observation requires a theory about your body as one physical object among others, but a physical object with the special function of channelling sensory input into your mind. So if you really were in the predicament described by Hume, you could not say that you had left your room and returned to it later and wondered whether your fire had continued to exist in the gap in your observation. For if you said that, you would be presupposing our ordinary theory of the world around us, which you would not yet be able to formulate.

It follows that there is no fault in the analogy at this point. Hume thinks that the ordinary gaps in his observation have the totally mysterious character of the gaps in the observations made by the people in the analogous world. However, he cannot have it both ways. If he identifies them as ordinary gaps in his observation he must have assumed that his fire and he himself, as observer, are situated in a common and continuous space, in which he moves away from it and returns to it. But this assumption is part of our ordinary theory of the world around us, which, given the pre-theoretical neutrality of his belief in objects, he is not even in a position to formulate. That is one horn of the dilemma that confronts him. Its other horn is that if he did distinguish between sense-impressions and objects and so did put himself in a position to formulate our ordinary theory, the gaps in his observation would cease to be totally mysterious. What the analogy does is to set up a situation in which there really would be gaps in people's observation as mysterious as he mistakenly takes the gaps in his observation of his fire to be. In that situation we really would be unable to believe, or even to understand, that our objects did, or did not, exist in the gaps.

That, of course, is what Hume does say in the end about the belief in the unobserved fire. But he has not earned the right to this conclusion, because he has not identified gaps with this mysterious character. He thinks that he has identified gaps of this kind, because his official view of this stage in our belief in the continued and distinct existence of objects is that it is categorially neutral. However, if it really were categorially neutral, our ordinary theory, which he uses when he iden- .tifies the gaps, would not be available. For our conception of a space containing our bodies among other physical objects would not yet have been achieved. The adoption of our ordinary criteria for the identities of physical objects would still lie in the future. Most important of all, the essential, Kantian distinction between changes attributable to the observer and changes attributable to the object of observation would be beyond us. To put the point the other way round, the mystery presented by Hume is presented in a way that presupposes resources which he could have used to solve it.

Consider the gap in his observation of the fire in his study. He describes it in the ordinary way in which we all describe such gaps: he leaves his room for a time and then returns to it. But this description presupposes our ordinary view of the relation between the circle of a given person's observation and the world extending beyond its circumference: his observation is like a moving spotlight on an otherwise dark stage, and its movement can be explained only if we distinguish the physical space, in which his body moves among other objects, from the 'inner space' of his visual field, in which his impressions come and go. Hume makes what passes out of the circle of observation mysterious by depriving us of that essential distinction. Or perhaps we should say that, because he describes his fire's exit from the circle of his observation in a way that tacitly relies on the distinction, he really has the resources needed to dispel the mystery. So he faces a dilemma: the gaps in observation that he describes are either not identified in our way or not mysterious.

However, that is not his official view. For, officially, he represents the explicable gaps in his observation in a way that makes them as mysterious as the gaps in the existence of the whole physical world in the drama that was introduced above as an analogy. He achieves this result by setting up his world as a world of 'perceptions', which, *at that initial stage of his presentation*, he refuses to specify either as sense-impressions or as their physical causes.

How then will he deal with the mystery? In order to get an answer to this question, we must now analyse his long account of the way in which imagination gives us our belief in the continued and distinct existence of our objects. It is developed in a passage in which he shows himself uncharacteristically unsure of himself, almost groping for a satisfactory solution within the framework of his Sophisticated Empiricism. His tentativeness and final lack of success are not really surprising. His treatment of causation had avoided all questions about the frontier between body and mind and the relations between them. Personal identity, at least when he was dealing with it in the chapter devoted to it in the *Treatise*, seemed to him to be a problem which could be tackled from within the mind. But our perception of the world around us is a subject which can hardly be discussed without the body's immediately reasserting itself and wrecking any attempt to manage without it.

Hume starts by saying that the explanation of our belief in the continued and distinct existence of certain impressions must be sought in qualities peculiar to those impressions. Some think that the qualities which produce our belief are involuntariness or 'superior force and violence'. However, he dismisses both these suggestions, because we do not attribute 'any existence beyond our perception' to 'our pains and pleasures' or to our 'passions and affections', in spite of their violence.[6]

Next he examines his own thought-processes when he leaves his room and his fire unobserved for a time. He rapidly concludes that the qualities of the impressions at either end of the gap in observation, which convince him that things continue to exist in it, are constancy and coherence. The impression that he gets of his room on his return is the same as when he left, except for the fire, which now yields an impression exactly appropriate to the point in its burning down that he would have seen it reach if he had observed it continuously.

The argument here is simple and almost banal. However, there is a hitch in it. Although the thought-process which goes on in his mind seems to be quite like causal inference, because ideas are brought into his mind by association and given vivacity by impressions, the similarity is largely illusory.

But tho' this conclusion from the coherence of appearances may seem to be of the same nature with our reasonings concerning causes and effects; as being deriv'd from custom, and regulated by past experience; we shall find upon examination, that they are at the bottom considerably different from each other, and that this inference arises from understanding, and from custom in an indirect and oblique manner. For 'twill readily be allow'd, that since nothing is ever really present to the mind, besides its own perceptions, 'tis not only impossible, that any habit shou'd ever be acquir'd otherwise than by the regular succession of these perceptions, but also that any habit shou'd ever exceed that degree of regularity. Any degree, therefore, of regularity in our perceptions, can never be a foundation for us to infer a greater regularity in

---

[6] *Treatise*, p. 194. He might have given the suggestion that the belief is based on involuntariness a fairer hearing. It was probably the source of his own treatment of the felt inevitability of causal inference. See also p. 110.

some objects, which are not perceiv'd; since this supposes a contradiction, *viz.* a habit acquir'd by what was never present to the mind.[7]

This piece of self-criticism throws a clear light on Hume's very strange formulation of the problem of unobserved objects. The trouble, as he sees it, is that it involves inferences to conclusions that are never verified. For example, he would complain that inferences from smoke to ships below the horizon always remain unverifiable.

The difference, as he sees it, between this kind of inference and causal inference lies in their conclusions: unobserved objects will never be observed — that is the implication of the word 'unobserved' — but many of the effects which are inferred because they have not yet been observed will be observed later.[8] This difference, he thinks, makes it legitimate to appeal to the association of ideas based on repeated observation when he is explaining our belief in causation, but illegitimate to explain our belief in the continued and distinct existence of unobserved objects in the same way. The passage just quoted continues in a way that makes the difficulty, as he sees it, absolutely clear:

But 'tis evident, that whenever we infer the continu'd existence of the objects of sense from their coherence, and the frequency of their union, 'tis in order to bestow on the objects a greater regularity than what is observ'd in our mere perceptions. We remark a connexion betwixt two kinds of objects in their past appearance to the senses, but are not able to observe this connexion to be perfectly constant, since the turning about of our head, or the shutting of our eyes is able to break it. What then do we suppose in this case, but that these objects still continue their usual connexion, notwithstanding their apparent interruption, and that the irregular appearances are join'd by something, of which we are insensible? But as all reasoning concerning matters of fact arises only from custom, and custom can only be the effect of repeated perceptions, the extending of custom and reasoning beyond the perceptions can never be the direct and natural effect of the constant repetition and connexion, but must arise from the co-operation of some other principles.[9]

So the next question is 'What does he think that these other principles are?'

---

[7] *Treatise*, p. 197.
[8] Hume's neglect of counterfactual causal inference magnifies this difference. See above, p. 82.
[9] *Treatise*, pp. 197–8.

Before we examine his solution to the problem, as he sees it, we must appreciate the strangeness of his way of seeing it, and we must try to understand how he came to adopt a point of view from which the problem of unobserved objects looks exactly like the problem introduced earlier to illustrate his line of thought—the problem that we would face if we did not distinguish between our sense-impressions and the objects that we observed with their aid, and if those objects occasionally, but completely unpredictably, vanished *en masse*, and then, after an interval, were restored to our observation.[10]

The mistake which gave Hume his strange point of view was mentioned briefly at the end of the previous chapter, but we are now in a position to describe it more fully and to take the diagnosis of it further. We may begin by repeating the earlier description of his mistake. It was that he failed to realize that 'whatever category the objects of perception are taken to exemplify, unobserved objects will not be a determinate species of objects in that category. To put it another way, there will not be a well-formed class of inferences to unobserved objects.'[11] This can now be amplified. First, we need to understand what induced him to construe the problem of perception in this mistaken way. Then we need to appreciate the ramified effects of the mistake.

There are three things that led him astray. The first, and most important, explanation of his error was the brilliant success of his treatment of causation. When he was working on that problem, he had not felt any need to specify the category of the causal processes that we observe around us, because his theory of causation seemed to work equally well, whether they were construed as occurrences of sense-impressions or as changes in physical objects. So he failed to see any reason why he should determine the category of the objects of perception before dealing with the problem presented by the gaps in our observation of them.

The second thing that contributed to his error was the confusion analysed at the end of the previous chapter. He failed to keep the following two questions distinct from each other: 'How can we make legitimate inferences to unobserved objects, whatever their category?' and 'How can we make legitimate inferences to unobserved objects, if we take them to be the inaccessible physical causes of our

---

[10] See above, pp. 169–73. [11] See above, p. 166.

sense-impressions?"[12] The second question is loaded in a way that may well have seemed to him to hold him down to the answer 'We cannot'. But it would not follow that he would have to give the same pessimistic answer to the first question.

The third contributory cause of his error is more subtle in its operation. He specifies the gaps in our observation of objects in the way that we specify them in the ordinary course of our lives: for example, he says that he leaves his room and later returns to it and notices the appropriately advanced combustion of the logs in his hearth. But what he then goes on to say about these gaps makes no use of the ordinary way in which he has specified them. For his specification of them presupposes that he has already distinguished his sense-impressions from physical objects, and that he already understands that the circle of his perceptions shifts in physical space, first illuminating this scene, but leaving others in the darkness and then moving on to illuminate another scene. However, when he tries to explain his inferences to things actually existing in the gaps in his observation, he reverts to a pre-theoretical consciousness which does not distinguish, and does not even ask if there is any distinction, between sense-impressions and physical objects. The consequence, already described, is that, though he introduces the question as a perfectly ordinary one about his fire in his absence from his room, he makes it as insoluble as the question about the objects in the analogy, which simply vanished *en masse* and then, later, were restored to our observation, without any available explanation of this extraordinary phenomenon in its immediate surroundings.

These three things which led Hume astray have all been mentioned before. However, it is worth reviewing them now in more detail, in order to exhibit the connections between them.

We may start with the first, and most general, of the three contributory causes. Hume's apparent success in dealing with the problem of causation in a way that was neutral between the two categories, the mental and the physical, must have encouraged him to approach the problem of perception in the same way. It did not seem to him to matter whether the constant conjunctions, on which he based the associations of ideas required for causal inferences, were conjunctions of two types of impression, or conjunctions of two types of physical event perceived with the aid of the impressions. Either way, the inter-

---

[12] See above, pp. 158 and 161–6.

nal impression of necessity would be projected outwards—in one case on to the sense-impressions, and in the other case on to the physical events beyond them.[13] So there seemed to be no need for him to answer, or even seriously to consider, the categorial question. His usual flat view of the phenomenal world struck him as completely satisfactory. Any depth in his perspective could be denied, or else allowed only as a temporary concession to a prejudice which would be examined later when he took up the problem of our perception of the world around us. Meanwhile, he could deal with the problem of causation without clouding the discussion with irrelevant vapour from the controversy about the category of the objects of perception. In fact, he did manage to deal with it with a striking degree of success on that basis.

Or so he assumed. The effects of his assumption were described in Chapter 6.[14] He never focused on to the problem of counterfactual inferences—for example, what would have happened if the white ball had hit the red ball marginally instead of squarely—and he certainly would not have treated that problem as a crucial one, or as the rock on which most theories of causal necessity founder.[15] The class of inferences with which he was concerned was the class of inferences from the observed to the *temporarily* unobserved. If some effects *remained* unobserved, or even were, by implication, unobservable, that did not worry him. For he lumped all causal inferences together in the same class, and, from a certain point of view, he was right to do so. A counterfactual inference about the contents of a person's visual field would presumably raise the same kind of problem for him as the parallel future factual inference to a conclusion anticipated by the person's death. In short, it seemed to him that, so long as he remained on a phenomenal plane which was either mental or else not categorially specified, he did not have to pay any special attention to counterfactual causal inferences. They did not extend the subject's picture of the world into gaps in his consciousness, but only into alternative scenes produced by the substitution of one sense-impression for another.

Naturally he was also aware that there are gaps in a person's consciousness, because his sensory fields are not continuous from birth till

---

[13] Of course, the second option would not be available in cases where a person made a causal statement about a process entirely confined to his mind, e.g. when he inferred the imminent occurrence of an idea in his mind from the present occurrence of an impression.

[14] See above, pp. 81–4.

[15] See above, p. 83.

death, but interrupted by sleep or fainting. However, he did not think
that those gaps presented any special problem for his treatment of
causation. The consideration of them could be postponed until his
later discussion of perception, in which, as we have seen, he was not
going to treat them differently from the other kind of gap, produced by
walking out of his room. As far as causation was concerned, the
problem of inferences that happened to be unverifiable struck him as
irrelevant.

He was certainly right to this extent: causal inferences that happen
to be unverifiable are not a well-formed class of inferences, some of
which really ought to be verified before we can believe any of them. So
this problem is unlike the problem of unobserved objects, *as he construes the problem of unobserved objects*. We can bring out the dis-
similarity, as he saw it, in the following way: if he had been a
phenomenalist, he could have covered any gaps in his observation by
using conditional sentences about sense-impressions; but, not being a
phenomenalist, he took the plain man to believe that something actually existed in the gaps—something of a special kind, which, therefore,
required inferences belonging to a well-formed class, based on their
own special kind of evidence.

When the two problems, causation and perception, are presented in
categorially neutral terms, as he presents them, it is easy to understand
his relative optimism about his treatment of the former and his relative
pessimism about his treatment of the latter. But was he even right to
present the problem of causation as if it made no difference to his
treatment of it, whether causal processes in our environment were
construed as conjunctions of physical events or as conjunctions of
sense-impressions?

Kant uses a well-known argument to demonstrate that the possession of the concept of causation depends on the ability to distinguish
between changes attributable to the physical objects under observation
and changes attributable to the observer.[16] We need not endorse, or
even examine, his complex development of this argument, because it is
enough for our purpose that the point from which it starts, simple
though it is, already contains a difficulty for Hume. For when Hume is
watching a game of billiards, he is presumably not running round the
table and giving himself the problem of distinguishing between real
changes in the position of the balls on the table and mere changes in

---

[16] Kant, *Critique of Pure Reason*, trans. N. Kemp Smith (London: Macmillan, 1929),
218–33 (Second Analogy).

the position of the related impressions in his visual field. Nor, on the other hand, is he always taking brief naps so that the conjunctions in his visual field sometimes break down. Nor are there small opaque clouds drifting through the room and producing a similar effect. However, that only shows that the simultaneous equation has been solved in this case, and not that it did not need to be solved. When the observer stands still and remains alert, we have a special case in which the solution to the equation happens to be easy. If Kant could have put Hume in a space capsule and asked him to report the flight paths and collisions of rockets, his story would have been very different, and Kant could have said 'I told you so.'

There is no need to pursue this point. There is evidently a strong case for concluding that Hume's theory of causation needs, but does not have available, the distinction between sense-impressions and the physical objects that are perceived with their aid. It is interesting to observe that this deficiency, which he does not notice, is related to the deficiency which he does notice, but does not correctly diagnose, in his theory of personal identity. In that case it proved to be impossible to separate one mind from another with the resources offered by the theory developed in the text of the *Treatise*. For the two relations between perceptions proposed by him for this task, resemblance and causation, were insufficient, because the causation involved did not require contiguity in place but only contiguity in time. It was argued above that a substitute was required for contiguity in place, and that the only available substitute was the attachment of minds to bodies.[17] So in that case it was his neglect of the body that made it impossible for him to solve the problem. Similarly, when he is dealing with the problem of causation, he gets into a different difficulty for the same reason: he refuses to consider the body, and, in particular, the movements of the observer's body among other physical objects.

It is worth observing that his neglect of the body and his determination to solve his three difficult problems with purely mental resources operate in different ways in the three cases, but produce a similar effect. Throughout most of his discussion of perception he refuses to formulate the categorial distinction between the objects of our perception which would have allowed him to make use of the movements of the observer's body. In his discussion of personal identity he is in a position to make use of the body, but he tries to get along without it. In

[17] See above, pp. 136–7 and 142–5.

his discussion of causation it is clear that the point made by Kant simply had not occurred to him. But the effect is the same in all three cases—a lame theory.

The second of the three contributory causes of Hume's mistaken presentation of the problem of interrupted observation[18] is a simpler matter and there is no need to say much more about it. It was shown in the previous chapter that, when he is examining our natural inferences to things existing in the gaps in our observation, he often abandons categorial neutrality.[19] Instead of leaving the category of the infilling unspecified, he often implies that it consists of physical objects lying beyond our sense-impressions and causing them. Given his unexamined assumption, that our sense-impressions would then operate as an opaque screen, it follows that the objects lying beyond them really would be mysterious. Of course, this does not make our inferences to the unobserved infilling a well-formed class of inferences, because there would be the same mystery about these objects even when they were actually giving us sense-impressions. But the looseness of Hume's writing at this point must have reinforced his tendency to treat unobserved objects as a specific, and so as a totally mysterious, class.

The third contributory cause of Hume's mistaken presentation of the problem of the gaps in our observation is more complex and it needs to be explained in more detail. The explanation given above[20] was that he specifies the gaps in his observation in a way that presupposes the distinction between the physical world and the sense-impressions which give him direct information about his momentary environment: but that he then makes no more use of the terms in which he has specified the gaps, and goes on to treat their infillings as totally mysterious—just like the infillings in the analogous world in which physical objects occasionally and unpredictably vanished *en masse* and were later restored to our observation.[21]

The first thing that is needed is a closer look at the analogous world. It is analogous only in this sense: it fits Hume's pessimistic description of our view of the gaps in our observation, but it does not fit his specification of the gaps, because he specifies them in a way which really supports a more optimistic description of our view of them.

The way in which this happens needs to be explained in two stages.

---

[18] See above, pp. 175–6.
[19] See above, pp. 158 and 161–6.
[20] See above, pp. 168–72.
[21] See above, pp. 169–70.

First, he specifies the gaps in our observation in terms that presuppose a distinction between sense-impressions and physical objects. We move in the physical world from one scene to another and that produces a change in our sense-impressions. However, the view of these changes that he ascribes to us makes no use of any distinction between sense-impressions and physical objects. But if we really made no use of the distinction, we would regard the changes merely as changes in our sensory fields. It would not even occur to us that they involved gaps in our observation.

We have to move to the second stage, in order to reintroduce the idea of gaps in our observation. We have to describe the analogous world, in which a subject's sensory fields occasionally became completely empty and yet he remained conscious.[22] If he asked himself whether anything continued to exist in one of these intermissions, he would have no reason for choosing between an affirmative and a negative answer, and if he did hazard an affirmative answer, he would have no reason for choosing one description of the infilling rather than another. He could say what the audience says when the curtain comes down in a theatre, 'The drama has stopped.' Or, if he insisted that it still continued, there would be nothing to give him any hint about how it continued. The actors could tell him nothing about the continuation of their performances which he persisted in imagining when the curtain was down.[23]

Hume specifies the problematical gaps in our observations of particular things in our world in exactly the same way as the utterly mysterious gaps in the analogous world. That is the point where the analogy fits. But it is only *his conception of our view* of the problematical gaps in our observations that it fits and not *our actual view* of them. We certainly do not regard their infilling as a special kind of thing, no examples of which are ever observable, and so we do not regard our inferences to their infillings as a well-formed class of unverifiable inferences. It is only Hume who does these two things.

There is a very clear reason for the divergence between our view and his conception of our view of the problematical gaps in our observations of particular things in our world. The mysterious intermissions in the analogous world are not framed by any actions of the observer, like leaving the room and returning to it. Nor are his sensory fields filled

---

[22] i.e. these would be extreme cases of sensory deprivation.

[23] There is, of course, only a partial similarity here, because a physical speculation is being used to throw light on a metaphysical one.

with any new sets of impressions. However, these two differences are ignored by Hume when he judges the problematical gaps in our world in the same way as the very different intermissions in the analogous world. What he fails to appreciate is that the problematical gaps in our world are not so mysterious.

He fails to appreciate this point, because he does not see that our ordinary specification of these gaps presupposes a distinction between the physical world and the changing perspective provided by the observer's impressions as he moves around in the physical world. This is, perhaps, his most fundamental error. He assumes that this distinction is not drawn by the plain man but foisted on him by philosophers, and that is an assumption which can be seen to be false as soon as it is formulated.

These mistakes produce ramifying effects. For example, they vitiate his appeal to constancy and coherence. In ordinary life, when we compare what we observe at the beginning and the end of a gap in observation, we really are impressed by constancy and coherence. But that is only because we have already drawn the distinction between the physical world and our impressions. If we had not yet drawn it, but put everything on the same level, we could not make any inferences from the constancy or coherence of what came before and after the gap. Of course, the stage reached in the combustion of Hume's logs would be *appropriate* to the length of the gap. But we would have no reason to suppose that that effect was produced by steady combustion in the interim. Our drama might just be interrupted and resumed at a point appropriate to the length of the interruption, like a play on the stage, with continuity carefully contrived to fit the lengths of the intervals. We would not need to imagine that an entirely different drama was being played out in a similarly coherent way in the intervals when the curtain came down on ours.

This criticism of Hume's presentation of the problem of the gaps in our observation is not intended as an *argument* for the plain man's realism. It is only intended to show that, if Hume surreptitiously presupposes what is in fact the plain man's view, he cannot make such a mystery of what he believes to be going on in the gaps in his observation.

He really should have retraced his steps and started again. Then he might perhaps have tried to specify the gaps entirely in terms of impressions, like a phenomenalist. However, the question whether he could have succeeded in that enterprise will not be pursued here. Alternatively, he might have conceded that the way in which he does specify the gaps makes them far less mysterious than he takes them to be. However, he does not do that either. He assumes that he has a real problem on his hands, and not just one created by his faulty formulation of it. So he soldiers on and tries to strengthen the support provided by the imagination for the continued and distinct existence of unperceived objects, but without any success.

This part of his argument is not very impressive and we need not dwell long on it. He assumes that the weakness that he has found in our inferences to the continued and distinct existence of unobserved objects shows that he has not yet given a sufficiently full account of the working of the imagination. But the supplementary account, which he then proceeds to give, is very unconvincing and presented in an uncharacteristically confused and rambling way. His heart does not seem to be in it. He alternates between two quite different attitudes to this part of his theory of the imagination. One attitude is a complacency which he could have expressed like this: 'I told you so: our belief in the existence of body is forced on us by nature, and if nature can succeed by such transparent intellectual tricks, that only goes to show that the force that she exerts on us is irresistible.' His other attitude is dismay:

I begun this subject with premising, that we ought to have an implicit faith in our senses, and that this wou'd be the conclusion, I shou'd draw from the whole of my reasoning. But to be ingenuous, I feel myself *at present* of a quite contrary sentiment, and am more inclin'd to repose no faith at all in my senses, or rather imagination, than to place in it such an implicit confidence. I cannot conceive how such trivial qualities of the fancy, conducted by such false suppositions, can ever lead to any solid and rational system.[24]

He then goes on to recommend 'carelessness and inattention': the only remedy is to stop analysing our 'belief in body', because it is not, in the end, intellectually defensible, and to show our commitment to it by getting on with our lives.

This famous passage is often taken as his comment on the entire range of his Sophisticated Empiricism, including its application to the problem of causal inference. But that is a mistake. The point that he is making here is that there is a *special weakness* in the foundations of our 'belief in body', which is not shared by the foundations of our causal inferences. Of course, there is something common to the two cases, namely that it is not reason but imagination that lays the foundations, and so it is only by a kind of insincere courtesy that these thought-

---

[24] *Treatise*, p. 217. This is part of the concluding passage of his chapter 'Of Scepticism with regard to the Senses'.

processes can be called 'rational'. But the difference between the two cases is that our system of causal beliefs really does deserve this courtesy title, because, though it is audacious,[25] it is, at least, based on observed constant conjunctions. But when Hume complains in this passage that, if imagination produces our 'belief in body' in the way that he has just described in his supplementary account, he cannot see how it 'can ever lead to any solid and rational system', he is *making a further criticism*: our ramshackle system of perceptual beliefs is not even rational by courtesy.

How does it get into such straits? His supplementary account can be summarized quite briefly. He tries to make a further use of constancy. What he has already done with constancy is to take it together with coherence and to use both of them to explain our belief in the continued and distinct existence of unobserved objects. What he now does is to single out constancy for a special role. He points out that, when an object is 'surveyed for any time without our discovering in it any interruption or variation, it gives us a notion of identity'.[26] The concept of identity, then, is based on two properties, *invariableness* and *uninterruptedness*: when an object possesses both these properties, it 'preserves a perfect identity'.[27] Now the difficulty which he ran into earlier was the difficulty of explaining why we believe that an object continues to exist unobserved. The question can now be posed like this: 'Why do we think that the object maintains its identity in the gap in our observation?', or like this, 'Why do we concede identity in a case like this, where there is *invariableness* but no *uninterruptedness*?'

Hume gives his answer in a famous simile: 'the imagination, when set into any train of thinking, is apt to continue even when its object fails it, and, like a galley put in motion by the oars, carries on its course without any new impulse'.[28] This is a nice comparison, but does it tell us anything more than that the mind is audacious, and, apparently, even more audacious in its belief in body than in its belief in causation? For if that is all that it tells us, no progress has been made towards a better explanation.

The literal meaning of the simile is given in one of Hume's characteristic footnotes:

---

[25] See above, pp. 78–9.
[26] e.g. the lump of matter which has no particle added to it or subtracted from it, and which is observed continuously. See above, pp. 123 and 138–9.
[27] *Treatise*, p. 203.
[28] Ibid. 198.

This reasoning, it must be confest, is somewhat abstruse, and difficult to be comprehended; but it is remarkable, that this very difficulty may be converted into a proof[29] of the reasoning. We may observe, that there are two relations, and both of them resemblances, which contribute to our mistaking the succession of our interrupted perceptions for an identical object. The first is, the resemblance of the perceptions: The second is the resemblance, which the act of the mind in surveying a succession of resembling objects bears to that in surveying an identical object. Now these resemblances we are apt to confound with each other; and 'tis natural we shou'd, according to this very reasoning. But let us keep them distinct, and we shall find no difficulty in conceiving the precedent argument.[30]

So the new resource that he finds in constancy is a pair of related resemblances. There is a resemblance between two sequences of impressions, one uninterrupted and the other interrupted: both exhibit invariableness. There is also a resemblance between the smooth operation of the mind when it observes the uninterrupted sequence and its only slightly less smooth operation when it constructs the missing segment of the interrupted sequence. In short, both in a case where an object is kept under continuous observation and found to be invariable, and in a case where it is not kept under continuous observation but re-emerges in our sensory field without any variation, there is a resemblance not only between the data presented to the mind, but also between its reactions to the data.

Does this represent progress? It does, if the task is merely to explain the actual performance of the mind, however acrobatic, when it encounters a gap in observation. But the problem which started Hume on this line of inquiry was that its performance in this case is much less justifiable than it is in the case of causation. So his further use of constancy ought to have contributed something to the justification of our belief in body. Of course, if justification could be achieved only by Naïve Empiricism or by Rationalism, then it could not be achieved in this case any more than it could be achieved in the case of causation. But if there is a less ambitious kind of justification, which is achieved by Hume for our causal beliefs, it has certainly not been achieved by his further use of constancy to explain our perceptual beliefs.

This is easily seen. The original problem, as Hume construed it, was ·that we are never able to verify any inferences which extend into the gaps in our observation. So his new strategy is, first, to broaden the

---

[29] He means 'an example which verifies it'.
[30] Ibid. 204 n. 1.

inquiry by bringing into it the case of the invariable object observed without interruption, and then to move up to a higher level from which he can survey this larger scene and compare the data available to the mind and its reaction to them in a case where observation is interrupted and a case where it is not interrupted. However, this contributes nothing to reducing the difference between the justifiability of our belief in body and the justifiability of our belief in causation. For all that has been changed is the level at which the problem is formulated. It starts on the ground-floor level as the problem posed by the unverifiability of inferences extending into gaps in our observation. Then it moves up to the next level, where it becomes the problem whether there are enough similarities between the data and the mind's reaction to them in a case of continuous observation and a case of interrupted observation.

There are two things wrong with this strategy, one of minor importance and the other really radical. First, it is clear that, whatever further use Hume makes of constancy, he could, and should, also make of coherence. For an object will very often not emerge completely unchanged at the end of a gap in observation: the constancy of his impressions of his fire-tongs may be impressive, but so too is the coherence of his impressions of his fire. There are evidently two distinctions in play here, one between 'genuine' and 'feigned' physical identity over time,[31] and the other between interrupted and uninterrupted observation. So his account of the way in which imagination fixes up our belief in body ought to cover not only cases of unobserved 'genuinely' identical objects, yielding constant impressions, but also cases of unobserved objects with 'feigned' identity, yielding coherent impressions. But when he makes his further move he only appeals to constancy. It is as if he thought that the work of the imagination when it fills the gap in observation is more justified when the result is a belief in genuine identity. But that is to confuse the two problems, one posed by 'imperfect' identity and the other by interrupted observation. Gaps in observation framed by coherent impressions are as important as, and more common than, those which are framed by constant impressions.

The radical fault in this part of Hume's strategy is that it fails to contribute to the justification of the working of the imagination in cases of interrupted observation—or, to lower the aim, it fails to make it look

---

[31] See above, pp. 138–9.

any less silly. It is, of course, a necessary part of his naturalistic programme to describe what the imagination does in such cases and, if strict justification is demanded, he makes no claim to supply it.[32] However, it is really not enough for him to describe what the imagination does in a way that makes it look positively silly. So when he falls back on the observation that the mind does in fact react in the same way to the data available in the two cases, continuous and interrupted observation, he must point to something in the two sets of data which, at least, makes the uniform reaction not unreasonable. This is what he fails to do, and the failure is a radical one.

What he does point out is that there is a similarity between the data available in the two cases. When an unvarying object is continuously observed, the smoothness of the transition from one impression to the next supports a judgement of genuine identity. When there is an interruption in the observation of an object, the constancy of the impressions that frame it facilitates an equally smooth transition. Of course, there is a gap in this case, but a gap is not as upsetting as a jolt produced by a variation between one impression and the next.[33] So, impressed by the similarity between the two cases, the mind reacts to them both in the same way.

But that is not good enough. The mind's reaction in both cases is based on an observed set of similar instances, the unvarying impressions. However, there is a difference in the use made of the set by the mind in the two cases. When observation of the unvarying object is uninterrupted, the mind makes a judgement of genuine identity which is based entirely on perception, because it involves no inference from impressions actually received. But when observation is interrupted, the mind makes an inference from the known to the unknown. Now this would be a scientific inference and so its scope ought to be limited to instances exhibiting the right kind of similarity. To put the point in another way, the set of instances over which such an inference can legitimately range should be *relevantly similar*. Or, to put it in yet another way, the inferences must belong to a well-formed class. But that is a condition which is not met when the problem of unobserved objects is formulated in Hume's way.

It is difficult to specify precisely what counts as a relevantly similar set of instances for a scientific inference. The specification would

---

[32] See above, pp. 95–9.
[33] But what about cases which only exhibit coherence? This whole argument concentrates rhetorically on the easier cases exhibiting constancy.

certainly rule out similarities of the kind exploited by riddles. But when we move in from that extreme towards the centre, it is notoriously hard to say what counts as a relevant similarity. The reason for this is probably that relevant similarities are simply those that yield successful scientific generalizations. However, we do not need to explore this difficult terrain any further at this point. For Hume, quite evidently, treats the inference from the observed to the unobserved as an inference that crosses a line dividing one relevantly similar set of instances from another. His whole problem is that it is an inference of a kind that can never be verified.[34]

It follows that it is not good enough for him to point out that the evidence available in the two cases, interrupted and uninterrupted observation, belongs to the same relevantly similar class. This is true, but it is not sufficient, because in the case of uninterrupted observation, there is no inference, and in the case of interrupted observation there is an inference which, *as he construes it*, crosses a boundary into another relevantly similar class, *the unobserved*.[35] It is, therefore, not surprising that he is not satisfied by the further use that he makes of constancy and finally admits that he 'cannot conceive how such trivial qualities of the fancy, conducted by such false suppositions, can ever lead to any solid and rational system'.[36]

The right remedy would have been to retrace his steps and question his treatment of the unobserved. That would have required him to distinguish impressions from physical objects at the beginning of his inquiry, and to concede that the plain man is familiar with this distinction and uses it to construct his picture of the physical world in which he moves around as observer enjoying an explicably changing sensory show.[37] However, he does not retrace his steps in this case or question his starting-point.

In fact, he piles on the agony. For, not satisfied with arguing that our belief in body is completely unjustifiable, he now goes on to show that there is something wrong with its content. This further argument is not unexpected, because his normal strategy is to develop two parallel critiques, one dealing with the justifiability and the other with the meaningfulness of a problematical belief. However, in this particular case the development does not conform to the normal pattern, because

---

[34] See above, pp. 166–7.
[35] See above, pp. 173–6.
[36] *Treatise*, p. 217, quoted above, p. 183.
[37] See above, pp. 168–73.

it makes very little use of his theory of meaning. This is a remarkable fact and, if we are not going to abandon the balanced interpretation which has been sustained so far in this book, we shall have to find some feature of the problem of perception which will explain why his theory of meaning plays such an inconspicuous role in this particular case.

First we need the details of this new turn in his argument. It is initiated by the belated question 'To what category do the plain man's objects really belong?' So far he has been taking our belief in body in its pre-theoretical form, with uncategorized objects and the question of their category not even asked. But he now asks it, and he argues that there are two possible answers to it and that each of them exposes our belief to the criticism that there is something wrong with its content. So this part of his inquiry presents a dilemma: either our objects are impressions, and it is impressions that we believe to continue to exist in the gaps in our observation; or else they are physical objects lying behind our impressions and causing them. But whichever alternative is chosen, the result is a flaw in the *content* of our belief, and there is no third answer worth considering.

Consider, first, the suggestion that we believe our impressions to continue to exist in the gaps in our observation. It was suggested above[38] that this analysis of our belief might be incoherent. In fact, we might well think that the notion that impressions can exist outside minds with nobody aware of them really involves what Hume in the case of personal identity calls 'a manifest contradiction and absurdity'.[39] However, in the discussion of personal identity, the point was made that this was certainly not his view. He believed that our perceptions 'may exist separately and have no need of anything else to support their existence'.[40]

So now, when he examines the first of the two interpretations of the plain man's belief, he does not argue that it requires a conceptual impossibility. He only argues that it is 'contrary to the plainest experience'.[41] For, he points out,

When we press one eye with a finger, we immediately perceive all the objects to become double, and one half of them to be remov'd from their common and natural position. But as we do not attribute a continu'd existence to both these perceptions, and as they are both of the same nature, we clearly perceive, that

---

[38] See p. 165.
[39] See above, p. 127.
[40] *Treatise*, p. 233, quoted above, p. 141.
[41] *Treatise*, pp. 210–11.

all our perceptions are dependent on our organs, and the disposition of our nerves and animal spirits. This opinion is confirm'd by the seeming encrease and diminution of objects, according to their distance; by the apparent alterations in their figure; by the changes in their colour and other qualities from our sickness and distempers; and by an infinite number of other experiments of the same kind; from all of which we learn, that our sensible perceptions are not possest of any distinct or independent existence.

The natural consequence of this reasoning shou'd be that our perceptions have no more a continu'd than an independent existence . . .[42]

We may find it strange that he should argue only for the weaker thesis, that it is physically impossible for our perceptions—in this case, impressions—to exist independently of our bodies, when most of us would find it more natural to argue for the stronger thesis, that it is conceptually impossible. However, there is no doubt that he only argues for the weaker thesis that the belief that our impressions exist in the gaps in our observation is physically incompatible with our other beliefs about them. It follows that its inclusion in the complete system of our beliefs would make the system incoherent, and this is a flaw in the content of the belief.

However, his exposure of this flaw does not rely on his theory of meaning. Even if he had argued that the belief that our impressions exist in the gaps in our observation is self-contradictory and, therefore, meaningless, he would still not have been relying on his special theory of the derivation of ideas from impressions, but only on the general thesis that beliefs with a self-contradictory content are meaningless. Anyway, he does not take this line, but merely argues for the weaker thesis that it is physically impossible for impressions to exist independently of our bodies. His choice of argument is understandable, given his general construal of the problem of individuating minds. If it really were like the problem of individuating constellations, there would be no conceptual incoherence in the supposition that the smallest unit, an impression, could exist on its own.[43] The strongest objection that could be made against it would be that it did not cohere with other scientifically established truths.

Here we have part of the explanation of the recessiveness of Hume's theory of meaning in this part of the *Treatise*. It is not that he is solely concerned with the weakness of the evidential support for the plain man's belief, when it is interpreted in the first way. It is, rather, that he

---

[42] *Treatise*, pp. 210–11.   [43] See above, pp. 140–5.

finds a flaw in the content of his belief, but, though the flaw is a feature of its meaning, its exposure has nothing to do with the theory of the derivation of ideas from impressions.

The passage incompletely quoted above goes on to deal with the alternative interpretation of the plain man's belief: what continues to exist in the gaps in our observation are the physical objects which lie beyond our impressions and cause them:

> ... and indeed philosophers have so far run into this opinion [that our perceptions have no more a continued than an independent existence], that they change their system, and distinguish, (as we shall do for the future) betwixt perceptions and objects, of which the former are suppos'd to be interrupted, and perishing, and different at every different return; the latter to be uninterrupted, and to preserve a continu'd existence and identity.[44]

He criticizes this hypothesis on the ground that it

> ... has no primary recommendation either to reason or to the imagination, but acquires all its influence on the imagination from the former [sc. from the other hypothesis, that our perceptions are our only objects, and continue to exist even when they no longer make their appearance to the senses].[45]

His claim that this alternative has 'no primary recommendation to reason' is supported by an argument quoted above:[46] we cannot argue a priori from our known impressions to their unknown causes. But what about the kind of reasoning that gets that title by courtesy, causal 'reasoning'? That too is of no avail in this case, because it is only the effect that is observed and never the cause. Then what about the more acrobatic operations of the imagination, which he has been describing at such length? We have already gathered his opinion of 'such trivial qualities of the fancy, conducted by such false suppositions'.[47]

These criticisms are directed not against the meaningfulness, but against the credibility of the thesis that it is physical objects that enjoy a continued and distinct existence in the gaps in our observation. This is very surprising, because there was an extremely simple argument that he could have used to show that the thesis is meaningless. Berkeley had argued, without any of the inhibitions that might have been expected, for the conclusion that we do not have a genuine idea of material substance. The argument, expressed in Hume's terms, would have

---

[44] *Treatise*, p. 211.
[45] Ibid., continuation.
[46] See above, p. 164.
[47] *Treatise*, p. 217, quoted above, p. 183.

been devastatingly simple: if all our (genuine) ideas are derived from impressions, then the idea of a physical object lying beyond the impression that it gives us and so, in a sense, screened by it must be spurious. Why did he not develop this argument here? What explanation can a supporter of the balanced interpretation of his strategy offer at this point?

First, he does use a similar argument elsewhere in the *Treatise*:

As every idea is deriv'd from a precedent impression, had we any idea of the substance of our minds, we must also have an impression of it; which is very difficult, if not impossible, to be conceiv'd. For how can an impression represent a substance, otherwise than by resembling it?[48]

It is true that this passage deals with a special case, mental substance, but he applies the same reasoning to physical substance arguing that it too is an 'unintelligible chimera',[49] and later, when he is speaking quite generally about substance, he says,

We have no perfect idea of any thing but of a perception. A substance is entirely different from a perception. We have, therefore, no idea of a substance.[50]

However, the argument used in these passages is not directed against the general thesis that we have an idea of any things lying beyond our perceptions and causing them (or, in the case of the mind, holding them together). It is directed against the special version of that thesis which takes those things to be substances, a version which introduces further problems of its own.[51] What we need to find are passages in which the argument is used against the general thesis.

The clearest passage and the one which uses the argument in the most uninhibited way has already been quoted:[52]

We may observe, that 'tis universally allow'd by philosophers, and is besides pretty obvious of itself, that nothing is ever really present with the mind but its perceptions or impressions and ideas, and that external objects become known to us only by those perceptions they occasion. To hate, to love, to think, to feel, to see; all this is nothing but to perceive.

Now since nothing is ever present to the mind but perceptions, and since all ideas are deriv'd from something antecedently present to the mind; it follows

---

[48] *Treatise*, pp. 232–3.
[49] Ibid. 222.
[50] Ibid. 234.
[51] See above, pp. 124–5.
[52] *Treatise*, pp. 67–8, quoted above, p. 157.

that 'tis impossible for us so much as to conceive or form an idea of any thing specifically different from ideas and impressions. Let us fix our attention out of ourselves as much as possible: Let us chance our imagination to the heavens or to the utmost limits of the universe; we never really advance a step beyond ourselves, nor can conceive any kind of existence, but those perceptions, which have appear'd in that narrow compass. This is the universe of the imagination, nor have we any idea but what is there produc'd.

Here we have part of the answer to the question why Hume in his chapter 'Of Scepticism with regard to the Senses' did not deploy his theory of meaning against the second interpretation of the plain man's belief: he had already carried out that task and did not need to repeat it.

It would still be surprising if the chapter contained no allusion to this use of his theory of meaning. But, in fact, there is an allusion. Consider this passage, which occurs near the beginning of the chapter:

That our senses offer not their impressions as the images of something *distinct*, or *independent*, and *external*, is evident; because they convey to us nothing but a single perception, and never give us the least intimation of any thing beyond. A single perception can never produce the idea of a double existence, but by some inference either of the reason or imagination. When the mind looks farther than what immediately appears to it, its conclusions can never be put to the account of the senses; and it certainly looks farther, when from a single perception it infers a double existence, and supposes the relations of resemblance and causation betwixt them.[53]

There is no actual reference back to his earlier use of his theory of the derivation of ideas from impressions, but surely there is an allusion: 'a single perception can never produce the idea of a double existence'. This production would be, in the first instance, the production of a genuine idea of each 'existence'. It is only after the idea of a physical object has acquired a meaning as an idea of an object beyond the impression that it can go on to figure in a belief. It may be surprising that Hume immediately concentrates exclusively on belief,[54] but it can not indicate any reluctance to use the simple argument from his theory of the derivation of ideas from impressions against the 'philosophical system' which postulates physical objects to fill the gaps in our observation.

So when he says '*that the philosophical system acquires all its influence*

---

[53] *Treatise*, p. 189.
[54] See above, pp. 33-4, for another example of his tendency to slur over meaning in his haste to get on to truth.

on the imagination from the vulgar one' and '*that it has no primary recommendation to reason or the imagination*',[55] he means that the philosophical system is cheating both about truth and evidence and about meaning. The 'vulgar system' assumes that our impressions continue to exist independently of our minds with the very same properties that they exhibit when they are present to our minds. What the philosophical system does is borrow those properties and project them on to physical objects which are never present to our minds. This violates the canons of meaningfulness as well as credibility.

However, the way in which it violates the canons of meaningfulness is not as straightforward as it might appear to be from the interpretation of Hume's position developed so far in this chapter. The complication is introduced by the sequel to the passage quoted above.[56] After saying, 'This is the universe of the imagination, nor have we any idea but what is there produc'd', Hume continues,

> The farthest we can go towards a conception of external objects, when suppos'd *specifically* different from our perceptions, is to form a relative idea of them, without pretending to comprehend the related objects. Generally speaking we do not suppose them specifically different; but only attribute to them different relations, connexions and durations. But of this more fully hereafter.[57]

Now the argument that has been developed in the last few pages is that Hume makes little use of his theory of meaning in his chapter 'Of Scepticism with regard to the Senses' because he has already made the very simple use that he needed to make of it in his treatment of perception, and there was not much more to be said. But these last remarks suggest that it may not be as simple as that.

They seem to hint at a more liberal theory of meaning than the one proposed in the first chapter of the *Treatise*. Perhaps a genuine idea of a physical object does not require the unavailable impression because it is a complex idea with something left unspecific in its formulation. This might allow a more relaxed style of thinking in which the ideas would not be tied down so closely to specific impressions. It might also provide a different explanation of the recessiveness of his original theory of the derivation of ideas—perhaps he no longer really believed

---

[55] *Treatise*, p. 213.
[56] Ibid. 67–8. See above, p. 157.
[57] i.e. in his later chapter 'Of Scepticism with regard to the Senses'.

in it, and so was free to discuss the more important issue, truth and evidence.

But before we run too far ahead with these suggestions,[58] it is worth asking whether Hume's remarks about relative ideas with something non-specific in their structures amount to a substantial change in his theory of meaning. Here it is instructive to start from Russell's very similar theory, because its logical formulation is so much clearer than Hume's psychological formulation.[59] Russell required every word that we can understand either to denote things with which we are acquainted or else to be defined in terms denoting things with which we are acquainted. But he also allowed that we can understand propositions about physical objects in spite of the fact that we are not acquainted with them. They are, of course, introduced as whatever causes our sense-data, and the quantification in this formula cannot be eliminated because the acquaintance that would be needed for its elimination is lacking.

When Russell countenances ineliminable quantification in the formula used to introduce physical objects, he is not abandoning his empiricist theory of meaning. He still requires a basis in acquaintance for the words in the formula used to specify physical objects, but he does not require acquaintance with physical objects themselves. In fact, he is working in a framework of assumptions which make acquaintance with them theoretically unattainable. They are not things that we merely happen not to have encountered.[60]

Hume takes the same line in his remarks about relative ideas with something non-specific in their structure. He too is not abandoning his empiricist theory of meaning, and he too regards physical objects as theoretically inaccessible. But if it is theoretically impossible to encounter them, and if we are never going to be in a position to ascribe any intrinsic properties to them, the line that we have on to them is extremely thin. Strictly speaking, we know them only as whatever causes our sense-impressions. Now since this is offered as the

---

[58] They are developed by E. O. Craig in *The Mind of God and the Works of Man* (Oxford: Clarendon Press, 1987). Similar suggestions about Hume's treatment of causal connections in the physical world have been made by G. Strawson in *The Secret Connexion: Causation, Realism, and David Hume* (Oxford: Clarendon Press, 1989), *passim*. See above, pp. 90–3.

[59] See above, pp. 3–4.

[60] Russell's most important use of his Theory of Descriptions occurs at this point in his construction of the world as we find it. See his 'Knowledge by Acquaintance, Knowledge by Description', in *Mysticism and Logic* (London: Longman, 1911).

definition of 'physical object', or the analysis of our idea of *physical object*, all sorts of extraneous ideas will immediately crowd in and give us the illusion of a richer concept. They must be dismissed. On this theory, physical objects are known *only* as whatever things cause our sense-impressions. But why does even this count as knowledge? Presumably, the word 'whatever' implies that something external causes our sense-impressions, but if we start from Hume's position or Russell's, then for all we know, our sense-impressions are caused by nothing lying beyond them. There may be absolutely nothing occupying the gaps between our sequences of sense-impressions, and absolutely nothing external causing them when they do occur. The accurate description of this kind of empiricist's world is the description of the imaginary world that was offered as an analogue at the beginning of this chapter.[61] It is not surprising that Hume does not think it worth mentioning this etiolated interpretation of the plain man's belief in his chapter 'Of Scepticism with regard to the Senses'.

His conclusion is that our belief in body is intellectually indefensible on either of the two alternative interpretations that he considers. For, whichever way it is taken, there is something seriously wrong not only with our reasons for holding it but also with its content. All the more credit to nature, which, nevertheless, forces us to hold it! There is an element of heroism in this solution to the problem of perception.

The point has been made more than once in this chapter that he should have retraced his steps and started again. For one of his most important errors occurs right at the beginning, when he assumes that the plain man's belief does not presuppose any distinction between his impressions and physical objects. This enables him to represent 'the opinion of a double existence' as the extravagant speculation of philosophers. However, we can now see that it would not have been enough for him to correct that mistake. For the line of reasoning sketched earlier,[62] which starts from its correction and ends with the realization that unobserved objects do not belong to a well-formed class, would immediately run up against his assumption that physical objects are not directly accessible to observation.

This too is a mistake and it can be corrected only by reversing his treatment of impressions and physical objects. He finds no difficulty in treating impressions as objects, but then he is at a loss to explain our

---

[61] See pp. 169–72. [62] See pp. 166 and 181–2.

cognitive relations with any physical objects beyond them. It would have been better to start with our acceptance of things in space as our objects and then to have treated our impressions as something less than another kind of object. But that is another story.

Postscript

THIS study of Hume's basic system has concentrated exclusively on *A Treatise of Human Nature* and neglected *An Enquiry concerning Human Understanding*. The reason for this procedure was not that the *Enquiry* throws no light on the matter. It was that the light that it does throw is softer and more diffuse, whereas the *Treatise* is a young man's book in which the structure of his thought emerges more starkly and with sharper outlines. In his first presentation of his system paradoxical implications are never blunted to reduce the shock of their impact.

If an excuse were needed for adding another book to the many that have been written on Hume, mine would be that it is still worth demonstrating that he did not face the dilemma 'Either Scepticism or Reductivism'; and, in the present climate of opinion about his work, it is even more worth demonstrating that he did not face another dilemma, 'Either argue from the theory of meaning or from the theory of truth and evidence'. He may not even have always distinguished between the alternatives in each pair. However, though that indicates confusions at certain points in his thinking, it allowed him to develop his ideas with subtleties and ramifications which otherwise might not have been possible.

Bibliography

BEAUCHAMP, T., and ROSENBERG, A., *Hume and the Problem of Causation* (Oxford: Clarendon Press, 1981).

CRAIG, E. O., *The Mind of God and the Works of Man* (Oxford: Clarendon Press, 1987).

DAVIDSON, D., 'Causal Relations', *Journal of Philosophy*, 64 (1967), 691–703; repr. in Davidson, *Essays on Actions and Events* (Oxford: Clarendon Press, 1980).

FREGE, G., 'Sense and Reference', trans. M. Black, in *Philosophical Writings of Gottlob Frege*, ed. P. Geach and M. Black, 2nd edn. (Oxford: Blackwell, 1960).

GOODMAN, N., *Fact, Fiction and Forecast* (London: Athlone Press, 1954).

HUME, D., *An Abstract of the Treatise of Human Nature*, in Hume, *A Treatise of Human Nature*.

——*An Enquiry concerning Human Understanding*, ed. L. A. Selby-Bigge, 2nd edn. (Oxford: Clarendon Press, 1982).

——*A Treatise of Human Nature*, ed. P. H. Nidditch (Oxford: Clarendon Press, 1989).

KANT, I., *Critique of Pure Reason*, trans. N. Kemp Smith (London: Macmillan, 1929).

KEMP SMITH, N., *The Philosophy of David Hume* (London: Macmillan, 1st edn. 1940, 2nd edn. 1949).

PEARS, D., 'Hume on Personal Identity', in *Questions in the Philosophy of Mind* (London: Duckworth, 1975).

——'Hume's Empiricism and Modern Empiricism', in Pears (ed.), *David Hume: A Symposium* (London: Macmillan, 1963).

PRICE, H. H., *Hume's Theory of the External World* (Oxford: Clarendon Press, 1940).

RUSSELL, B., 'Knowledge by Acquaintance, Knowledge by Description', in *Mysticism and Logic* (London: Longman, 1911).

——'The Philosophy of Logical Atomism', in *Logic and Knowledge: Essays 1901–1950*, ed. R. C. Marsh (London: Allen and Unwin, 1956).

——*The Problems of Philosophy*, 1st edn. (London: Oxford University Press, 1950).

STRAWSON, G., *The Secret Connexion: Causation, Realism, and David Hume* (Oxford: Clarendon Press, 1989).

STROUD, B., *Hume* (London: Routledge and Kegan Paul, 1977).

WITTGENSTEIN, L., *Philosophical Investigations*, trans. G. E. M. Anscombe, 3rd edn. (Oxford: Blackwell, 1958).

——'Some Remarks on Logical Form', *Proceedings of the Aristotelian Society*, suppl. vol. 9 (1929), 162–71; repr. in *Essays on Wittgenstein's* Tractatus, ed. R. Beard and I. Copi (London: Routledge and Kegan Paul, 1966).

Index